Jahrbuch für Europäische Geschichte. European History Yearbook

Jahrbuch für Europäische Geschichte
European History Yearbook

Herausgegeben von Johannes Paulmann
in Verbindung mit Markus Friedrich und Nick Stargardt

Edited by Johannes Paulmann in cooperation with
Markus Friedrich and Nick Stargardt

Band / Volume 16

Mobility and Biography

Herausgegeben von
Sarah Panter

DE GRUYTER
OLDENBOURG

Herausgegeben am Leibniz-Institut für Europäische Geschichte von Johannes Paulmann
in Verbindung mit Markus Friedrich und Nick Stargardt

Gründungsherausgeber: Heinz Duchhardt

ISBN 978-3-11-041515-5
e-ISBN (PDF) 978-3-11-041516-2
e-ISBN (EPUB) 978-3-11-042393-8
ISSN 1616-6485

Library of Congress Cataloging-in-Publication Data
A CIP catalog record for this book has been applied for at the Library of Congress.

Bibliografische Information der Deutschen Nationalbibliothek
Die Deutsche Nationalbibliothek verzeichnet diese Publikation in der Deutschen
Nationalbibliografie; detaillierte bibliografische Daten sind im Internet über
http://dnb.dnb.de abrufbar.

Titelbild: Harvepino/iStock/Thinkstock
Satz: PTP-Berlin, Protago-TEX-Production GmbH, Berlin
Druck und Bindung: CPI books GmbH, Leck
♾ Gedruckt auf säurefreiem Papier
Printed in Germany

www.degruyter.com

Contents

Sarah Panter, Johannes Paulmann and Margit Szöllösi-Janze

Mobility and Biography: Methodological Challenges and Perspectives

Abstract: *This introductory article discusses methodological challenges for and perspectives related to a field of study that has only recently gained importance in historical research: transnational lives. For a long time, methodological nationalism had slowed down or even prevented investigations of individual or collective life-courses that were characterised by a high degree of mobility and internationality. We argue that a critical engagement with concepts from the social sciences related to the current interest in processes of globalisation and transnational phenomena can open up new perspectives on "mobility and biography". In doing so, we first explore how focusing on lives that crossed political, social or cultural boundaries can bring aspects of individual agency together with larger structural settings as explanatory factors. In the second part, this article attempts to conceptualise transnational lives for historical research. Introducing our own concept of "cosmobilities", we demonstrate how engaging with two sociological strands, "rooted cosmopolitanism" and "mobilities", might provide a fresh impetus for analysing transnational subjects and their practices.*

In 1849, Lorenz Brentano, today an almost forgotten activist during the European Revolutions of 1848/49 in the Grand Duchy of Baden, set sail with his wife via Switzerland for the United States. Almost thirteen years later, in 1862, this son of a merchant from Mannheim with family roots in Tremezzo (Lombardy) was finally granted an amnesty. Nonetheless, Brentano, who by then had settled in Chicago and acquired US citizenship, would not return to Germany for good. Only during his term as American consul in Dresden from 1872 to 1876 did he resettle for an extended period in Germany.[1] At first glance, then, and in particular as displayed in dictionaries of national biography like the *Neue Deutsche Biographie* and the *American National Biography*, Brentano seems to have lived two separate lives: as

1 On the history of the Brentano family, see Manfred Beller: Die Familie Brentano – Vom Comer See zum Rhein. Migration, Assimilation und die Folgen, in: Bernd Thum and Thomas Keller (eds.): *Interkulturelle Lebensläufe*. Tübingen 1998, 159–169; Konrad Feilchenfeldt and Luciano Zagari (eds.): *Die Brentano. Eine europäische Familie*. Tübingen 1992.

a failed revolutionary he had to flee German territory, only to achieve success as a journalist and politician in the US.[2]

This division is problematic because it not only simplifies a life's course unduly but also because it shows a bias towards national narratives. Analysing such biographies as "nationalised" lives ignores the transnational dynamics and entangled practices shaping their agency. For such transgressive life stories were not bound to one territory or one nation-state but rather marked by a high level of mobility and internationality, especially if one keeps in mind larger group relations, like family or business networks.[3] Bringing research on aspects of "mobility and biography" during different epochs and in various spatial dimensions together, this issue of the *European History Yearbook* intends to open up new perspectives on the emerging field of transnational lives.

Transnational Lives: A New Perspective on Writing Biographies?

The subject of transnational lives has only recently gained importance in historical research, for instance in the study of imperial biographies and careers or diasporic minorities.[4] This seems surprising given that during the last two de-

2 Both assertions have also had a deep impact on the historiography of the so-called "Forty-Eighters" – a term that is highly problematic in itself. Wolfgang Hochbruck: Einführung. Das offene Ende einer Revolution, in: id. (ed.): *Achtundvierziger – Forty-Eighters. Die deutschen Revolutionen von 1848/49, die Vereinigten Staaten und der amerikanische Bürgerkrieg.* Münster 2000, 12–28; Sonja Maria Bauer: Lorenz Brentano – Vom Advokaten und Revolutionär in Baden zum Journalisten und Politiker in den USA, in: Hans-Peter Becht, Kurt Hochstuhl and Clemens Rehm (eds.): *Baden 1848. Bewältigung und Nachwirkung einer Revolution.* Stuttgart 2002, 217–238. On transnational approaches that avoid this dilemma, see in particular Sabine Freitag (ed.): *Exiles from European Revolutions. Refugees in mid-Victorian England.* New York 2003; ead.: *Friedrich Hecker. Two Lives for Liberty*. St. Louis 2007; and more recently Hélena Tóth: *An Exiled Generation. German and Hungarian Refugees of Revolution, 1848–1871.* Cambridge, MA 2014.

3 Elizabeth Buettner: *Empire Families. Britons and Late Imperial India.* Oxford 2004; Simone Derix: Transnationale Familien, in: Jost Dülffer and Wilfried Loth (eds.): *Dimensionen internationaler Geschichte.* München 2012, 335–352.

4 Desley Deacon, Penny Russell and Angela Woollacott: Introduction, in: eaed. (eds.): *Transnational Lives. Biographies of Global Modernity, 1700–Present.* Basingstoke 2010, 1–14; David Lambert and Alan Lester (eds.): *Colonial Lives across the British Empire. Imperial Careering in the Long Nineteenth Century.* Cambridge 2006; Malte Rolf (ed.): *Imperiale Biographien.* Special Issue of *Geschichte und Gesellschaft* 40, no. 1 (2014), esp. 5–21; Clare Anderson: *Subaltern Lives. Biographies of Colonialism in the Indian Ocean World, 1790–1920.* Cambridge 2012. On recent,

cades, history as a discipline has been increasingly marked and reshaped by the so-called "transnational turn". What are the main reasons for this hesitant reception, only gradually producing spill-over effects on the *analysis* and *writing* of biographies? If we follow the analyses of sociologists, one important reason seems to be that, despite programmatic claims of change, "methodological nationalism" (Ulrich Beck) or "methodological territorialism" (Neil Brenner) continues to dominate in the social sciences – and, one might add, in the humanities.[5] Yet through the lens of this volume's topic one can identify another obstacle, pertaining more to the practical sphere of the historian's profession and everyday business: the difficulty of finding and gaining access to relevant sources for analysing transnational lives due to their fragmented existence, scattered across different national and local archives. This challenge increases even further if we include historically marginalised groups (e.g. women and religious or ethnic minorities) in our analyses. For in most cases, they have neither consciously left traces of their lives behind nor have they been identified by researchers as subjects worth pursuing.[6] Hence, it is safe to assume that there are many more "hidden" transnational lives yet to discover.

The reluctance which has so far been shown to make transnational lives a prominent research subject has also been reinforced by a more general discourse on the merits of the biographical approach itself. Especially among German historians, writing biographies was for a long time overshadowed first by historicism and then by negative connotations the genre of biography carried to later generations of scholars.[7] A main argument of earlier critics against the biographical approach was that it lacked not only analytical strength but also reinforced

partly converging attempts to re-explore the transnational dynamics of "Germans abroad", see H. Glenn Penny and Stefan Rinke: Germans Abroad. Respatializing Historical Narrative, in: iid. (eds.): *Rethinking Germans Abroad*. Special Issue of *Geschichte und Gesellschaft* 41, no. 2 (2015), 173–196.

5 Ulrich Beck and Natan Sznaider: Unpacking Cosmopolitanism for the Social Sciences. A Research Agenda, in: *British Journal of Sociology* 57 (2006), 1–23, esp. 2; Neil Brenner: Beyond State-Centrism? Space, Territoriality, and Geographical Scale in Globalization Studies, in: *Theory and Society* 28 (1999), 39–78, esp. 46.

6 On these challenges in a colonial and global context, see Hannes Schweiger: Postcolonial Studies, in: Christian Klein (ed.): *Handbuch Biographie. Methoden, Traditionen, Theorien*. Stuttgart 2009, 408–413, esp. 409; Deacon, Russell and Woollacott, Introduction, 1–14; Hannes Schweiger and Deborah Holmes: Nationale Grenzen und ihre biographischen Überschreitungen, in: Bernhard Fetz and id. (ed.): *Die Biographie – zur Grundlegung ihrer Theorie*. Berlin 2009, 385–418.

7 For general reflections on the genre of historical biography, see Simone Lässig: Die historische Biographie auf neuen Wegen?, in: *Geschichte in Wissenschaft und Unterricht* 60 (2009), 540–553.

the dominance of heroic, "great men" narratives. Over the last decades, however, and partly due to the "cultural turn" and its impact on the humanities, biography as a genre has been re-evaluated. The insight has gained ground that one of its strengths is to link the "individual" with "society", thereby turning such biographies into valuable sensors for general trends and changes in society.[8] Emphasising the relationship between subject and context, individuals are no longer portrayed as acting completely independently of their social context. Out of this reflexive process a "new biography"[9] has emerged that attempts to avoid the pitfalls of past biographies. The writing of transnational lives has to take these recent advances even further, because such an approach must take into account several contexts in which individual and collective lives were entangled.

Conceptualising Transnational Lives for Historical Research

Closely linked to the aforementioned historiographical trends is the heightened interest in the agency of transnational (or global) subjects.[10] Given the specific perspective of this volume, two questions arise: How can we conceptualise actors if

8 Peter Alheit: Biographie und Mentalität. Spuren des Kollektiven im Individuellen, in: Bettina Völter et al. (ed.): *Biographieforschung im Diskurs*. Wiesbaden 2005, 21–45; Thomas Etzemüller: *Biographien. Lesen – erforschen – erzählen*. Frankfurt 2012, 8–13; Hans Erich Bödeker: Annäherungen an einen gegenwärtigen Forschungs- und Diskussionsstand, in: id. (ed.): *Biographie schreiben*. Göttingen 2003, 9–64, esp. 19–20; Volker R. Berghahn and Simone Lässig (eds.): *Biography between Structure and Agency. Central European Lives in International Historiography*. New York 2008; Margit Szöllösi-Janze: Lebens-Geschichte – Wissenschafts-Geschichte. Vom Nutzen der Biographie für Geschichtswissenschaft und Wissenschaftsgeschichte, in: *Berichte zur Wissenschaftsgeschichte* 23 (2000), 17–35; Volker Depkat: The Challenges of Biography. European-American Reflections, in: *Bulletin of the German Historical Institute* 55 (2014), 39–48; Levke Harders: Legitimizing Biography. Critical Approaches to Biographical Research, in: ibid., 49–56; Andreas Gestrich: Einleitung. Sozialhistorische Biographieforschung, in: id., Peter Knoch and Helga Merkel (eds.), *Biographie – sozialgeschichtlich*. Göttingen 1988, 5–28, esp. 14–17.

9 Jo Burr Margadant: Introduction. Constructing Selves in Historical Perspective, in: ead. (ed.): *The New Biography. Performing Femininity in Nineteenth-Century France*. Berkeley, CA 2000, 1–32.

10 Johannes Paulmann: Regionen und Welten. Arenen und Akteure globaler Weltbeziehungen seit dem 19. Jahrhundert, in: *Historische Zeitschrift* 296 (2013), 660–699; Madeleine Herren: Inszenierung des globalen Subjekts. Vorschläge zur Typologie einer transgressiven Biographie, in: *Historische Anthropologie* 13 (2005), 1–18; Bernd Hausberger: *Globale Lebensläufe. Menschen als Akteure im weltgeschichtlichen Geschehen*. Wien 2006; Tobias Weger (ed.): *Grenzüberschreitende Biographien zwischen Ost- und Mitteleuropa. Wirkung – Interaktion – Rezeption*. Frankfurt 2009.

we want to acknowledge the dynamics of their multiple identities and, at the same time, give due consideration to their specific, localised links, with the goal in mind to avoid defining them solely as individuals or groups who crossed boundaries? And given that we do not view them as "heroes" acting autonomously with regard to larger structural settings, how can we explain their agency in its complexity and ambiguity? Trying to cope with both the methodological challenges as well as the perspectives that manifest themselves in these questions, we propose an approach to "mobility and biography" that brings two sociological strands – "rooted cosmopolitanism" and "mobilities" – together with a historical research agenda. We subsume this approach under the term "cosmobilities". We think that this offers a stimulating impetus for analysing transnational lives. We have developed our own approach initially with dictionaries of national biography in and across Europe in the long nineteenth century[11] in mind but its applicability reaches further in time and space.

Applying "Rooted Cosmopolitanism" to Historical Research

In the fields of philosophy and political thought, the term *cosmopolitanism* is primarily used in a normative sense to describe an ideal of world citizenship that corresponds with a harmonious understanding of individuals or groups, crossing geographical, national, cultural or social boundaries. This understanding rests on the further assumption that a cosmopolitan identity can overcome "difference" caused by particularistic notions of belonging.[12] Hence, the meaning of cosmopolitanism overlaps in part with the logics of universalism (inclusion) and

---

11 Although some of the dynamics connected to our approach of "cosmobilities" are not peculiar to the nineteenth century, mobility was, as Jürgen Osterhammel and others have pointed out, one of the century's main features. Jürgen Osterhammel: *Die Verwandlung der Welt. Eine Geschichte des 19. Jahrhunderts*. München 2009, 1290–1291; Christopher A. Bayly: *The Birth of the Modern World, 1780–1914. Global Connections and Comparisons*. Oxford 2004, 1–22. For the changing semantics of mobilities in different historical epochs, pointing also to the fact that mobility in the early modern period often existed independently of spatial movement, see Wolfgang Bonß and Sven Kesselring: Mobilität am Übergang von der Ersten zur Zweiten Moderne, in: Ulrich Beck and Wolfgang Bonß (eds.): *Die Modernisierung der Moderne*. Frankfurt 2001, 177–190.

12 Out of the vast body of literature, see Jeremy Waldron: What is Cosmopolitan?, in: *Journal of Political Philosophy* 8 (2000), 227–243, esp. 238; Carol A. Breckenridge et al.: Cosmopolitanisms, in: ead. et al. (eds.): *Cosmopolitanism*. Durham 2002, 1–14, esp. 12; Andrea Albrecht: *Kosmopolitismus. Weltbürgerdiskurse in Literatur, Philosophie und Publizistik um 1800*. Berlin 2005, 1–9; Pauline Kleingeld and Eric Brown: "Cosmopolitanism", in: Edward N. Zalta (ed.): *The Stanford Encyclopedia of Philosophy* (Fall 2013 Edition). URL: *http://plato.stanford.edu/archives/fall2013/entries/cosmopolitanism/* (23 Apr. 2015); Mike Featherstone: Cosmopolis. An Introduction, in:

particularism (exclusion) – a conceptual pair that has been applied on different levels in the social sciences as a category for the analysis of "difference".[13] Nonetheless, because of its strong normative overtones, most historians still prefer to treat cosmopolitanism as a contemporary phenomenon or descriptive category. And although this catchy label has made a lasting impression on studies of transnational, transcultural and global phenomena, it has only rarely been credited with explanatory power or heuristic value as a concept for critical analysis.[14]

In the social sciences, however, the situation is quite different. Since the 1990s, large-scale attempts, especially among sociologists, have increased to re-define and operationalise cosmopolitanism as an analytical concept. Picking up this trend and embedding it in his own theory of reflexive modernisation, Ulrich Beck in particular became a leading proponent of a "cosmopolitan turn" in the social sciences.[15] Despite the persuasiveness of Beck's arguments, he clearly developed them mainly against the background of challenges for sociological analysis related to the present and not – as is important from a historian's perspective – to the past. In contrast, Sidney Tarrow's concept of "rooted cosmopolitanism"[16] seems to offer a more concrete starting point for historical analyses: On the one hand, Tarrow characterises cosmopolitans as those who strive for world citizenship. Hence, humanity as a whole serves as a central point of reference for their way of being in the world. On the other hand, he argues that cosmopolitan actors are rooted in transnational social relationships, linking them to multiple contexts. Thus distancing his concept from the stereotypical notion

Theory, Culture & Society 19 (2002), 1–16, esp. 8; Garrett W. Brown and David Held (eds.), *The Cosmopolitanism Reader*. Cambridge 2010.

13 Mark Currie: *Difference*. London 2004, 1–20 and 105–126; Ernesto Laclau: *Emancipation(s)*. London 1996, 20–35; Chris Lorenz: Representations of Identity. Ethnicity, Race, Class, Gender and Religion. An Introduction to Conceptual History, in: Stefan Berger and id. (eds.): *The Contested Nation. Ethnicity, Class, Religion and Gender in National Histories*. New York 2008, 24–59, esp. 25.

14 Julia Horne and John Sluga: Cosmopolitanism. Its Past and Practices, in: *Journal of World History* 21 (2010), 369–374, esp. 369–370. On first attempts in this direction, see the workshop on "Kosmopolitismus: zum heuristischen Mehrwert eines wissenschaftlichen Modekonzepts" (organised by Bernhard Gißibl and Isabella Löhr), 12.09.2013–13.09.2013 Mainz, in: *H-Soz-Kult*. URL: *http://www.hsozkult.de/event/id/termine-22553* (24 Apr. 2015).

15 Beck and Sznaider, Unpacking, 1; Ulrich Beck, Wolfgang Bonß and Christoph Lau (eds.): *Entgrenzung erzwingt Entscheidung. Was ist neu an der Theorie reflexiver Modernisierung?* Frankfurt 2004; Ulrich Beck: Mobility and the Cosmopolitan Perspective, in: Weert Canzler, Vincent Kaufmann and Sven Kesselring (eds.): *Tracing Mobilities. Towards a Cosmopolitan Perspective*. Aldershot 2008, 25–36.

16 Sidney Tarrow: Rooted Cosmopolitans and Transnational Activists, in: id. (ed.): *Strangers at the Gates. Movements and States in Contentious Politics*. Cambridge 2012, 181–199. For an earlier version, see id.: *The New Transnational Activism*. Cambridge 2005, 35–56.

of "rootless cosmopolitans", Tarrow stresses that transnational actors remain "rooted" in – i.e. connected to – particular localities and networks.[17]

There are several advantages of such an approach to transnational actors: First, the entanglements between local, national and global contexts in which their agency was shaped and constructed are put into focus. Second, acknowledging the complex dynamics of the lives of such "rooted cosmopolitans" challenges us to pay equal attention to the question of how they coped with their respective situations of transnational mobility and of connectedness in multiple societal environments. As a consequence, "rooted cosmopolitans" could be mediators of transnationalism and internationalism[18] but did not necessarily have to take on this role. For the challenge of finding one's way and place in different contexts could also put transnational actors into a marginalised position and possibly strengthen local attachments and particularistic attitudes. A nuanced approach to those multiple biographies, then, can open up new perspectives on how individuals and groups crossing boundaries negotiated their agency in the past in varying political, social, and cultural circumstances.

"Rooted Cosmopolitans" and Mobility: Movements, Networks and "Motility"

Closely linked to debates about cosmopolitanism and globalisation are the developments in the field of mobility studies. Starting with the programmatic first issue of the journal *Mobilities* in 2006, a "new mobilities paradigm" has been emerg-

17 Id., Rooted Cosmopolitans, 183–185. On a similar argument, yet for the phenomenon of network transnationalism, see Janine Dahinden: "Wenn soziale Netzwerke transnational werden". Migration, Transnationalität, Lokalität und soziale Ungleichheitsverhältnisse, in: Markus Gamper and Linda Reschke (eds.): *Knoten und Kanten. Soziale Netzwerkanalyse in Wirtschafts- und Migrationsforschung*. Bielefeld 2010, 393–420.

18 Our usage of the terms *trans*nationalism and *inter*nationalism points to different nuances in relation to the concept of "nation" as well as "nationalism". Whereas the first term implies a going beyond the "nation" in a rather cultural and non-governmental sense, the second puts more emphasis on boundary crossings that lead, for example, to forms of cooperation between actors representing different "nations" and political interests in an international arena or in intergovernmental organisations, like the League of Nations. Both concepts and the dynamics associated with them overlap, however, on many levels and are furthermore not without ambiguities of their own. On the question of how to define internationalism see, pars pro toto Johannes Paulmann and Martin H. Geyer: Introduction. The Mechanics of Internationalism, in: iid. (eds.): *The Mechanics of Internationalism. Culture, Society, and Politics from 1840 to the First World War*. Oxford 2001, 1–26.

ing.[19] There are obvious points of contact between the fields of mobilities studies and transnational history. Nonetheless, and contrary to recent developments in the fields of cultural studies and anthropology[20], its methodological aspects have not yet been widely received by historians.[21] Mobility studies focus especially on the current increase in migration due to globalisation, interacting systems of mobility and the associated political issues and questions of governance. From a historian's perspective, however, it is not these processes as such but only their current manifestations and practices that seem to be *new* phenomena. But the analytical potential of the field of mobility studies from which historians may benefit becomes clear when looking at Weert Canzler's, Vincent Kaufmann's and Sven Kesselring's proposed division of "mobility" into three sub-components: "movements", "networks" and "motility".[22] While the first two components are rather widely used terms in transnational studies, "motility" – i.e. the capability to become spatially or socially mobile – points to structural prerequisites as well as the intentionality behind individual and collective boundary crossings.

"Motility" therefore relates on the one hand to capabilities and opportunity structures – like education, social status, gender, religion, ethnicity or capital – on which individuals and groups depend in order to move spatially, socially or culturally between different localities and contexts. On the other hand, it also comprises the motivations, strategies and socio-economic or political restraints of actors – i.e. the question of why such movements occur or why transnational and transcultural networks start to exist and which purpose they serve. Hence not only commodities, people and ideas should be taken into account when analys-

19 Kevin Hannam, Mimi Sheller and John Urry: Editorial. Mobilities, Immobilities and Moorings, in: *Mobilities* 1 (2006), 1–22; Tim Cresswell: *On the Move*. London 2006, 1–24; John Urry: Moving on the Mobility Turn, in: Canzler, Kaufmann and Kesselring, Tracing Mobilities, 13–24; Canzler, Kaufmann and Kesselring: Tracing Mobilities – An Introduction, in: ibid., 1–12; Peter Adey et al. (eds.): *The Routledge Handbook of Mobilities*. Hoboken 2014; Bonß and Kesselring, Mobilität am Übergang, 177–190.

20 Silke Göttsch-Elten: Mobilitäten – Alltagspraktiken, Deutungshorizonte und Forschungsperspektiven, in: Reinhard Johler, Max Matter and Sabine Zinn-Thomas (eds.): *Mobilitäten. Europa in Bewegung als Herausforderung kulturanalytischer Forschung*. Münster 2011, 15–29; Johanna Rolshoven (eds.): *Mobilitäten!* Berlin 2014 (= Voyage 10).

21 One exception is, for example, Valeska Huber: Multiple Mobilities. Über den Umgang mit verschiedenen Mobilitätsformen um 1900, in: *Geschichte und Gesellschaft* 36, no. 2 (2010), 317–341; ead.: *Channelling Mobilities. Migration and Globalisation in the Suez Canal Region and Beyond, 1869–1914*. New York 2013.

22 Canzler, Kaufmann and Kesselring, Tracing Mobilities, 3–4. Cresswell, in turn, argues that whereas "movement" is rather an "abstract and scientific conception", pointing to a linear understanding of the relationship between time and space, "mobility is thoroughly socialized" and includes aspects of power and social representation. Cresswell, On the Move, 20.

ing the agency of such "rooted cosmopolitans", but also the impact of opportunity structures[23] and the question of how individuals or groups perceived their chances of mobility. Additionally, and most importantly, focusing on mobility instead of "the nation", without denying that the latter might have been an important – or even the most important – reference point for contemporaries, reveals aspects of those transnational life-courses that otherwise would remain hidden.[24] In such a research setting, it is not only the reflexive side of mobility – i.e. the subjectivity and construction of worlds by those who managed to become spatially or socially mobile – but also its moorings[25] and transformations in time and space[26] that this volume addresses as a whole.

Spatial Dimensions in a "Cosmobile" Research Setting

"Boundaries" and "borders", whose meanings are both comprised by the German *Grenze/Grenzen*, are terms related to multiple dynamics of mobility, encompassing such different phenomena as geographically, politically, socially and culturally coded crossings. Consequently, "boundaries" and "borders" are terms often used in a very broad sense. Although such an openness allows for a flexible and dynamic usage of the concept, it also complicates locating exactly *what* "boundaries" and "borders" transnational subjects are either crossing or have already crossed and how they experienced these multiple mobilities.[27]

Furthermore, "boundaries", "borders" and "space", even when they seem to be politically and territorially fixed categories, are not *per se* powerful but unfold their meaning only through concrete social practices. As Georg Simmel

23 Jürgen Mackert: Opportunitätsstrukturen und Lebenschancen, in: *Berliner Journal für Soziologie* 20 (2010), 401–420.

24 Deacon, Russell and Woollacott, Introduction, 2.

25 Hannam, Sheller and Urry, Editorial, 2.

26 Vincent Kaufmann and Bertrand Montulet: Between Social and Spatial Mobilities. The Issue of Social Fluidity, in: Canzler, Kaufmann and Kesselring, Tracing Mobilities, 37–56, esp. 40–42.

27 On the challenge of conceptualising boundaries and borders, see, for example, Jürgen Osterhammel: Kulturelle Grenzen in der Expansion Europas, in: *Saeculum* 46 (1995), 101–138; Stefan Böckler: Grenze. Allerweltswort oder Grundbegriff der Moderne?, in: *Archiv für Begriffsgeschichte* 45 (2003), 167–220; Monika Eigmüller and Georg Vobruba (eds.): *Grenzsoziologie. Die politische Strukturierung des Raumes*. Wiesbaden 2006; Étienne François, Jörg Seifarth and Bernhard Struck: Einleitung. Grenzen und Grenzräume. Erfahrungen und Konstruktionen, in: iid. (eds.): *Die Grenze als Raum, Erfahrung und Konstruktion. Deutschland, Frankreich und Polen vom 17. bis zum 20. Jahrhundert*. Frankfurt 2007, 7–32; Hans Medick: Grenzziehungen und die Herstellung des politisch-sozialen Raumes. Zur Begriffsgeschichte und politischen Sozialgeschichte der Grenzen in der Frühen Neuzeit, in: Eigmüller and Vobruba, Grenzsoziologie, 37–51.

already pointed out in 1908, in his *Inquiries into the Construction of Social Forms*: "boundar[ies]" – to pluralise his definition – are not "spatial fact[s] with sociological effects, but a sociological reality that is formed spatially."[28] Particularly for such historical settings as East Central Europe, where "boundaries" and "borders" have historically been difficult to define because of the region's multi-ethnic composition, recent studies have shown how phenomena of de- and re-territorialisation can make us overcome pitfalls of the imperial past(s). In such a scenario it is no longer the implementation of the nation-state model but the dynamic and complex entanglements between regional, national, imperial and global levels that are put into the analytical focus.[29] This, in turn, connects to our understanding, which views "mobilities" as both infrastructural prerequisites for actors going beyond borders and influential factors in (re-)shaping and (re-) negotiating boundaries. Furthermore, it is why a dynamic understanding of space is necessary if one-dimensional and static narratives are to be avoided.

This, in turn, also implies that the main features of "rooted cosmopolitanism" and "mobility" which we used as a starting point to conceptualise "cosmobilities" are not self-explanatory when it comes to "boundaries" and "borders", but need to be part of larger reflections about "space" – a category that has gained new interest among historians in the context of the so-called "spatial turn"[30]. Taking these reflections on "space" into account, "cosmobilities" proposes to connect local rootedness, transcultural orientations and global entanglements with insights on mobility and its three defining features: movements, networks and "motility". In doing so, this approach is particularly suitable for putting forward a multi-sided perspective on transnational lives that avoids the pitfalls of merely constructing a new master narrative, as one-dimensional as the binary ones we seek to overcome (e.g. *nation* and *cosmopolitanism*).

---

28 Georg Simmel: *Sociology. Inquiries into the Construction of Social Forms. Vol. 2* (translated and edited by Anthony J. Blasi, Anton K. Jacobs and Mathew Kanjirathinkal). Leiden 2009, 551.

29 Steffi Marung and Katja Naumann: Einleitung, in: eaed. (eds.): *Vergessene Vielfalt. Territorialität und Internationalisierung in Ostmitteleuropa seit der Mitte des 19. Jahrhunderts*. Göttingen 2014, 9–44.

30 On the spatial turn, see Doris Bachmann-Medick: *Cultural Turns. Neuorientierungen in den Kulturwissenschaften*. Reinbek bei Hamburg 2006, 284–328; Matthias Middell: Der Spatial Turn und das Interesse an der Globalisierung in der Geschichtswissenschaft, in: Jörg Döring and Tristan Thielmann (eds.): *Spatial Turn. Das Raumparadigma in den Kultur- und Sozialwissenschaften*. Bielefeld 2009, 103–123; Frithjof Benjamin Schenk: *Russlands Fahrt in die Moderne. Mobilität und sozialer Raum im Eisenbahnzeitalter*. Stuttgart 2014.

Mobility and Biography in and across Europe: An Interdisciplinary Panoply of Transnational Lives

Given the broad subject matter of this volume, the individual articles focus on a wide array of aspects and themes connected to "mobility and biography". Hence, most of the articles either combine both aspects or – if perfect symmetry cannot be maintained – focus on one aspect and reflect on the other along the way. Networks, movements and the capacity to become socially or spatially mobile in and across Europe are not only analysed as structural factors but rather seen as connected to concrete practices of mobility among different groups in the spheres of business, politics and the arts: from Jewish merchants via legal and financial advisors all the way to musicians.

The articles can be grouped around three sub-themes of "mobility and biography", though cross-references exist in most articles: hidden transnational lives and the role of networks, multiple contexts and "rooted cosmopolitans", and, finally, opportunity structures and mobility. Furthermore, the sample represented in this volume has been chosen in a way that each one of the three sub-themes includes a case study that either precedes forms of mobility before the modern nation-state emerged as a leading category or that addresses aspects of "mobility and biography" from an alternative disciplinary perspective, i.e. that of a non-historian.

Hidden Transnational Lives and the Role of Networks

With her case study of members of the Ashkenazic mercantile elite between Warsaw, Frankfurt (Oder) and Amsterdam, *Cornelia Aust* focuses on the role of commercial and familial connections across eighteenth-century Europe. In this context, she discusses what historians have long disregarded: how Jewish merchants shaped these networks, and the strong position of women within them. While networks and boundary-crossings furthered Jewish mercantile interests, they also had an impact on cultural and social practices, like marriage patterns. Combining "mobility and biography" from the perspective of Jewish history in the early modern period, this article points to new insights at the intersection of economy and culture, before the age of Jewish mass migration from Central and Eastern Europe set in during the nineteenth century.

Rainer Liedtke, in turn, views the agents of the Rothschild dynasty as important nodes within an information network characteristic of the nineteenth century. In doing so, he discusses how they placed their mobility at the service of the business success of the Rothschild family. Far from being a homogeneous group, the Rothschild agents, who were located at places where the banking house had not yet established a permanent presence, included Jews as well as non-Jews. Hence, the main selection criterion for employment as an agent in the service of the Rothschilds was not so much, as one might have expected, the factor of shared religious belonging but rather trustworthiness and the willingness to uproot oneself and become spatially and culturally mobile.

Addressing aspects also present in both preceding articles, *Simone Derix* asks how to identify and conceptualise historical actors who have so far remained hidden from the historian's agenda. Focusing on the first half of the twentieth century, her programmatic contribution reflects on how connecting a biographical approach with infrastructures of wealth and mobilities shifts the focus to the central role of legal and financial advisors of the Thyssen family. Though working in the background and thus not attracting much public attention, these "hidden helpers" were decisive brokers of capital for the Thyssens. As experts with very specific transnational knowledge on how to move money in and between different contexts, they occupied a central position in the field of wealth management. Exploring legal as well as illegal means for saving taxes and finding tax havens, they furthered both their employers' as well as their own interests.

Multiple Contexts and "Rooted Cosmopolitans"

Nico Randeraad's contribution considers new insights on transnational knowledge exchange by tracing mobilities among social reformers participating at international congresses between 1840 and 1914. Discussing two overarching topics prevalent in debates about social reform around the turn of the century, he demonstrates that overlapping dynamics between local, national and international contexts shaped the multiple agencies of this sample group. In this context, he makes biographical sketches of four social reformers from different social, political and cultural backgrounds. Whereas aspects of mobility and internationality are permanent companions of the analysed life-courses and professional careers, his study makes us aware of the different logics and dynamics that have to be taken into account when studying the lives of "activists beyond borders".

Approaching this volume's topic from a political science perspective – and hence from a methodological starting point quite different to that of the historical case studies –, *Lucas Geese, Wolfgang Goldbach* and *Thomas Saalfeld* address the relationship between mobility and parliamentary representation in the British House of Commons between 2001 and 2015. They focus in particular on the question of how the voting behaviour of legislators with a "Black or Asian Minority Ethnic" background was influenced by their geographical origin. Whereas more recent immigrants tend to focus strongly on issues connected to transnational mobility, the second generation shows a greater concern for issues of social mobility within Britain and their local constituencies. Analysing parliamentary questions for written answer, this article demonstrates not only the diversity among immigrant legislators, but also when and why they still rely on networks that are marked by ethnicity. In doing so, the authors join biographical distance and transnational mobility with the wider framework of democratic representation in the British House of Commons over the last fifteen years and provide an alternative avenue of how to approach "mobility and biography".

Opportunity Structures and Mobility

Gesa zur Nieden's article discusses the relationship between musicians as an occupational group and their paths of migration in early modern Europe. Her case study focuses in particular on Glückstadt (in today's Schleswig-Holstein), a city that was founded by Christian IV of Denmark and Norway in 1616, and on the biography of Johann Jakob Froberger, a harpsichord player, organist and composer, travelling in the service of the Viennese court across Europe. Hence, it provides insights into the question on what resources musicians could rely on in order to become mobile. This case study is in particular of added value for this issue, for it focuses on historical subjects who lived in a pre-modern setting where mobility was a rather negatively connoted phenomenon that often meant a complete exclusion of vagrant groups from early modern society. Yet even in the case of musicians for whose careers movement and migration played an important role, the attitudes towards such life-courses were in many respects ambivalent, too. Hence, immobility could sometimes be a more promising choice for those musicians who strove to further their social status in a particular locality or to settle in a permanent and stable manner.

The final contribution on opportunity structures by *Alix Heiniger* and *Thomas David* examines the activities of French philanthropists in Geneva during the Belle Époque, widening our understanding of practices to control and restrict migration before the First World War. In doing so, it discusses aspects of spatial as well as of social mobility among French immigrants. Compared to the situation of many other groups of immigrants, their difference was based on citizenship and even more so on the question of social rights and not on language. The authorities of Geneva, notably the police, tried to keep groups who could not provide for their own means of living from staying permanently. In this context, such "undesirable" – mostly unmarried male – immigrants who did not have the capacities to further their social mobility were considered a threat to the interests of the French elite in Geneva as well as to the general public. Pointing to the ambivalent aims of multi-sided philanthropic activities, the article examines also the relationship between the French elite who took care of the immigrant community and the recipients of their philanthropic support.

Whereas we propose "cosmobilities" in our introductory article as a way to operationalise "mobility and biography", in particular for the long nineteenth century, this volume's strength lies in its temporal, spatial and methodological spread. Coming therefore from divergent disciplinary backgrounds (history, music and political science), the selected case studies which start in the early modern period and end in the present address "mobility and biography" from multiple perspectives. It is exactly from this intellectual diversity that we hope to gain impulses for future concretisations of our "cosmobilities" approach.

Acknowledgements

We would like to thank the Fritz Thyssen Foundation for funding our feasibility study *"Cosmobilities" – Transnational Lives in Dictionaries of National Biography across Europe during the Nineteenth Century*. For the year of its duration, we explored how combining historical research questions regarding "mobility and biography" with instruments and methods of the digital humanities can lead to new insights on transnational lives. In this context, and as part of a use case co-developed by members of DARIAH-DE located at the Leibniz Institute of European History in Mainz (Michael Piotrowski) and the Chair of Media Informatics in Bamberg (Andreas Henrich and Tobias Gradl), we have started to develop our own tool for identifying transnational dynamics in national biographies (URL: *http://search.de.dariah.eu/cosmotool/search*).

The concrete idea for this volume, by contrast, stems mainly from insights, challenges as well as perspectives coming up during an explorative workshop that took place in Mainz on January 23–24, 2015; for a conference report, see URL: *http://www.immigrantentrepreneurship.org/article.php?rec=54* (5 Aug. 2015).

We are grateful to the anonymous reviewers whose critical comments helped much to improve the volume as a whole as well as the individual articles. Special thanks go to Joe Kroll (Mainz) for carefully copy editing all articles in this edition of the *European History Yearbook*.

Cornelia Aust

Jewish Mobility in the Eighteenth Century: Familial Networks of Ashkenazic Merchants across Europe

Abstract: *The mobility of the Jewish population in the early modern and modern period is usually taken as a given, though much historical research is, nevertheless, done according to political boundaries. This article examines the possibilities to link biographical studies of members of the Jewish mercantile elite in eighteenth-century continental Europe with a transgeographical approach to mobility. Using examples of Ashkenazic merchant families from Amsterdam, Frankfurt (Oder) and Warsaw, the article looks at the creation of familial and commercial connections among merchants, the role of women in these networks, and the influence of this geographical mobility in the cultural realm. It argues that the study of transgeographical connections – familial, commercial and otherwise – of families or groups of merchants will allow for new insights into the strategies of network building and mobility beyond the highest strata of the Jewish population, like early modern Court Jews.*

The topics of travelling and migration – and thus of spatial mobility more generally – are not new to Jewish history. Living in Jewish communities across Europe and beyond, Jews in the early modern period are usually considered to have been exceptionally mobile in comparison to much of the local population. Individual merchants, rabbis and students, as well as groups of political, religious or economic refugees, made their ways across Europe as well as to the Ottoman Empire and into the "New World". David Ruderman has recently pointed out that "migration was an essential condition of the shaping of Jewish culture in early modern Europe,"[1] and thus can be described as one of the five central elements in early modern Jewish history. This individual and collective mobility not only led to the growth of small Jewish communities and the establishment of many new ones, but also to numerous encounters between Sephardic Jews from Spain, Italian Jews, Ashkenazim moving from central Europe eastward and, from the mid-seventeenth century onward, back to central and western Europe and as far as to the Ottoman Empire. These encounters sometimes caused social tensions but also enabled the

1 David B. Ruderman: *Early Modern Jewry. A New Cultural History*. Princeton, NJ 2010, 24. The other four central elements according to Ruderman are communal cohesion, knowledge explosion, the crisis of rabbinic authority and the emergence of mingled identities.

transfer and juxtaposition of a whole array of different religious and cultural concepts and practices.[2]

Though transregional and transcultural approaches to Jewish history in the early modern period are not new, they still are much less prevalent in actual research than one might expect. Already in 1985, Jonathan Israel not only defined for the first time an early modern period in Jewish history but also emphasised the European component of this history by approaching mainly economic and political developments in early modern Jewish communities across political boundaries.[3] This, however, has not been the standard approach in subsequent decades. Transgeographical[4] approaches of nineteenth-century historians as well as nationalist and/or Zionist approaches to Jewish history emphasised the unity of world Jewry and marginalised local circumstances. Moreover, as Moshe Rosman has pointed out, older transgeographical approaches paid little attention to mobility and connections but rather automatically assumed a commonality among Jews all across the world.[5] Rejecting such approaches, local and regional studies organised – often unconsciously – Jewish history according to political geography, adding a whole array of new and important information on local Jewish communities and their existence within a specific political framework.[6] These studies usually took into account the mutual influence between Jews and non-Jews, which yielded important findings, but equally has its limitations as it often neglects transregional and transgeographical connections. Thus, the importance both of local conditions and influences as well as of phenomena that developed within the Jewish world across early modern political boundaries should be taken as an argument for writing a relational Jewish history. One of the fields that is highly suitable to

2 Ibid., 23–55.

3 Jonathan Israel: *European Jewry in the Age of Mercantilism, 1550–1750*. London [3]1998.

4 Here and in the following I use Moshe Rosman's very general term transgeographical to describe connections that crossed early modern political borders as transnational is an anachronistic term applicable to the modern period only. Other terms can define transgeographical connections more closely. Transregional fits connections across political borders in a rather limited space, such as the Prussian-Polish border region. The term transcultural, in contrast, carries a much more complicated baggage as it makes assumptions about the quality of a contact across political, religious or ethnic borders. For a discussion of cross-cultural trade, see Francesca Trivellato: *The Familiarity of Strangers. The Sephardic Diaspora, Livorno, and Cross-Cultural Trade in the Early Modern Period*. New Haven, CT 2009, 1–3.

5 Moshe Rosman: Jewish History across Borders, in: Jeremy Cohen and id. (eds.): *Rethinking European Jewish History*. Oxford 2009, 15–29, esp. 17–21.

6 Ibid., 22–23.

this approach is that of Jewish economic history and, in particular, the history of commerce and trade[7], which will be at the core of this article.

Biographical approaches are equally not new to Jewish history. Especially in the German-Jewish tradition of the nineteenth century, the biographies of important rabbis and scholars were central to this literary history (*Literaturgeschichte*); often enough, epochs were named after their most important protagonists,[8] though the focus was obviously not on their quite mobile life-courses but on their intellectual and literary achievements. Beyond these prominent figures, the writing of biographies of Jewish men and women in the early modern period suffers from the same problems that all historians face regarding biographical writing: a lack – or at least a relative lack – of suitable sources. Few people left ego-documents or even autobiographical narratives behind, and these are usually not enough to write an individual's biography. This is especially true for those who did not belong to religious or economic elites.[9] The rather well-known autobiographical writings of Glikl bas Yehuda Leib, Jacob Emden, Ber of Bolechov, Salomon Maimon, from the eighteenth century provide important glimpses into those individuals' experiences and into early modern Jewish life more broadly. With Glikl's memoirs we even have extensive writing from a woman and thus biographical material from "the margins".[10] Nevertheless, even with Glikl we need to keep two things in mind. Despite the fact that Glikl as a woman and as a

---

7 For the modern period the work of Sarah Abrevaya Stein has demonstrated the high degree of mobility and interconnectedness of Jews from Europe, North America and South Africa in the ostrich feather trade. Sarah Abrevaya Stein: *Plumes. Ostrich Feathers, Jews, and a Lost World of Global Commerce*. New Haven, CT 2008. Adam D. Mendelsohn's recent book traces the rise of Jewish rag dealers into the clothing trade business in America and the British Empire. Adam D. Mendelsohn: *The Rag Race. How Jews Sewed Their Way to Success in America and the British Empire*. New York 2015. For the early modern period, see in addition to Trivellato, Familiarity of Strangers: Lois Dubin (ed.): *Port Jews of the Atlantic*. Special Issue of *Jewish History* 20, no. 2 (2006); David Cesarani and Gemma Romain (eds.): *Jews and Port Cities, 1590–1990. Commerce, Community and Cosmopolitanism*. London 2006 (= *Jewish Culture and History* 7, no. 1–2 (2004)); Jonathan Israel: *Diaspora within a Diaspora. Jews, Crypto-Jews and the World of Maritime Empires*. Boston 2002.

8 For example in Heinrich Graetz's *History of the Jews*, where one finds the "Epoch of Maimuni (Maimonides)" or "The Mendelssohn Epoch". Rosman, Jewish History across Borders, 18.

9 An example for transgeographical lives difficult to trace is that of refugees after the Chmielnicki uprisings in the Polish-Lithuanian Commonwealth in 1648/49. Adam Teller: Jewish Women in the Wake of the Chmielnicki Uprising. Gzeires Tah-Tat as a Gendered Experience, in: Richard I. Cohen et al. (eds.): *Jewish Culture in Early Modern Europe. Essays in Honor of David B. Ruderman*. Pittsburgh 2014, 39–49.

10 Natalie Zemon Davis: *Women on the Margins. Three Seventeenth-Century Lives*. Cambridge, MA 1995, 5–62. On Glikl, see also Michael Stanislawski: *Autobiographical Jews. Essays in Jewish

Jew can be considered at the margins of historians' view for over two centuries,[11] one should not forget that she – wealthy and articulate – did indeed belong to a small Jewish mercantile elite.[12]

One possibility to at least partly circumvent these problems and to integrate a wide array of sources beyond the individual level might be collective biographies. Aimed not at following an individual's life from beginning to end but rather analysing a group of individuals related by family, geography or occupation – to mention just a few possibilities –, collective biographies allow for the exploration of shared features, views, and mentalities within such groups.[13] In this article, I try to suggest some ways of combining collective biography with the analysis of commercial networks, though these are neither complete life stories nor a network analysis as would be the case in the social sciences. My approach takes merchants and their families, their business partners and clients rather into account as a tightly or more loosely woven web of relations.

Based on an analysis of commercial and familial networks of Jewish mercantile families located in Amsterdam, Frankfurt (Oder) and Warsaw from the mid-eighteenth to the early nineteenth century,[14] I will suggest three topics worthwhile considering when connecting "mobility" and "biography" in historical studies of the transitional decades between the early modern and the modern period. The examples also focus on Ashkenazic Jews instead of Sephardim, who are usually considered more mobile. Though many Sephardic merchants – whether in Amsterdam or Livorno, around the Mediterranean or in the "New World" – overcame longer distances or traded higher volumes, Ashkenazim involved in trade across the European continent or transregionally were nevertheless crucial to supplying the local population, local authorities and armies. In what follows, I will discuss network strategies of those merchants, the role of female family members in those commercial networks, and the impact of those connections on the cultural sphere.

Self-Fashioning. Seattle 2004, 32–53; Monika Richarz (ed.): *Die Hamburger Kauffrau Glikl. Jüdische Existenz in der Frühen Neuzeit*. Hamburg 2001.

11 On the exclusion of those not belonging to the male Christian western elite, see Levke Harders: Legitimizing Biography. Critical Approaches to Biographical Research, in: *Bulletin of the German Historical Institute* 55 (2014), 49–56, esp. 52–53.

12 Moreover, the reliance on a single autobiographical source for the reconstruction of historical conditions and statements about general circumstances of daily life proves to be problematic at least. Robert Liberles: "She sees that her merchandise is good, and her lamp is not extinguished by nighttime". Glikl's Memoir as Historical Source, in: *Nashim. A Journal of Jewish Women's Studies and Gender Issues* 7 (2004), 11–27, esp. 15. See also Stanislawski, Autobiographical Jews, 5–6.

13 Harders, Legitimizing Biography, 53.

14 Cornelia Aust: *Commercial Cosmopolitans. Networks of Jewish Merchants between Warsaw and Amsterdam, 1750–1820* (Ph.D. thesis, University of Pennsylvania, 2010).

Familial and Commercial Connections

Kinship, shared religion and ethnicity were crucial in the formation of early modern business connections, not only among Jewish merchants. Armenians, for instance, formed commercial networks based on shared ethnic origins, while Dutch or Scottish merchants sent their sons to Russia and northern Europe to establish businesses. They maintained their commercial networks based on religion and place of origin. In many cases, however, Christian merchants acculturated to their new domiciles, often via intermarriage with local families of the mercantile elite.[15] Thus, merchants usually were *per se* a highly mobile group.

Jews from across Europe regularly married into other Jewish communities near and far, though, in general, business connections based on marriage ties seem not to have lasted for more than two generations. Marriage among families of the Jewish mercantile elite in central Europe were orchestrated for a variety of reasons, including the increase of a firm's assets, the geographical extension of commercial networks, entry into new branches of business, and the circumvention of state-imposed legal marriage restrictions. Moreover, marriage decisions were made based on social status and economic ability and were central to commercial cooperation.[16]

Though much better known for its Sephardic community, Amsterdam constituted an important hub for Ashkenazic merchants and their commercial networks, especially as a central place for the trade in bills of exchange and for the provision of credit.[17] Familial connections within the Netherlands and across Europe played an important role as the marriage patterns of the Symons family, one of the leading families of Ashkenazic merchant-bankers in Amsterdam show. The two brothers Benjamin and Samuel Symons, whose ancestors had lived in

15 See, for example, Sebouh David Aslanian: *From the Indian Ocean to the Mediterranean. The Global Trade Networks of Armenian Merchants from New Julfa*. Berkeley, CA 2011; Steve Murdoch: *Network North. Scottish Kin, Commercial and Covert Associations in Northern Europe, 1603–1746*. Leiden 2006; Jan Willem Veluwenkamp: Familienetwerken binnen de Nederlandse koopliedengemeenschap van Archangel in de eerste helft van de achttiende eeuw, in: *Bijdragen en mededelingen betreffende de geschiedenis der Nederlanden* 108 (1993), 655–672.

16 Rotraud Ries: Status und Lebensstil. Jüdische Familien der sozialen Oberschicht zur Zeit Glikls, in: Richarz, Kauffrau Glikl, 280–306, esp. 292–295. See also Cornelia Aust: Between Amsterdam and Warsaw. Commercial Networks of the Ashkenazic Mercantile Elite in Central Europe, in: *Jewish History* 27, no. 1 (2013), 41–71.

17 On Amsterdam, see Jan De Vries and A.M. van der Woude: *The First Modern Economy. Success, Failure, and Perseverance of the Dutch Economy, 1500–1815*. Cambridge 1997, 136; Peter Spufford: From Antwerp and Amsterdam to London. The Decline of Financial Centres in Europe, in: *De Economist* 154 (2006), 143–175.

Amsterdam since the early seventeenth century, were mostly involved in trade in diamonds and bills of exchange and provided financial services.[18] They belonged to the small affluent elite of the community, although the volume of their business activities was not comparable to those of the most affluent Sephardic merchants and bankers. In 1743, Benjamin Symons was listed among the ten wealthiest taxpayers in the Ashkenazic community, and his sons Abraham and Emmanuel Symons continued the business in the 1770s after the death of Benjamin and his brother Samuel.[19] The marriage strategies of the Symons family included marriages among close relatives to secure the family firm, multiple marriages into one geographically close family to enhance their shared business and to gain additional capital, and marriages over longer distances to create new business opportunities and broaden their commercial networks.

In an attempt to keep the family business together Benjamin Symons married his son Abraham to Veronica, the daughter of his business partner and brother Samuel Symons. Consanguineous marriages were not uncommon, and among Sephardic Jews they were the norm rather than the exception. For Benjamin and Samuel Symons the cohesion and strength of their shared business was surely the most important incentive for the marriage between their children, though similar marriage arrangements were probably not uncommon in families where capital played a smaller role. The couple's marriage contract, preserved in a Dutch version, stipulated a clear division of the couple's assets, but points to the expectation that both would share their business and the income resulting from it. Veronica Symons brought a dowry of 17,000 Dutch guilders in cash plus various movable goods into the marriage, a hint at the wealth of the family and the importance of dowries for raising liquid capital.[20]

The closest marriage connections were forged between the Symons family and the Boas family in The Hague. Tobias Boas' father was a Polish immigrant dealing in textiles, jewellery and precious metals, and thus was involved in similar fields of trade as the Symons family. Tobias Boas (1696–1782) succeeded in turning the

---

18 J.C.H. Blom, R.G. Fuks-Mansfeld and Ivo Schöffer: *The History of the Jews in the Netherlands*. Oxford 2002, 92 and 100–102. On the immigration of Ashkenazic Jews to Amsterdam in the seventeenth century, see Yosef Kaplan: Amsterdam and Ashkenazic Migration in the Seventeenth Century, in: *Studia Rosenthaliana* 23 (1989), 22–44. On the Jewish involvement in the diamond trade in Amsterdam and London in the eighteenth century, see Gedalia Yogev: *Diamonds and Coral. Anglo-Dutch Jews and Eighteenth-Century Trade*. New York 1978, 110–182.

19 For the economic activities of Amsterdam Jewry in general, see Herbert Ivan Bloom: *The Economic Activities of the Jews in Amsterdam in the Seventeenth and Eighteenth Centuries*. Williamsport, PA 1937, 177–178.

20 Aust, Commercial Cosmopolitans, 96–100.

business into a large-scale banking house of international standing, a career similar to that of many of the more affluent Ashkenazi merchants in the Netherlands.[21] Tobias Boas was married to Sara Symons (b. 1704), the sister of Benjamin and Samuel as well as of Berend Symons (b. 1708), who also was a successful merchant banker. After the death of his first wife, Samuel Symons married Mietje Boas, a daughter of Tobias Boas. Two more children of Boas married children of Benjamin Symons. Thus, the two families were closely linked by marriage ties. These close connections also found expression in the business ties of the two families.

The marriage strategies of the Symons family were closely mirrored by the way they structured their business undertakings. While Emmanuel Symons became responsible for the family's business in Western Europe and the Mediterranean, Abraham Symons took over the Central and East European part of the business. For the commercial venture into Central and Eastern Europe, the Symons family used an additional marriage strategy. Abraham Symons' uncle Berend Symons sent two of his sons away, one of them to Frankfurt (Oder), where he married Hendele, daughter of the affluent merchant Pincus Moses Schlesinger, in 1758. This marriage tie was advantageous for both sides. Simon Symons began a shared business with his brother-in-law Levin Pincus Schlesinger. While the Schlesingers gained easier access to the credit market in Amsterdam, the Symons family extended its ties to one of the most important Jewish families in the textile trade in Prussia. The familial ties of the Schlesingers to Amsterdam were strengthened further with an additional marriage arrangement. In 1763, Levin Pincus Schlesinger travelled with his father to Amsterdam, where he married Margolia Elias Daniels. Two years later, his business partner Simon Symons, whose first wife and only son had passed away, went to Amsterdam to marry Mitje Elias Daniels, a sister of Margolia. The additional financial capital that these weddings brought into the shared business of Levin Pincus Schlesinger and Simon Symons may have provided them with the financial power to offer their services to the Polish king, who made them court suppliers in 1765, the year of Simon Symons' wedding with Mitje Elias Daniels. The ties established through these marriages proved to be strong. Even the quarrels that broke out between Simon Symons and the father-in-law from his first marriage Pincus Moses Schlesinger in the 1780s could not disrupt these ties completely. After Simon Symons' death in Warsaw in 1793, his wife did not return to Amsterdam or follow her brothers to London but remained in Frankfurt (Oder) until her death in 1811. Pincus Moses Schlesinger even bought

21 B.W. de Vries: *From Pedlars to Textile Barons. The Economic Development of a Jewish Minority Group in the Netherlands*. Amsterdam 1989, 41; Blom, Fuks-Mansfeld and Schöffer, Jews in the Netherlands, 102.

a special privilege that allowed her to stay in the city.[22] Though it is difficult to explore the merchants' perceptions of their multiple spatial identities, this example seems to show that both Simon Symons and his wife may have developed a certain feeling of belonging to the Jewish community in Frankfurt.

Economic considerations, however, were not the only reason for Jewish merchants to arrange marriages of their children in different towns, which may be one of the features that distinguishes them from fellow Christian merchants and their commercial and familial networks. Legal restrictions on Jewish communities by the Prussian state aimed at a strict limitation of population growth among Jews. Although a privileged protected Jew (*ordentlicher Schutzjude*), Pincus Moses Schlesinger was originally allowed to pass this status on to only one child. Evidence suggests that matches made for his children and particularly his sons were driven not only by economic considerations but by the need to secure their privileged status. One can trace the paths of four of Pincus Moses Schlesinger's sons.[23] While he passed on his privilege to his oldest son Levin Pincus, who married the aforementioned Margolia Elias Daniels from Amsterdam, solutions for Levin's siblings had to be found.

The most common solution was to emigrate and to find a match in another city, preferably one that provided new economic opportunities as well. Both Alexander Pincus and Abraham Pincus moved to Königsberg in the 1760s. There, Isaac Mendel, the brother-in-law of Pincus Moses Schlesinger, had carried on an extensive wholesale trade with Poland and Russia until his death in 1765. Alexander Pincus Schlesinger received his residence privilege through his marriage to the daughter of the local privileged Jew (*Schutzjude*) Abraham Seeligmann. While the brothers' move to Königsberg solved the problem of their residence privilege, it also was of great importance for their father's business in the city, where they continued their uncle's business.[24] The example of the Schlesinger family fits with a generally large immigration of Jewish men to Königsberg. In the second half of the eighteenth century nearly every second groom came from outside the city, mostly from Brandenburg but also from Silesia, Poland, and the settlements outside of Danzig, as well as from Russia after the first partition of Poland in 1772.[25] This

22 Aust, Commercial Cosmopolitans, 100–104.

23 The register of Jews in Frankfurt (Oder) lists eight children of Pincus Moses Schlesinger, five sons and three daughters. Judentabellen der Stadt Frankfurt (Oder), 1748–1759, Abteilung I, VII, 107 (Stadtarchiv Frankfurt/Oder), 144v–145.

24 Aust, Commercial Cosmopolitans, 104–105.

25 Rolf Straubel: *Die Handelsstädte Königsberg und Memel in friderizianischer Zeit. Ein Beitrag zur Geschichte des ost- und gesamtpreußischen "Commerciums" sowie seiner sozialen Träger (1763–1806/15).* Berlin 2003, 304–305.

underlines the high degree of mobility of Jewish families, many of which were involved in commerce.

Nevertheless, Pincus Moses Schlesinger was not able to marry off all his sons successfully at the appropriate age. The youngest of the male siblings, David Pincus, remained in Frankfurt (Oder) and his age of 43 years at the time of his marriage is suggestive. Neither the Prussian records nor the translation of his prenuptial contract mention any earlier marriage, thus he probably had to wait until a suitable opportunity arrived. When Gittel, the only child of the privileged protected Frankfurt (Oder) Jew Isaac Herz Reiss, turned 20 – her father had died in 1782 when she was 12 – the marriage between her and David Pincus was decided. Thus, David Pincus Schlesinger received the privilege of the first child that had been passed on from Isaac Herz Reiss to his only daughter Gittel.[26] For David Pincus Schlesinger it was a prestigious marriage, but also a very late one.

Marriage strategies of the Jewish mercantile elite took various forms and were driven by multiple motivations. Through marriage ties these merchant families secured their social and economic position, and extended their networks into new places or branches of trade. Moreover, marriage could secure or enlarge the financial assets of a business and open new market opportunities. Finally, marriage was also a means to secure the right of settlement and legal status in places like Prussia where these rights were seriously limited. Though the familial connections described here were often at the core of business undertakings, this does not mean that these commercial networks were restricted to family members or to Jews in general. Both the Symons and the Schlesingers had numerous Christian business partners and regular Christian customers. Similarly, in her memoir the Hamburg female merchant Glikl repeatedly describes reliable Christian business partners of her husband and herself, while not shying away from denouncing unreliable Jewish business partners.[27] Nevertheless, the reconstruction of marriage connections tied to business connections allows us to see a widely woven net of travel and migration across Jewish communities in Europe in more detail than the general claims often made about Jewish connectedness and mobility. Though the example of the Symons and the Schlesinger family put a focus on marriage strategies, the available data concerning their commercial activities, their travels and their involvement in communal matters would allow for a more extensive collective biography tying together the mobility patterns of multiple family member across time and space. Moreover, it is also possible to trace their connections to

---

26 Aust, Commercial Cosmopolitans, 106.

27 Chava Turniansky (ed.): *Glikl Zikhronot. 1691–1719*. Jerusalem 2006, 208–214, 220–222 and 290–296.

other Jewish and Christian merchants at least to some extent and thus to map wider commercial networks.

The Role of Female Family Members

With the case of Glikl as an active merchant with – and later without – her husband, one might inquire in more detail about the role Jewish women played in the framework of their familial and commercial connections. As Glikl's case suggests, women were more than just nodal points in these networks and played important roles in running businesses. However, it is much more difficult to examine their roles within business, including in the cases of the Symons and the Schlesinger families, where we find them only as marriage partners, even if it is very likely that they assumed an active role in business as well.

In the early modern period, women were an inseparable part of the family's economic activities. Commercial and trade laws in Central Europe did not exhibit exclusively patriarchal structures. In urban environments, many Jewish and non-Jewish women were active in retail trade, either as part of their husband's business or on their own. In Polish towns, women, among them many single women, were involved in retail trade, innkeeping, brewing and small-scale moneylending, while noble women took part in running estates.[28] Only towards the end of the early modern period were women increasingly excluded from retail and wholesale trade.[29]

---

28 Merry E. Wiesner: *Women and Gender in Early Modern Europe*. Cambridge ³2008, 101 and 116. See also, Maria Bogucka: *Women in Early Modern Polish Society Against the European Background*. Aldershot 2004, 31–52. Cezary Kuklo: Kobiety w życiu społeczno-gospodarczym miast polski przedrozbiorowej, in: *Kwartalnik Historii Żydów* 207, no. 3 (2003), 391–402, esp. 392 and 401. On the numbers and status of single women in eighteenth-century Poland in general, see Cezary Kuklo: *Kobieta samotna w społeczeństwie miejskim u schyłku Rzeczypospolitej szlacheckiej. Studium demograficzno-społeczne*. Białystok 1998, 117–143 and 219–221. On the noble woman Elżbieta Sieniawska who ran an estate, see Moshe Rosman: *The Lords' Jews. Magnate-Jewish Relations in the Polish-Lithuanian Commonwealth during the Eighteenth Century*. Cambridge, MA 1990, 147–184. On a female Jewish leaseholder on Sieniawska's estate, see Janusz Nowak: Feyga Lejbowiczowa. Arendarka w końskowoli Sieniawskich. Z dziejów gospodarczej aktywności kobiet żydowskich w początkach XVIII wieku, in: *Rocznik Biblioteki Naukowej PAU i PAN w Krakowie* 48 (2003), 211–236.

29 Susanne Schötz: *Handelsfrauen in Leipzig. Zur Geschichte von Arbeit und Geschlecht in der Neuzeit*. Köln 2004, 26–28, 42, 70, 217 and 422–434; Daniel A. Rabuzzi: Women as Merchants in Eighteenth-Century Northern Germany. The Case of Stralsund, 1750–1830, in: *Central European History* 28, no. 4 (1995), 435–456.

Jewish women were similarly, if not more, involved in the economic activities of their families. In German-speaking lands, Jewish women took part in various kinds of commerce, although here as elsewhere most women who appeared in tax registers were widows.[30] One can assume, nevertheless, that they had already been active in commerce during the lifetime of their husbands. If not, it is hard to imagine how they would have been prepared for commercial undertakings. Glikl recounted her regular travels to fairs including one to Leipzig, where she was accompanied only by her 15-year-old son Moses.[31] Beyond autobiographical accounts, archival documentation strengthens the assumption that women regularly accompanied their husbands to fairs. The standardised and printed slip of paper to register Jews entering the city of Leipzig to attend the fair had a space for "wife".[32] Among the various members of the Schlesinger family from Frankfurt (Oder) who travelled regularly to Leipzig to conduct business it was not unusual for their wives to accompany them.[33] Though the registers of Jews attending the Leipzig fair do not show a large number of women travelling to the fairs independently, Pincus Moses Schlesinger travelled to five different Leipzig fairs with his wife Bela during the 1750s.[34]

In the Polish-Lithuanian Commonwealth, eighteenth-century sources suggest that married women pursued their own business in retail trade on noble estates.[35] The will of the wealthy Cracow merchant David Todros Kozuchowski from the mid-seventeenth century also adds to this picture as he "appointed his [...] wife as overseer, power, executrix and governor over the entire estate from the smallest to the greatest item, as of today, for all the days of her life. [...] Thus she will conduct all business as she sees fit and as she desires as she always has [...]."[36]

30 Michael Toch: Jewish Women Entrepreneurs in the 16th and 17th Century Economics and Family Structure, in: *Jahrbuch für Fränkische Landesforschung* 60 (2000), 254–256.

31 Turniansky, Glikl Zikhronot, 416, 454, 472, 484 and 496.

32 Acta die von verschiedenen auswärtigen Handelsjuden über den ihnen zeithero versagten Durchgang durch die Pleißenburg [...] betreffend, 1790, Tit. LI 23, (Stadtarchiv Leipzig), 17.

33 Acta den Handelsjuden Markus Levin Schlesinger aus Frankfurt (Oder) betr. anno 1787, Tit. LI 18 (Stadtarchiv Leipzig), 1, 9.

34 Judenverzeichnisse 1742–1764, 10024 Geheimer Rat (Geheimes Archiv), Loc. 9482/3 (Sächsisches Hauptstaatsarchiv Dresden), 143, 205, 210v, 218v and 224. For more details on travel to fairs, see Aust, Commercial Cosmopolitans, 110–113 and 137–145.

35 Adam Teller: *Kesef, koah, ve-hashpa'ah. Ha-Yehudim ba-ahuzot bet Radzivil be-Lita ba-me'ah ha-18*. Jerusalem 2006, 210–216; Gershon David Hundert: The Role of the Jews in Commerce in Early Modern Poland-Lithuania, in: *Journal of European Economic History* 16, no. 2 (1987), 245–275, esp. 266.

36 Moshe Rosman: How Family Wealth and Power Are Organized. The Will of David Theodore [Todros] Kozuchowski, in: *Early Modern Workshop. Jewish History Resources. Volume 3. Gender,*

A figure similar in many ways to Glikl but different in the outstanding trans-geographical extent of her involvement in business, is Judyta Jakubowiczowa, daughter of Levin Buko, born in Frankfurt (Oder) around 1750. She was born into one of the wealthiest and most influential merchant families of the city. While Glikl, despite travelling to Amsterdam and spending the last years of her life in Metz, was very much rooted in the German-speaking lands, Judyta crossed political and cultural borders. Via her family and business connections she and her business can be seen as an extension of the commercial networks of the Symons and Schlesinger families, who both equally established ties to Warsaw.

Most likely following already established connections between Jewish mercantile families in Frankfurt (Oder) and in or around Warsaw,[37] Judyta moved there in the late 1770s to marry the much older Szmul Jakubowicz Zbytkower. Until his death in 1800, both were closely involved in trade, the processing of agricultural products and army supplying. In the following three decades Judyta continued her and her husband's business on her own and, unlike Glikl, did not remarry, which was rather unusual at the time. Until the end of the Napoleonic Wars she was especially active in army supplying, serving Polish, Prussian, Russian and French troops. To do so, she kept close relations to family members and fellow Jewish merchants from Frankfurt (Oder), among them her brother Philip Levin Buko, who resided in Grodno and after 1812 in the Prussian town of Memel (now Klaipeda in Lithuania). One of her closest business partners, especially in financial matters, became the army supplier and banker Jacob Herz Beer in Berlin, son of Herz Beer, the wealthiest Jewish merchant and one of the communal leaders in Frankfurt (Oder) in the second half of the eighteenth century. Only after the end of the Napoleonic Wars and the creation of the Kingdom of Poland in 1815 did Judyta move into banking, and she continued using her business connections primarily to Prussia and Russia with the support of her family and already existing commercial networks.[38]

Family, and Social Structures. Middleton, CT 2006, 57–58. URL: *http://wesscholar.wesleyan.edu/cgi/viewcontent.cgi?article=1036&context=emw* (15 June 2015).

37 Due to a privilege *de non tolerandis Judaeis* Jews were not allowed to settle in the city of Warsaw since 1527. Only in the second half of the eighteenth century did an increasing number of Jews settle in the estates of Polish nobles (*jurydiki*) around the city or in Praga, a then independent town on the other side of the Vistula. Some settled in Warsaw illegally. Artur Eisenbach: The Jewish Population in Warsaw at the Turn of the Eighteenth Century, in: *Polin* 3 (1988), 46–77; Hanna Węgrzynek: Illegal Immigrants. The Jews of Warsaw, 1527–1792, in: Glenn Dynner and François Guesnet (eds.): *Warsaw. The Jewish Metropolis. Essays in Honor of the 75th Birthday of Professor Antony Polonsky*. Leiden 2015, 19–41.

38 For more details, see Cornelia Aust: Merchants, Army Suppliers, Bankers. Transnational Connections and the Rise of Warsaw's Jewish Mercantile Elite (1770–1820), in: ibid., 42–69, esp. 55–59.

In general, as in the case of Judyta Jakubowiczowa, it is only widowhood that allows a closer look at women's economic role. Aside from a few letters that Judyta wrote and signed herself during her husband's lifetime and most likely while he was travelling, she appears as economically active only after his death. However, one can assume that women would not have been able to take over these activities unprepared upon the death of their husband, but were only able to do so because they had been closely involved in them beforehand. The example of Judyta Jakubowiczowa not only confirms the active involvement of Jewish women in business beyond being marriage partners and nods in family networks, but provides an unusual insight into a transgeographical biography of such a women.

The Cultural Sphere

It was mainly money, but also diamonds and much more mundane goods such as cloth, meat, wood, vodka and grain that were moved along the commercial networks examined here, which were largely but not exclusively run by Jewish merchants, many of them belonging to extended families. Though hard to quantify, it is comparatively easy to identify these goods. However, it is much more complicated to point to the ideas, habits and lifestyles that were negotiated and exchanged along those connections. These multi-directional and often transcultural connections among Jews from across Europe as well as between Jews and non-Jews created a cultural sphere that is difficult to dissect.[39] As Francesca Trivellato has shown, close commercial connections especially in cross-cultural settings did not naturally lead to close cultural interaction or influence: "The cosmopolitan language of business letters did not automatically spawn cosmopolitan feelings of tolerance, mutual respect, curiosity and appreciation of differences."[40]

Despite much greater geographic proximity than among long-distance merchants, cultural differences were felt and expressed even among Jews from the Holy Roman Empire and the Polish-Lithuanian Commonwealth. In the anonymous Yiddish polemical poem *Di Baschraybung fun Aschkenaz un Polak* (A description of Ashkenazim and Polish Jews) the supposedly Polish-Jewish author describes the cultural differences that he experienced during his flight and wan-

39 On the connection between cultural transfer and family connections, see Dorothea Nolde and Claudia Opitz-Belakhal: Kulturtransfer über Familienbeziehungen – einige einführende Überlegungen, in: eaed. (eds.): *Grenzüberschreitende Familienbeziehungen. Akteure und Medien des Kulturtransfers in der Frühen Neuzeit.* Köln 2008, 1–14.
40 Trivellato, Familiarity of Strangers, 17.

derings following the Chmielnicki uprisings in the mid-seventeenth century. With polemical exaggeration he depicts differences in dress, eating habits, economic behaviour, and the use of leisure time.[41] Though the polemical nature of the poem probably exaggerates the differences between the two groups, the text nevertheless points to the fact that the differences between Ashkenazim from German-speaking lands and those from Poland went beyond differences in legal matters (*Halakhah*), customs (*minhagim*) and liturgy.[42]

To return to Judyta Jakubowiczowa, who had moved from Frankfurt (Oder) to Warsaw in the late 1770s, we unfortunately do not know much about how she dealt with the probably drastic change in her cultural environment. Growing up in the Jewish community of Frankfurt (Oder) she was certainly influenced by the inclinations of the wealthy community members towards the early writings of the *Haskalah*, the Jewish enlightenment. Members of the aforementioned Schlesinger family and Judyta's brother subscribed to the 1791 Berlin edition of Psalms with Moses Mendelssohn's German translation and commentary, the Pentateuch edition edited by Aaron Wolfson and Joel Brill (1789) as well as to the 1798 edition of *Sefer ha-Gedarim* (Book of Definitions) published by the *maskil*, follower of the Jewish Enlightenment, Isaac Satanov.[43] In contrast, Judyta Jakubowiczowa's future husband Szmul grew up in a traditional Jewish family in Poland and developed leanings toward Hasidism.[44] When Judyta married her much older husband, he had already been married twice and had four children, who grew up in his household. They most likely spoke some form of Yiddish to each other, though Judyta was fluent in German and wrote passable French, a fact that was important to the extension of their shared business, especially as army suppliers. In the historiography, however, their marriage is often described in rather negative terms, either depicting Szmul as a simple-minded and strictly religious person or Judyta as an arrogant and selfish woman who did not respect her husband and eventually was responsible for the conversion of some of her children.[45]

---

41 Max Weinreich: Tsvey yidishe shpotlider oyf yidn, in: *Filologishe Shriftn. Shriftn fun Yidishn Visnshaftlekhn Institut* 3 (1929), 537–554.

42 See, for example, Moshe Rosman: Innovative Tradition. Jewish Culture in the Polish-Lithuanian Commonwealth, in: David Biale (ed.): *Cultures of the Jews. A New History*. New York 2002, 217–268.

43 See Aust, Commercial Cosmopolitans, 284–285.

44 On the Hasidic leanings among Warsaw's Jewish mercantile elite, see Glenn Dynner: *Men of Silk. The Hasidic Conquest of Polish Jewish Society*. Oxford 2006, 89–116.

45 Most vividly, this narrative is found in the work of the Polish-Jewish historian Ezriel N. Frenk: *Meshumadim in Poilen in 19ten yohrhundert*. Warsaw 1923, 22–32.

Even after the death of her husband in 1800, in the nearly three decades in which she ran the business by herself, she had to manoeuvre among her family members and her Jewish and non-Jewish business partners in a complex cultural field. Her Hasidic stepson Szmul Berek (Bergsohn) as well as her convert son-in-law, the banker Samuel Antoni Frankel, were close business partners. As far as we know, she held a salon in Warsaw in the second and third decade of the nineteenth century following the model of the Jewish salon women in Berlin. Due to her close business contacts with Jacob Herz Beer, originally from Frankfurt (Oder), and her regular travels to Berlin she was also familiar with Beer's wife Amalie, who held a salon in Berlin in the 1820, while her husband was a patron of the early religious reform movement. During her regular visits in Berlin she surely was introduced to this cultural environment.

In Warsaw, by contrast, she was also closely linked to the traditional Jewish community and to Hasidic circles. Though she may not have opposed the conversion of one of her three daughters, her step-daughter, and some grand-children she personally kept ties to the *Hevra Kadisha* (burial society) in Praga, a town outside of Warsaw on the other side of the Vistula (today part of Warsaw). The land that her husband had purchased to establish a Jewish cemetery in Praga in 1780 remained in Judyta's possession after her husband's death. A contract, written in German with Hebrew letters, confirms this in 1810. It is the only preserved document that she has signed with Gitl, the Yiddish form of her name. The contract itself left administration of the cemetery, as well as the profits from selling burial plots, to the *Hevra Kadisha*. In return, the burial society had to pay an annual rent to Judyta and her descendants and to maintain the cemetery properly. This case shows not only how Judyta carried on her and her husband's business after his death, but also that she was sufficiently attached to the Praga Jewish community to remain involved with its traditional-minded leadership.[46]

Judyta's property list and her last will provide a mixed image of her attitudes toward religion and tradition. Upon her death, in 1829, Judyta was one of the wealthiest women in Warsaw, and the state administration promptly ordered an inventory of all her property for tax purposes. This long list appears to confirm that she held highly acculturated attitudes. With the exception of "five pieces of silverware with religious depictions," not a single item is listed that appears to have been a ritual object, nor are there any books, though one must keep in mind that books and ceremonial objects may have been handed down from her husband directly to his sons. She did, however, own a copper engraving of the Russian tsar

46 Aust, Commercial Cosmopolitans, 295.

Alexander I and a painting of the Polish Prince Josef Poniatowski, items that mark her close connection to the government and possible admiration for Alexander I.[47]

Judyta's last will complicates the image of an acculturated woman as much as it confirms it. She penned, in German, two different but fairly similar versions of her will shortly before her death.[48] Among her family members, she divided her assets without regard to the religion of the descendants. Similarly, Judyta assigned considerable amounts to charity, dividing them between Jews and Christians, although the sum for Jewish institutions was about one third higher than that for non-Jewish institutions. Even more surprisingly, she stipulated a gift of 5,000 gulden to be distributed to the poor "without regard to religion" during her burial. Giving to the poor in one's will was customary in Judaism, but giving to Christians, much less "without regard to religion," was decidedly not.

In contrast, Judyta's stipulations in her will regarding her own burial suggest a close affinity to Praga and to the cemetery she and her husband Szmul had purchased. She decided that the cemetery was to be transferred to the burial society of Praga or of Warsaw a year after her death. Although a new Jewish cemetery had been opened in Warsaw in 1806 and a number of family members, including her step-son Berek Szmul, were buried there, she insisted on being laid to rest at the old Praga cemetery:

> I ask to be buried quietly at my churchyard [sic] in Praga. [...] Moreover, three learned men shall pray for me for one year in my synagogue no. 150 in Praga; each of them will receive three hundred gulden for the year, and another three hundred gulden shall be given for the light to burn for a whole year.[49]

Her wish emphasised her close affinity to her and her husband's property in Praga beyond its mere material value – a marker of a possible local identity –, since she insisted on being buried in her cemetery and being prayed for in her synagogue, though she had probably not attended the latter on a regular basis. She observed the Jewish tradition of having learned men pray for her after her death and light a candle in her memory. Yet her use of the word "churchyard" (Kirchhof) for the Jewish cemetery suggests a high degree of acculturation. Judyta Jakubowiczowa certainly belonged to the most acculturated group of Warsaw Jewry, but she remained

47 Artur Eisenbach and Jan Kosim: Akt masy spadkowej Judyty Jakubowiczowej, in: *BŻIH* 39 (1961), 88–143, esp. 102 and 115.

48 The first version is dated February 27th, the second March 5th 1829. The differences between them are minimal. Kancelaria Kowalewskiego, syg. 8, no. 675 (Archiwum Państwowe, Warsaw), 159–163v.

49 Kancelaria Kowalewskiego, syg. 8, no. 675, 162v–163. The synagogue was situated in one of the houses that belonged to Judyta's property.

attached to essential Jewish customs, at least with regard to her own burial. These limited insights into the life of Judyta Jakubowiczowa and her environment in Warsaw suggest a high degree of cultural adaptation and flexibility among those Jewish merchants and Jewish travellers in general who regularly crossed not only political but also cultural boundaries within continental Europe at the turn from the eighteenth to the nineteenth century.

Conclusion

The examples of familial and commercial contacts between Jewish merchants across the European continent examined here can only provide a glimpse into the complex questions of network building, mobility and belonging. Though in general not different from other Christian or Jewish familial and (on this basis) commercial networks, the connections and spatial mobility of Ashkenazic merchant families exhibit some peculiarities. Ethnicity played a role in so far we do not find any intermarriage into Sephardic families, though in Amsterdam, where Ashkenazim and Sephardim lived in close proximity, shared business was common, as were Christian business partners and clients. Nevertheless, it seems that the Ashkenazic merchants examined here less frequently had Christian business partners than did their Sephardic coreligionists.[50] Moreover, legal restrictions on Jews played a crucial role in decisions about spatial mobility. Though economic considerations were important in forging marriage ties, legal considerations were no less so. Finally, these Ashkenazic merchant families moved mostly eastward, a fact that counters the common narrative of Jewish westward migration in eighteenth-century Europe, even though they were numerically in the minority.

Merchant families are just one field for examining the mobility of individuals and groups in collective biographical studies, but they constitute a particularly rewarding one. Trade and commerce are especially suitable for the study of transgeographical mobility in early modern and modern Jewish history, although similar studies for rabbis and students should prove to be equally fruitful. The merchants' mobility included the crossing of political as well as of cultural borders and led to regular contact not only between Jews of different social and geographical backgrounds, but also between Jews and Christians, men and women. A biographical study of numerous family members spread across Europe including if possible also unrelated Jewish as well as Christian business partners casts

50 For Sephardic connections with non-Jewish trading partners, see Trivellato, Familiarity of Strangers, 194–223.

a wider view of these commercial networks. In the cases examined here, it shows the families outside their local contexts. Such an approach may also allow historians to move away from biographical considerations of the upper class, in this case often Court Jews, who made up only a very small minority of the Jewish population. Though the families examined here still belonged to the Jewish mercantile elite, it should nevertheless be possible to inquire into the lower levels of Jewish society by examining the movements and familial connections of Jewish retail traders or the wandering poor.

Having followed Jewish merchant families from Amsterdam in the west to Warsaw in the east at the turn from the early modern to the modern period, we have still seen primarily issues linked to early modern mercantile mobility. The establishment of commercial connections via marriage was central and legal aspects, in the sense of circumventing legal restrictions aimed at Jews, played an important role. If we look at the most important banking houses of nineteenth-century Warsaw – most of which had Jewish owners or owners who had converted to Christianity[51] – new parameters appear. The ancestors of most of these families had immigrated to Warsaw around the turn of the century from both towns and villages close by, from the Prussian-Polish borderlands or, in a few cases, from as far as Amsterdam. However, they now found themselves in a setting much more characterised by the aspirations of an emerging Polish national movement and to some extent considered themselves Polish Jews. Nevertheless, they were part and parcel of the transnational banking scene of the nineteenth century and connected by business and family with other Jewish and Christian banking houses across Europe.[52] However, they have hitherto been recognised and researched mainly as Polish-Jewish bankers without taking their transnational mobility and connections into consideration.

---

51 François Guesnet: Banking, in: *YIVO Encyclopedia of Jews in Eastern Europe*. URL: *http://www.yivoencyclopedia.org/article.aspx/Banking* (5 Aug. 2015).

52 For transnational ties among nineteenth-century Jewish banking houses, see Rainer Liedtke's article in this volume.

Rainer Liedtke

Agents for the Rothschilds: A Nineteenth-Century Information Network

Abstract: *This article discusses information transfer in nineteenth-century European merchant banking by analysing the leading banking dynasty of the age, the Rothschilds. The gathering, transfer and utilisation of information happened through people who were constantly crossing borders, sometimes physically but more often culturally. This was particularly true of the rather abstractly named "business agents", a highly heterogeneous group of people who were based in locations where the Rothschild banks did not have a permanent presence. There they carried out business transactions for their principals and at the same time gathered and forwarded a great variety of news and information, which enabled the Rothschilds to make decisions.*

Introducing the Rothschilds

Information – fast and in particular reliable information – was and is the key to decision-making in the financial world. This is as true now as it was for the emerging merchant bankers of Tuscany in the thirteenth century, the trading companies of the Holy Roman Empire and the merchants of seventeenth-century Amsterdam, who introduced bills of exchange as their prime financial instrument. The more transregional and transnational financial interactions became, the more complex was the task of gathering information. When merchant houses of Western Europe developed into fully fledged private banks from the late eighteenth century onwards, they also turned towards financing states and governments, which emphasised the need for consistent and reliable political intelligence. This article discusses information transfer in nineteenth-century European merchant banking, as exemplified by the leading banking dynasty of the age, the Rothschilds. The gathering, transfer and utilisation of information happened through people who were constantly crossing borders, sometimes physically but more often culturally. This was particularly true of the rather abstractly named "business agents", a highly heterogeneous group of people who were based in locations where the Rothschild banks did not have a permanent presence. There they carried out business transactions for their principals and at the same time gathered and forwarded a great variety of news and information, which enabled the Rothschilds to make decisions.

After a brief introduction to the history of the Rothschild banking houses of the nineteenth century, the agents' network will be looked at in more detail. Of particular interest are whether there were guiding concepts for its formation and maintenance and what kind of selection criteria were applied for employing agents. The day-to-day working of the information network leads to the question of the issue of mobility in the agents' biographies. This study is based mainly on source material. The Rothschild Archive London has ample holdings containing the correspondence of more than one hundred business agents working for the different Rothschild houses, mainly during the nineteenth century. However, the nature of the material entails that such correspondence is often incomplete. Moreover, we only have sparse information about the correspondence of the Rothschilds with their various agents, since letters leaving the Rothschild houses were usually not kept in copy and cannot be found elsewhere anymore. Some of the agents left behind a variety of sources themselves, in particular those who had at some point in time been bankers in their own right. Most, however, vanished without a trace, and the letters to the Rothschilds are often the sole documents of the existence of a fair number of individuals.

Five Rothschild banking houses, working in close cooperation with each other, dominated European banking between the 1820s and the 1870s, when the much larger joint stock banks generally broke the hegemony of private banks over European (and for that matter world) finance.[1] The origin of the business was a merchant house built up by Mayer Amschel Rothschild in Frankfurt from the 1770s onwards which, as was the trend of the time in merchant banking, increasingly turned towards financial transactions. In order to cut out the middleman in the profitable cloth trade within the British market, in 1798 the company patriarch sent one of his five sons, Nathan Mayer Rothschild, to Manchester. Some years later he moved to London and founded his own merchant bank there. In particular through bullion speculation and the facilitation of financing British continental military exploits during the Napoleonic Wars, *N M Rothschild & Sons* soon became one of the dominating financial forces in London. Arguable the most important component in explaining its lasting success was the fact that Nathan's four brothers were likewise heading private banking houses in four other European locations. All five cooperated closely with each other for decades to come: Amschel Mayer Rothschild, the oldest brother, took over the Frankfurt house after the father's death in 1812. James Mayer, the youngest, settled in Paris in 1810 and ran *De Rothschild Frères & Cie*. In 1821 Salomon Mayer went to Vienna

1 This brief outline follows the definitive general Rothschild history to date: Niall Ferguson: *The World's Banker. The History of the House of Rothschild*. London 1998.

to direct *S. M. von Rothschild & Söhne*, while Carl Mayer, the second-youngest brother, travelled to Naples in the wake of an Austrian military intervention in the capital of the Kingdom of the Two Sicilies and set up a banking house there. This, however, was handled not so much as an independent business than a branch of the Frankfurt parent house. Apart from conducting the traditional bills of exchange business, all houses engaged in issuing government bonds for practically all European and a number of Latin American countries, were active in financing industrial enterprises and railways, bought and sold specie and traded in a great variety of commodities. Though nominally independent, the houses arranged many transactions together, helped each other through temporary liquidity problems and, most importantly, through extremely regular correspondence shared political and economic intelligence practically on a daily basis.

The Information Network and the Role of Agents

It is important to note that the agents' network did not develop according to a master plan,[2] but evolved according to changing business interests of the Rothschilds and the opportunities and markets available to them. In doing so, it was not a static but a dynamic phenomenon, pointing to the mutual influences of situational factors and larger structures. The network's origins can be found in the later years of the Napoleonic period. One has therefore to bear in mind that the Rothschild family itself built up an international network of nominally independent banking houses during the first quarter of the nineteenth century, with which their agent network developed in tandem. The earliest permanent contacts are recorded in Flanders and the Netherlands. Rotterdam, Dunkirk, Amsterdam, Antwerp and Brussels were early nodes in a network in which the Rothschilds predominantly traded in "English goods". Political intelligence during the first decade of the century was merely a by-product of the agents' correspondence, which focused very much on market and stock prices. Towards the end of the Napoleonic wars, Hamburg rose quickly in importance as an additional focal point of the network. At this time, we also find the first transcontinental agencies, namely in Rio de Janeiro. During the French occupation of Portugal, the Portuguese government had been relocated to Brazil, which at the time was one of the world's biggest producers of gold. The company *Samuel & Philips* went to Rio with the court and government and dealt in precious metals with various European houses, but pre-

2 This account is a brief summary of Rainer Liedtke: *N M Rothschild & Sons. Kommunikationswege im europäischen Bankenwesen im 19. Jahrhundert*. Cologne 2006, passim.

dominantly with the Rothschilds. One of the partners, Moses Samuel, had married a sister of Nathan Rothschild's wife Hannah.

At the time of the rapid rise of the Rothschilds from around 1820, the agents' network enlarged enormously. Further North Sea ports were added and a large number of agencies founded in France and the Mediterranean, and also in Eastern Europe. This was the time when the Rothschilds became a truly pan-European and, to an extent, global financial force. Agents were placed in locations which were central to certain businesses, usually ports, but also in political decision-making centres of which there were many, reflecting the political fragmentation of the European continent at the time. This was particularly true of pre-unification Italy, but also for France and Spain. The German states were comparatively underrepresented, presumably because Amschel Rothschild in Frankfurt was controlling most of the financial dealings there himself. Several years before 1820, the Rothschilds began with the emission of government loans for a number of European states. This business kept growing and required particularly reliable political information.

In Latin America, the cities of Salvador (Bahia), Valparaiso and Havana joined Rio as focal points of Rothschild agencies. Here, trade in commodities such as cotton, sugar and tobacco, but also silver and gold, was in the foreground, not the provision of financial services. Hence, depending on the context, the business activities of the Rothschilds took on different shapes and furthered different goals.

From the 1830s to the 1850s, the network did not grow very much in size but it transformed its character, often in accordance with changing business requirements. Some of the agents, such as Weisweiller in Madrid, Bleichröder in Berlin or *Morpurgo & Parente* in Trieste, became more important nodes in the network and also corresponded intensively among each other. Generally speaking, many agents included a lot more political intelligence in their despatches to the various Rothschilds than during the earlier part of the century. In particular the development and spread of the electric telegraph and news agencies from the 1840s onwards decreased the value of pure business information, since they were common knowledge at least for those who subscribed to the required services, as all bankers did. Now, the evaluation of the course of business and in particular strategic counselling on the likely course of political events were the kind of high-value information the principals expected from their agents.

Finding and Keeping Agents

Various paths led to an appointment as a business agent to the Rothschilds. In the same way as the entire network of agents was not built up according to a strategic plan, there was also no clear-cut recruiting scheme for its individual members. One very obvious way of finding people who informed the Rothschilds on a regular basis was to turn to business partners with whom one or several of the houses had longer-standing relationships and ask them to regularly forward political and business intelligence. Sometimes they started by simply conveying stock exchange prices and later became more and more detailed. These were usually bankers and merchants in their own right who hoped for Rothschild commissions and therefore provided the family with all kinds of information about their place of residence they judged to be useful. What is important to note is that the judgement whether an agent of this kind was to be trusted was left to one of the Rothschild family members who made the initial contact. If one Rothschild house confirmed its reliability, others also accepted advice from such a source. It was quite unusual for such agents to feed regular intelligence into the Rothschild information network. If there were any noteworthy political developments, they included them in their briefs. If not, they may not have written at all or they limited themselves to regular stock exchange movements.

When it comes to the many agents specifically appointed and sent out by the Rothschilds, recruitment was usually far more elaborate. Here, the family placed the utmost importance on trust, and there were two principal ways of earning it before becoming an agent: through being a relation of the family or through having worked for one of the houses for a considerable amount of time. In some instances this was combined. Mayer Davidson, one of the early agents, came to London from Germany in 1803 and some years later began working for Nathan Rothschild there. In 1816 he married a sister of Nathan's wife Hannah, of the highly influential Barent Cohen family.[3] During the late Napoleonic period Davidson was sent to Amsterdam to coordinate a complex smuggling operation for procuring continental coins for British troops on the Iberian Peninsula. Nathan had been charged with this task by the British government and needed trustworthy middle-

3 Hannah was the daughter of Levy Barent Cohen, London's leading diamond trader in the late eighteenth century, who was also one of the pre-eminent leaders of the city's Ashkenazi Jewish community. Details about the marriage arrangement can be found in Herbert Kaplan: *Nathan Mayer Rothschild and the Creation of a Dynasty. The Critical Years, 1806–1816*. Stanford 2006, 8–10.

men to execute this dangerous but highly profitable business.[4] In later decades several other agents, who had usually started as clerks in one of the banking houses of the Rothschild dynasty and went on to represent the family's interests in certain locations, married Rothschild offspring or other more distant relations. It must be emphasised, however, that such men never gained access to the decision-making circle of the family but instead maintained their own business interests separately, albeit profiting significantly from contacts to the Rothschild network.

Several of the agents also married among each other. The best examples are the families Weisweiller and Bauer of Madrid and Morpurgo and Landauer of Trieste. While Weisweiller was the son of a Jewish money changer from the Frankfurt ghetto of the eighteenth century who had good contacts to the Rothschilds, Bauer – who identified culturally as a German – was a Hungarian with whom the Rothschilds had business contacts and who joined Weisweiller in the 1830s as their representative in Madrid.[5] Their families soon intermarried, and both became important Spanish bankers in their own right. During the 1850s and 1860s various Bauer relations married, at the explicit instigation of James de Rothschild from the Paris house, into the Rothschild agency *Morpurgo & Parente* of Trieste. Such strategies ensured that their business interests in Madrid and Trieste, two highly important business locations without a permanent Rothschild presence, were covered in the long run by trustworthy representatives.[6]

Some of the earlier agents, who had faithfully worked for the Rothschilds, also introduced their sons to the information network. That was true for Mayer Davidson, whose sons Lionel, Nathaniel and Benjamin (the two older children obviously being named for Rothschild family members) worked for decades as agents in various locations. An extreme case of an agent "dynasty" was the Cullen family, originally from the port of Folkestone. They were so-called "forwarding agents" who cared for speedy and discrete shipping of goods and information across the English Channel for the Rothschilds. Several generations of family members were in service with the English branch of the family, usually in subservient positions. In the twentieth century, some Cullens appeared as porters or butlers at the bank in the City of London.[7]

---

4 Rothschild Archive London (RAL): XI/112/20, Mayer Davidson, London to J.C. Herries, London (15 Dec. 1815); Ferguson, World's Banker, 94–96.

5 For a detailed account of Rothschild activities in Spain, see Miguel A. López-Morell: *The House of Rothschild in Spain, 1812–1941*. Farnham 2013.

6 Alfonso de Otazu: *Los Rothschild y sus socios en España*. Madrid 1987, 445–446. See also the interesting account of the extremely close interpersonal relationships with the Jews of the Frankfurt ghetto in Amos Elon: *Der erste Rothschild. Biographie eines Frankfurter Juden*. Reinbek bei Hamburg 1996, 11–62.

7 RAL: 000/921, Herbert Elton: *The Best Club in London*, Manuscript, undated c. 1930.

Family relations merited trust, although if they did not perform well, they were quickly excluded from important positions within the information network. Only born Rothschilds were always trusted, and the quintessential criterion for having a Rothschild bank in a certain location or not was whether a Rothschild was willing to move there. St. Petersburg, then the Russian capital, and New York, the emerging financial capital of the Americas, were cases in point. The former city held no appeal for a Rothschild because of the blatant anti-Jewish attitudes within much of Russian society but also its political elite and leaders, not to mention the uncomfortably cold weather.[8] In the case of the US, a lack of business judgement prevented the setup of a house, because no Rothschild found the American market important enough to settle there, until it was too late and the scene was dominated by other private and later the joint stock banks.[9]

In New York we also find the only real failure of the agents' network. Here distance and poor personal judgement combined to the disadvantage of the family. The German-born August Schönberg, who had joined the Frankfurt house as a clerk at the age of fifteen in 1813, was sent to New York in 1837 to sort out some financial dealings which had become disorderly during a trading crisis. Afterwards he was supposed to sail on to Havana to attend to Rothschild interests in Spanish-Cuban trade. However, Schönberg had other plans. He changed his name into Belmont, rented an office on Wall Street and told everybody there that he was acting as a Rothschild agent from now on. The various Rothschild houses were furious about this, yet they could not intervene or control such an event due to the enormous geographical as well as communicative distance. They were forced to put up a brave front, since Belmont had started discounting papers in their name. Having established himself in the market, Belmont converted to Christianity, since this gained him entry into New York society. He began to get involved in Democratic Party politics up to a very high level, married into a "good local family" and continued having business with and for the Rothschilds, although he had clearly emancipated himself from them at a very early stage.[10] The family always complained about him in their letters, yet they never dissociated themselves completely from Belmont, since the North American market at the time worked well enough for them and played second fiddle to their European and Latin American engagements.

8 Liedtke, N M Rothschilds & Sons, 106–107 and 168–185.

9 This process is being described in Lance E. Davis and Robert E. Gallman: *Evolving Financial Markets and International Capital Flows. Britain, the Americas, and Australia, 1865–1914*. Cambridge 2001, esp. chapter 3.

10 Irving Katz: *August Belmont. A Political Biography*. New York 1968.

Payment for Information

There are scarce indications in the sources that the Rothschilds payed their agents. Obviously those agents who also had businesses in their own names did not receive any remuneration. But the appointed agents sometimes did, and they all had certain amounts at their disposal to cover costs. And they also could trade in their own name, albeit on a much smaller scale. At the time this was perfectly normal, not only for agents but also for clerks working at the bank. What today would be called insider trading was commonplace in nineteenth-century finance and part of the salary package of employees of financial institutions.[11] All agents profited from having business relations with the Rothschilds, and did so in three ways. First, Rothschild agents enjoyed a tremendous reputation. Being in regular contact with the preeminent financial dynasty of its time boosted everybody's credibility. Second, the agents not only sent information to the Rothschilds but also received information from them. They were thus part of the whole network of intelligence. The depth of involvement varied, but there cannot be any doubt that agents were able to tap into the pool of (usually privileged) economic and political news to which others could not have had such easy access. Third, agents were favoured by the Rothschilds with business deals. That could include loan emissions or a simple deal in goods which went through their destination. In the long run, the quality and volume of such deals was certainly sufficient to boost the finances of any agency. Therefore, payment for information as a positively connoted way of capital leverage cannot always be traced directly but, as this example shows, at least indirectly.

Interesting is the Rothschilds appraisal of the earning potential of their agents and, for that matter, their employees. The family was confident that well-remunerated staff were likely to be motivated and, much more importantly, loyal. Amschel Rothschild, the principal of the Frankfurt house, wrote in 1816 to his brother James in Paris about Friedrich Gasser, their future representative in St. Petersburg:

> You may take Gasser with you to St. Petersburg when the time is right. He is a [...] person. I allowed him to earn 400 thalers here. He has received a brokerage fee from the Seehandlung in London, where I have bought back something. This brings about friendship[12], and

11 See Jehanne Wake and Kleinwort Benson: *The History of Two Families in Banking*. Oxford 1997, 68.

12 The word "friendship" (*Freundschaft* in the original *Judendeutsch*) is a commonplace term which does not denote emotional attachment but is rather used as a synonym for "trust".

> it is better I let him earn something openly than through stealing. One must let him earn something because one cannot do business without people like him.[13]

Agency costs, an important consideration when running a multinational business operation, must have therefore been kept relatively low. This is a mere assumption: we lack the hard data to prove it, since there are few records detailing remuneration, expense accounts and costing for running agencies. Agency costs fall into two categories. One is the straightforward payment of agents and taking care of their business expenses. The other is more difficult to ascertain because it concerns the amount of money agents make on the side *without* the consent of their principals.[14] It can be assumed that in particular this second type of costs was kept at a minimum in the case of the Rothschild network. The simple reason behind this was expediency. Someone employed by the Rothschilds or with regular business contacts to them would have been rather foolish to risk jeopardising this relationship, since throughout much of the nineteenth century, the family had no equal in the sheer volume of its financial transactions or political leverage. In that sense, the Rothschilds can hardly be investigated as a "typical" financial dynasty of their time; their information network was not the norm in banking, but was exceptionally well developed. This puts a clear limit to using findings from the history of the Rothschilds to explain European financial history.

Blurring Religious Boundaries? Jewishness as a Selection Criterion for Agents

The Rothschilds were Jews, and it was unthinkable to them to marry non-Jews. Although the original five brothers and their offspring varied in their standards of religious observance, none of them ever contemplated conversion as a vehicle for social advancement. The obvious question is whether religion played an important role in their selection of business partners and in particular of their representatives. One could expect that in a world where Jews were often rejected, disadvantaged or even persecuted, a coreligionist would be someone to put trust in. Ethnicity, after all, might be considered a highly reliable characteristic when it

---

13 RAL: XI/109/5A, Amschel von Rothschild, Frankfurt to James de Rothschild, Paris, undated, approximately late 1816. Translation by the author.

14 An elaboration of "agency costs" can be found in Ann M. Carlos and Stephen Nicholas: Agency Problems in Early Chartered Companies. The Case of the Hudson's Bay Company, in: *Journal of Economic History* 50, no. 4 (1990), 853–875, esp. 856–857.

is assumed to be a stable and unchangeable feature. Especially in the nineteenth century, people of the same ethnic or ethno-religious background usually shared similar origins, moved in the same circles and shared many values.[15] However, while a fair number of the business agents of the Rothschilds were Jews, many others were not. The fact that a disproportionately high number of men involved in banking and finance in nineteenth-century Western and Central Europe were Jews is definitely responsible for a high proportion of the agents being Jewish. Nevertheless, it would have been easy for the Rothschilds exclusively to deal with and employ Jews, yet they did not do so. Trying to find an answer to why this was not the case, two reasons can be identified: First of all, it was clear to the Rothschilds that honesty and loyalty were not necessarily functions of one's ethnic or religious background. There are countless letters written by various Rothschilds in which they complained bitterly about "this Jewish crook" or that "miserable Jewish rascal" when evaluating a poor or even disloyal performance of a business relation or agent. The above-mentioned August Schönberg/Belmont of New York was a case in point. Second, and this seems more important, an exclusively Jewish network of information gatherers would have been much more limited in its scope and in its ability to procure intelligence. It would have been far more self-referential than a network which was heterogeneous in as many respects as possible, so that its members had access to various circles of people and in turn to their information.[16]

---

15 Frederik Barth: *Ethnic Groups and Boundaries*. Boston 1969, 15. With reference to Barth, the discussion of Jewish "ethnicity", especially in nineteenth-century Europe, has progressed further. Till van Rahden has suggested the valuable concept of "situative ethnicity", meaning that being part of an ethnic group has a changeable significance which depends on concrete life situations or social contexts. See Till van Rahden: Weder Milieu noch Konfession. Die situative Ethnizität der deutschen Juden im Kaiserreich in vergleichender Perspektive, in: Olaf Blaschke and Frank-Michael Kuhlemann (eds.): *Religion im Kaiserreich. Milieus – Mentalitäten – Krisen*. Gütersloh 1996, 409–434, esp. 420–421. A comparative study of Jewish self-perceptions in France and Germany has convincingly established that already in the late eighteenth and early nineteenth century Jews identified primarily as an ethnic group, or rather that they generated a multitude of ethnic concepts. See Philipp Lenhard: *Volk oder Religion. Die Entstehung moderner jüdischer Ethnizität in Frankreich und Deutschland, 1782–1848*. Göttingen 2014, esp. 23. The Jewish Rothschild agents demonstrated that while their Jewishness might have mattered a great deal for their private social life and contacts, it held preciously little significance in the business sphere.
16 The classic study elaborating on this factor is Mark Granovetter: The Strength of Weak Ties, in: *American Journal of Sociology* 78 (1973), 1360–1380.

The Agents' Sources of Information

Where did the agents get their information? Obviously a lot of business details and some political intelligence were out in the open and available from stock exchange rate sheets or newspapers. Before the invention of the electric telegraph and even for some time afterwards, for such information one needed people on the ground at distant locations to send them on to decision-making principals. This was the bread-and-butter business of most agencies. However, it was particularly the more privileged and less easily obtained information that the Rothschilds and all other bankers and decision-makers were after. Two key factors helped agents in obtaining it: First, access to politicians and business people of rank. Although many agents were of rather humble origin themselves, the fact that they represented the most important bankers of their time virtually guaranteed them the attention of the highest levels of society in their various locations. That included the relevant government officials and sometimes even the rulers themselves. Second, the Rothschilds and their agents assumed, as did everybody in business and finance at the time, that especially ministerial personnel divulged important information or favoured one with state business. Yet it came at a price, for bribes were expected and freely given. Rare exceptions to that rule were duly noted. Christian von Rother, Prussia's plenipotentiary for disbursing French indemnity payments after 1815 was such a case. Amschel von Rothschild wrote to his brothers that "Rother has his system and we cannot do anything about that because Rother is not a man who can be bribed".[17] For almost everybody else, bribery, at least in the case of the Rothschilds and their staff, usually did not mean the payment of certain sums as cash in hand but maybe the arrangement of a favourable credit, help with the purchase of something or inclusion in lucrative future business undertakings.

Mobility and the Functioning of the Information Network

Today we naturally see the financial sector as a global player in a globalised economy. Globalisation was an incomplete concept in nineteenth-century Europe, evident only on the fringes of politics and in parts of the economy, particularly where overseas colonies were involved. However, banks and bankers operating on a scale as the Rothschilds did were already thinking and acting globally. They

17 RAL: XI/109/13/1/248, Amschel von Rothschild, Frankfurt to his brothers, 23 Dec. 1829.

were thus dependent on fast and reliable information from all over the world. The information network of the Rothschilds was an extremely international operation. For analytical purposes it is helpful to once more draw attention to the simple fact that the Rothschild family had transcended national borders at a very early stage. With Nathan's move to Manchester in the 1790s and at the latest with the trans-European smuggling operation conducted by the entire family during the Napoleonic period and the ensuing foundation of houses in Paris and Vienna, the family had made its home in several European states. While the original five brothers could be described as transnational Europeans – with the possible exception of Amschel, the eldest, who stayed in Frankfurt practically all his life – their children and grandchildren had become citizens of their respective homelands. They formed allegiances with German states, Britain, France and Austria, yet their loyalty to each other, also through wars, remained steadfast. And they continued to cross borders with ease through constant travel, something only a tiny proportion of the population did at the time.

The internationality of the information network the Rothschilds had formed is self-evident. Mobility was a key factor in its success. Many agents who were being sent to various posts in Europe and overseas had no prior connection with their new residences. Often they did not even know the languages being spoken there. Some agents therefore initially employed the services of an interpreter, although many were able to use French, the *lingua franca* of diplomacy, when dealing with political dignitaries. Many agents also changed positions across borders several times. Benjamin Davidson, for example, after a rather unsuccessful stint in St. Petersburg, where he had been denied permanent residency on account of his Jewishness, went across the Atlantic. Via the West Indies, Panama, Chile, Peru and Mexico he finally reached San Francisco, where he established a permanent agency for the Rothschilds.[18]

Every day the various Rothschild houses received letters in a number of languages. Until the 1830s German – or rather *Judendeutsch* (a Western Yiddish dialect) – was the dominant language of the agents' correspondence, including letters received by the London or Paris houses. In later decades English became more and more important, although some of the long-established agents such as all the Hamburg correspondents, Bleichröder in Berlin, Fraenkel in Warsaw and Meyer in St. Petersburg wrote exclusively in German up to the 1870s. It did not matter whether they were addressing the principals in France, England or one of the German-speaking cities. Most Southern European agents wrote in French. All the male Rothschilds of the second and many of the third generation mastered Ger-

18 Liedtke, N M Rothschild and Sons, 183.

man, English and French well enough to correspond in these languages. Between each other, the Rothschilds usually wrote in *Judendeutsch*, essentially German of the nineteenth century, sometimes interspersed with Hebrew words and always written in Hebrew characters. This language of inter-family correspondence only lost its significance when four of the five brothers of the first generation had died, i.e. in the mid-1850s.[19] Some Jewish agents occasionally used Hebrew characters for some words in their correspondence, not to keep matters secret from the prying eye of a third party but rather, one may assume, to evoke a sense of familiarity with their principals.

Being "foreign" (not only in a legal and political but also in a cultural sense) held both advantages and disadvantages for Rothschild agents in many locations. At least initially, they were not part of the established local business elite with long-standing political connections. This was something most of them had to work their way into, which could take some time. However, the reputation of Rothschilds speeded up that process tremendously. Moreover, not being part of an established set could also be seen as an advantage, since such agents were open for offers from all bidders and not steeped in local intrigues and animosities. Finally, being "foreign" ensured, at least to a degree, that agents had no established loyalties to the governments or ruling entities of their respective locations and retained some kind of independence. With time, they could develop new ones, but there was a good chance that their prime loyalties remained with their principals abroad, something that could not be valued highly enough in international finance.

Conclusion

It can be argued that the transnational mobility of the agents was one of the factors which strengthened the information network of the Rothschilds. However, they were not the only banking dynasty that had correspondents and agents abroad, although this has not been studied in great detail.[20] Overall it seems that not only the diversity but also the sheer size of the network, in particular the size of the Rothschild banks and their financial operations, should be regarded as a prime reason

19 Ibid., 59–60.

20 Studies on three of the main Rothschild competitors in the London market make only passing remarks on the importance of business correspondents. While all of these houses must have had agents' systems at least somewhat similar to that of the Rothschilds and sometimes shared the same agents, nobody seems to have studied these in any greater detail. See Philip Ziegler: *The Sixth Great Power. Barings, 1762–1929*. London 1988, esp. 131–132; and ibid., 169–170 for Barings

for their extreme success. The reputation of the bankers extended to their representatives, who owed to it a more privileged access to decision makers worldwide. As for loyalty, very few business partners or agents dared to cross the Rothschilds. Some of the older, more established agents took the liberty to carefully criticise particular business decisions or suggest alternatives. As long as this was done in a constructive way, and it always was, the various Rothschilds seemed to have welcomed that. Disloyalty, however, was an extremely rare occurrence when it came to the relationship between agents and principals, because almost nobody wanted to put an usually profitable relation with the foremost financial dynasty of its time at risk.

contacts to Stieglitz in St. Petersburg and Weisweiler in Madrid; Kathleen Burk: *Morgan Grenfell, 1838–1988. The Biography of a Merchant Bank.* Oxford 1989; Jehanne Wake: *Kleinwort Benson. The History of Two Families in Banking.* Oxford 1997.

Simone Derix

Hidden Helpers: Biographical Insights into Early and Mid-Twentieth Century Legal and Financial Advisors

Abstract: *This article sets out to encourage historical attention to the men who enabled wealthy people to keep and increase their fortune. In the twentieth century, the ultra-affluent had to rely on legal and financial experts in the management of their properties in times of economic and political crisis as well as in family conflicts. Furthermore, legal and financial advice was needed for practices of asset diversification on an international level. Despite their pivotal importance for the history of social inequality and its astonishing constancy, these hidden helpers open up a largely neglected field of historical research. Though these legal and financial advisors moved professionally in a rather masculine field of activity and were in this respect not a marginalised group, their transnational life stories have yet to be discovered as an eminent element of the infrastructures of wealth.*

Wealth in Focus

In recent times, there has been "a broad uprising in the level of public attention given to wealth and to the ways it is distributed" which reflects on the "growing gaps of income and wealth between the wealthiest 1 per cent and the balance of population."[1] In particular, following the Global Finance Crisis, the mass media has become more and more interested in bankers' bonuses and financial support for distressed banks, questioning their adequacy and legitimacy. The Occupy Wall Street Movement ("We are the 99 per cent") established the street as a stage for voicing criticism about social – i.e. economic – inequality. At the same time, academic research on wealth and wealthy people was suddenly given special attention. Almost overnight, the French economist Thomas Piketty found himself centre stage in a public debate representing academia's voice on the super-rich and global inequality. Based on more than a decade of research, Piketty's bestseller *Capital in the Twenty-First Century* sketches out how rich families have been

---

1 Iain Hay: Establishing Geographies of the Super-Rich. Axes for Analysis of Abundance, in: id. (ed.): *Geographies of the Super-Rich*. Cheltenham 2013, 1–25, esp. 1–2.

able to concentrate the major share of private wealth in their hands since the beginning of the industrial revolution.[2]

Looking back at the past, the twentieth century has more than once witnessed a heightened interest in the wealthy. Examples include critical investigations into the lives and living conditions of wealthy families, ranging from Thorstein Veblen's *Theory of the Leisure Class* at the turn of the century to Pierre Bourdieu's *Distinction. A Social Critique of the Judgement of Taste*, published in French in 1979.[3] Simultaneously, the focus has, however, not only been shifted to people themselves but also to their property. Rankings of estimated wealth either on a national or a global level can be found not only in the present but also at the beginning of the twentieth century.[4] Despite such continuities, recent research and public debate have added some rather new details to the picture by investigating the whereabouts of affluent people's assets, studying tax havens and exploring the legal and illegal ways of avoiding taxes.[5]

In this developing field of research, historians have up until now tended to refrain from intervening. Yet the infrastructures of wealth are a genuinely historical topic that lacks an in-depth analysis of its twists and changes and which encompasses more aspects than assets and owners. In this article I will focus historical attention on legal and financial advisors. These often invisible men operating behind the scenes can not only be considered a key to the personnel dimension of

2 Thomas Piketty: *Capital in the Twenty-First Century*. Cambridge, MA 2014; among the praising reviewers of Piketty's book are the economists Paul Krugman and Joseph E. Stiglitz as well as the professor of law Jedediah Purdy. For an account of these reviews, see URL: *http://www.hup.harvard.edu* (24 June 2015) and Bill Gates, URL: *http://www.gatesnotes.com/Books/Why-Inequality-Matters-Capital-in-21st-Century-Review* (24 June 2015).

3 Thorstein Veblen: *The Theory of the Leisure Class. An Economic Study of Institutions*. New York 1899; Pierre Bourdieu: *Distinction. A Social Critique of the Judgement of Taste*. Cambridge, MA 1984. For a newly emerging interest, see Hay, Geographies.

4 See for such historical accounts, e.g., Rudolf Martin: *Das Jahrbuch der Millionäre Deutschlands in 20 Bänden*. Berlin 1911–1914; Eva Maria Gajek: Sichtbarmachung von Reichtum. Das Jahrbuch des Vermögens und Einkommens der Millionäre in Preußen, in: *Archiv für Sozialgeschichte* 54 (2014), 79–108; for the present and the more recent past, see also the Forbes list, "The World's Billionaires", which was first published in 1987. URL: *http://www.forbes.com/billionaires/list/#version:static* (24 June 2015).

5 See the "Investigative Projects" of the International Consortium of Investigative Journalists, URL: *http://www.icij.org/projects* (24 June 2015); Martin Paldam: Safe Havens in Europe. Switzerland and the Ten Dwarfs, in: *European Journal of Comparative Economics* 10, no. 3 (2013), 377–396; Ana Margarida Raposo and Paulo Reis Mourão: Tax Havens or Tax Hells? A Discussion of the Historical Roots and Present Consequences of Tax Havens, in: *Financial Theory and Practice* 37, no. 3 (2013), 311–330; Adam H. Rosenzweig: Why are There Tax Havens?, in: *William & Mary Law Review* 52, no. 3 (2010), 923–996.

wealth management, but also provide insights into the entanglements between economics, mobility across places and borders, and the shaping of biographies. Thus, investigating the lives and actions of financial and legal experts can help us refine our concept of transnational subjects and their agency. For in the twentieth century, managing the assets of the ultra-affluent meant to think on an international level and to ignore national borders. Therefore, the advisors can be understood as men moving money, acting on a global level, embedded in transnational networks. Yet, as the article will show, it would be too simple to conceptualise the hidden helpers as independent actors following their own strategies autonomously as well as seeing and grasping their opportunities – thereby echoing the concept of "homo oeconomicus" on a secondary level. Although they knew how to benefit from opportunity structures, they were also men moved by money. In practice, the taking care of other people's money or their money matters affected the lives of these men deeply and often required a high level of commitment to the needs of their clients, including frequent changes of place and sometimes even of citizenship. Nonetheless, to focus only on their spatial mobility would create a false impression. For their capacity to move and act across borders inconspicuously strongly depended, as wealth management often does, on a visible local rootedness.

Men Moving Money: The Role of Legal and Financial Advisors in Wealth Management

In the first half of the twentieth century, private wealth management took shape as a professional field involving genuine specialists in the legal and financial dimensions of property and investment issues. From the 1880s to the beginning of the First World War in 1914, finance experienced a first era of globalisation, thereby creating new opportunities to invest and raise capital across borders.[6] Simultaneously, due to fortunes made during the era of industrialisation, a small group of entrepreneurs and entrepreneurial families turned into affluent and ultra-affluent families. Being affluent and ultra-affluent meant that they no longer had to depend upon earned income and were thus able to finance their cost of living exclu-

6 For a general account that stresses the continuities of economic integration even throughout the First World War, see Christof Dejung and Niels P. Petersson (eds.): *The Foundations of Worldwide Economic Integration. Power, Institutions, and Global Markets, 1850–1930*. New York 2013.

sively with capital gains.[7] Although the effects these developments had on private capital and its owners have not been studied in a satisfactory manner, recent research on wealthy families demonstrates that there was a growing need for legal and financial advice.[8]

There are three principal, interrelated fields of activity to be distinguished: Firstly, legal and financial specialists took on the task of administrating and managing assets and arranging an investment across national borders. Especially in times of political and economic crisis or under circumstances of political measures enforced to prevent capital flight, it was this group of experts who invented ways to move money quite inconspicuously using vehicles that non-experts would neither know nor understand. Secondly, legal and financial advice was needed when it came to orchestrating the transnational way of life of their clientele – for the ultra-affluent by and large tended to move as freely across borders as their assets. Legal and economic advisors helped not only to solve the issue of identifying real properties tailored to the individual needs of the purchaser, but also negotiated the conditions of purchase and drew up the sales contracts. Furthermore, they were in charge of all fiscal matters and, if necessary, assisted their clientele in their efforts to change citizenship. Thirdly, they played an important role in accompanying transfers of assets within families, e.g., apanages, gifts *inter vivos*, inheritances, and in moderating family conflicts concerning property issues, e.g., in divorce proceedings. One of the most important positions a legal or financial advisor could achieve was the appointment as executor. As legal historians in particular have pointed out, the executor's office can be considered the prototype of

---

7 There is no consistent academic terminology of wealth. Scholars tend to distinguish wealth that is based on earned income versus affluence that originates from capital assets; for an overview, see Wolfgang Lauterbach and Miriam Ströing: Wohlhabend, Reich und Vermögend – Was heißt das eigentlich?, in: Thomas Druyen, id. and Matthias Grundmann (eds.): *Reichtum und Vermögen. Zur gesellschaftlichen Bedeutung der Reichtums- und Vermögensforschung*. Wiesbaden 2009, 13–28. In the World Wealth Reports, published regularly since 1998 by the management consulting corporation Capgemini in cooperation with different partners, a distinction is made between affluent investors with more than 100,000 US dollars, "High Net Worth Individuals" (HNWI) holding investable finance in excess of one million US dollars and "Ultra-High Net Worth Individuals" (UHNWI) with liquid financial assets exceeding the 30 million US dollars, URL: *https://www.us.capgemini.com/worldwealthreport07/State_of_the_World_Wealth_2007.pdf* (10 July 2015); see also Jonathan V. Beaverstock, Sarah J. E. Hall and Thomas Wainwright: Overseeing the Fortunes of the Global Super-Rich. The Nature of Private Wealth Management in London's Financial District, in: Hay, Geographies, 43–60, esp. 45–47.

8 The following is based on my exhaustive research in Simone Derix: *Die Thyssens. Familie und Vermögen*. Paderborn, forthcoming. For an account of today's private wealth management and its sectors of activity, see Beaverstock, Hall and Wainwright, Overseeing.

private wealth management, bringing into focus numerous questions relating to the complex linkage of family and fortune.[9]

The above tasks required a wide spectrum of professional skills and specialist knowledge in different areas of expertise. Hence, depending on the subject, wealthy clients could rely on proven experts and their highly specialised knowledge. From the point of view of the clients, the more experts got involved with the complex of family and asset matters, the greater the need for generalists to keep a full overview of any legal and economic activity. Based on evidence from the ultra-affluent industrialist family Thyssen and its legal and financial advisors, the growing need for targeted advice seems to correspond with the emergence of a small circle of men entrusted with the management and control of the dozens of advisors and their activities: they recruited the experts, evaluated the experts' work from different countries and interpreted its results. Hence, they held a superior position and acted as representatives as well as aides. These men could be considered the real creators and enablers of wealth management across borders – and across front lines within families – and, therefore, as important actors in matters of capital flight and camouflage. In line with these observations, it becomes clear that "advisor" better describes a specific type of relationship than a clearly defined profession. From the client's perspective, advisors were powerful men in two respects. Firstly, their advisors had relevant knowledge that was missing. Secondly, while working, the advisors had access to quite sensitive information, thereby extending not only their knowledge, but also their power. Particularly the men who took on a variety of assignments for a single client or a whole family could easily exceed their clients' knowledge of the structure and the whereabouts of their assets and thereby strengthen their dominant position. On a more general level, historical research on financial advice appears to underline the power of advisors and consultants by emphasising their eminent role for their clients and, in a more diachronic perspective, also for the history of the twentieth century because financial advising and consulting are considered to be ever-increasing fields of activity.[10]

That said, it may come as a surprise that there has not yet been intensive historical research on private wealth managers and advisors.[11] While historians have

9 Rolf Sethe: Historische Entwicklung der Vermögensverwaltung, in: id., Frank A. Schäfer and Volker Lang (eds.): *Handbuch der Vermögensverwaltung*. München 2012, 20–33, esp. 21.

10 Matthieu Leimgruber, Daniela Saxer and Aline Steinbrecher: Ratschlag und Beratung, in: *traverse* 18, no. 3 (2011), 15–18.

11 For an account on contemporary "big men" in finance, see Horacio Ortiz: Financial Professionals as Global Elite, in: Jon Abbink and Tijo Salverda (eds.): *The Anthropology of Elites. Power, Culture, and the Complexities of Distinction*. New York 2013, 185–205.

analysed a broad range of different fields of expertise which must be taken into account when contextualising the men (and women) of the twentieth century as protagonists in their own time,[12] they have apparently avoided examining economic expertise and consulting. When taking an interest in economic knowledge in historical perspective, the focus has been merely on the impact of experts on economic policies and the public sphere.[13]

Money Moving Men: The Mobile Lives of Legal and Financial Advisors

Though the power of legal and financial advisors has yet to be fully discovered, it is only one side of the coin. If we investigate the power advisors had over ultra-affluent families and their assets, we may also want to examine the ways in which clients and their financial matters shaped the lives of their advisors. As we take a careful look at the advisors' ways of life, the blurring of boundaries unfolds as a main characteristic in two respects: Firstly, we can observe a blurring of boundaries in the relationship between advisor and client that can be illustrated by some examples taken from the Thyssen family.[14] Legal and financial advisors got deeply involved with family matters: In 1913, while litigating in court with his father over assets, a Thyssen son challenged his father's most important legal advisor to a duel. In 1919, one of the family's financial experts in the Netherlands was singled out not only to take responsibility for its private financial assets, but also to accompany some Thyssen children on their travels from the Ruhr area to The Hague. Apparently, when an advisor attained a certain level of trust, his area of potential responsibility was extended to all matters concerning the family. There were no limits of subject and time.

Secondly, the blurring of boundaries refers to a spatial dimension. As the assets of the ultra-affluent tended to create criss-cross mobility patterns throughout the transatlantic region and beyond, the men who were in charge of overseeing these movements became geographically mobile themselves. Their business

---

12 Peter-Paul Bänziger et al. (eds.): *Fragen Sie Dr. Sex! Ratgeberkommunikation und die mediale Konstruktion des Sexuellen*. Frankfurt 2010; Sabine Maasen et al. (eds.): *Das beratene Selbst. Zur Genealogie der Therapeutisierung in den "langen" Siebzigern*. Bielefeld 2011.

13 Marc Flandreau (ed.): *Money Doctors. The Experience of Financial Advising 1850–2000*. Abingdon 2003; Alexander Nützenadel: *Stunde der Ökonomen. Wissenschaft, Expertenkultur und Politik in der Bundesrepublik 1949–74*. Göttingen 2005.

14 Derix, Thyssen.

travel consisted of meeting up with clients or consulting colleagues. Sometimes business travel was quite literally linked up with capital transfer. As advisors occasionally personally delivered suitcases full of cash, sensitive legal documents, security papers or other valuable objects, like jewellery. Furthermore, they escorted transports of valuable goods, like gold bars, which they could not carry on their own. From this perspective, international capital flows[15] seem to obtain a physical and social dimension that can shed light on the biographical repercussions of economic practices in capitalist societies. In cases where advisors received a proxy for the assets in a specific country or region, sometimes a permanent change of residence was required or a change of citizenship might have seemed opportune. Even their holidays reflected their transnational professional activities. Often they chose locations potential clients preferred, like St. Moritz in winter, the Riviera in summer or specific resorts *à la mode*. These places allowed for mingling with so-called "international people" thus making new acquaintances and cultivating the ones they had already made.[16] In so doing, the men themselves – occasionally accompanied by their families and/or close associates – not only developed specific short- and long-term mobility patterns across regional boundaries and national borders, but also acquired their own private fortunes. There is evidence that they used the safes, strong rooms and depositories belonging to their clientele and, in addition, that they created their own holdings inside the webs of financing they had spun for their ultra-affluent clients. Looking more thoroughly at the case of the legal and financial advisors will strengthen our understanding of how various forms of movement are intricately intertwined and relate to mobility as a whole.

In recent years, a new mobility paradigm has been playing an increasingly important role in how we look at migration, tourism, transport and any other spatial activity.[17] Its main characteristic is its ability to establish a dialogue between the various fields of research on people, ideas and things on the move. The mobility

---

15 Mack Ott: International Capital Flows, in: *The Concise Encyclopedia of Economics*. 2008. Library of Economics and Liberty. URL: *http://www.econlib.org/library/Enc/InternationalCapitalFlows.html#lfHendersonCEE2-093_footnote_nt281* (29 June 2015).

16 Alexa Geisthövel: Promenadenmischungen. Raum und Kommunikation in Hydropolen, 1830–1880, in: Alexander Geppert, Uffa Jensen and Jörn Weinhold (eds.): *Ortsgespräche. Raum und Kommunikation im 19. und 20. Jahrhundert*. Bielefeld 2005, 203–222; Jill Steward: The Spa Towns of the Austro-Hungarian Empire and the Growth of Tourist Culture, 1860–1914, in: Peter Borsay, Günter Hirschfelder and Ruth-Elisabeth Mohrmann (eds.): *New Directions in Urban History. Aspects of European Art, Health, Tourism and Leisure since the Enlightenment*. Münster 2000, 87–124; John K. Walton: Seaside Resorts and International Tourism, in: Eric G.E. Zuelow (ed.): *Touring Beyond the Nation. A Transnational Approach to European Tourism History*. Farnham 2011, 19–36.

17 John Urry: *Sociology Beyond Societies. Mobilities for the Twenty-First Century*. London 2000.

approach can help researchers transcend disciplinary boundaries and methods, thus providing insights into the practices and infrastructures of everyday life, shedding light on the interrelation between the material and the social. Thereby it becomes clear that networks are not only built through social relations but also through material infrastructures and interactions between human beings and things. For a long time, academic discourse has cultivated a profound enthusiasm for mobility and mobile ways of life "romanticising" and "idealising" movement in itself, as critics pointed out.[18] The fascination with individual transnational or transboundary life-courses[19] could lead to overlooking the fact that "[m]obilities also are caught up in power geometries of everyday life", and that the "[r]ights to travel are highly uneven."[20] These critics contemplate not only the spatial implications of mobility but also the social implications thereof. Sociologists have proposed the term "motility" as a theoretical concept that highlights the interdependence of spatial and social mobility. Motility is defined "as the capacity of entities (e.g. goods, information or persons) to be mobile in social and geographic space". As "individual actors, groups and institutions differ in access, competence and appropriation", it is argued that the potential of socio-spatial mobility "may be considered an asset", thereby correlating mobility and social inequality.[21]

Based on these considerations, legal and financial advisors may be regarded as the ideal personification of this peculiar asset, thus supporting the idea that the "mobility paradigm can be linked to a 'bourgeois masculine subjectivity' that de-

18 Kevin Hannam, Mimi Sheller and John Urry: Editorial. Mobilities, Immobilities, and Moorings, in: *Mobilities* 1 (2006), 1–22, esp. 3.

19 For different accounts of lives across borders, see David Lambert and Alan Lester (eds.): *Colonial Lives Across the British Empire. Imperial Careering in the Long Nineteenth Century*. Cambridge 2006; Bernd Hausberger (ed.): *Globale Lebensläufe. Menschen als Akteure im weltgeschichtlichen Geschehen*. Wien 2006; Tony Balantyne and Antoinette Burton (eds.): *Moving Subjects. Gender, Mobility, and Intimacy in an Age of Global Empire*. Urbana, IL 2008; Angela Woollacott, Desley Deacon and Penny Russell (eds.): *Transnational Lives. Biographies of Global Modernity, 1700–Present*. New York 2010; Madeleine Herren: Between Territoriality, Performativity and Transcultural Entanglement (1920–1939). A Typology of Transboundary Lives, in: *comparativ* 23, no. 6 (2013), 99–123; Johannes Paulmann: Regionen und Welten. Arenen und Akteure regionaler Weltbeziehungen seit dem 19. Jahrhundert, in: *Historische Zeitschrift* 296 (2013), 660–699.

20 Hannam, Sheller and Urry, Editorial, 3.

21 Vincent Kaufmann, Manfred Max Bergman and Dominique Joye: Motility. Mobility as Capital, in: *International Journal of Urban and Regional Research* 28, no. 4 (2004), 745–756, esp. 750 and 754.

scribes itself as 'cosmopolitan'",[22] as studies on contemporary financial advisors suggest.[23] In fact, in today's context, mobility is strongly linked to power, social distinction and global competition, not only between companies but also between the men at the top. Spatial mobility appears to provide evidence for freedom of movement being a strongly limited political, social, and economic privilege. As this is true for the present and the past, large parts of the history of mobile ways and conditions of living of legal and financial experts, as well as of the twists and changes in their mobility patterns, are yet to be examined. From a historical perspective, one may assume that, especially during the high tide of nationalism in the first decades of the twentieth century and in times of international conflicts, mobile lifestyles could entail considerable burdens and challenges for those whose private and work lives extended across national borders. In these times, men and money attempted to be as inconspicuous as possible while crossing borders.

Challenges in Studying the Inconspicuous I: Names and Traces

Obviously, taking action in the most discreet and confidential manner possible is a fundamental challenge confronting historians of wealth and wealth management. While in the course of the twentieth century visibility has assumed an ever greater significance in politics and society,[24] affluent people and their advisors rather prefer to stay in the background. They also remain opaque in academic studies. From a political scientist's perspective, "[t]he rich inhabit spaces not easily accessible to researchers. They restrict access: part of their power is neither to be intimidated by, nor overly impressed by academic researchers, who invariably have a lower income level and occupy a less vaunted position in the social hierarchy."[25] The infrastructures of abundance are not easily accessible to historians either. Men who did not want to leave any traces and sometimes actually tried to erase them usually had no intention of handing over their private papers to a public archive and thereby disclosing secret information. Hence, historical study of

22 Hannam, Sheller and Urry, Editorial, 3 (quoting Beverly Skeggs: *Class, Self, Culture*. London 2004, 49).
23 Ortiz, Financial Professionals.
24 John B. Thompson: *Media and Modernity. A Social Theory of the Media*. Cambridge 1995.
25 John Rennie Short: Economic Wealth and Political Power in the Second Gilded Age, in: Hay, Geographies, 26–42, esp. 26.

those who wanted to remain in the shadows can be arduous, as it requires extensive research in various historical archives. It is also risky and potentially frustrating, as the outcome is uncertain. However, this situation can also prove helpful, particularly in increasing our recognition of the scant information we have and to the constructive character of historical research itself. For historiography is not an accurate depiction of the past but merely an interpretation which is aware of its specific perspective and of its blind spots. Therefore, single or collective biographies can never – and are never meant to – grasp the entire life or personality of a man or a woman, but they can provide biographical insights and investigate fragments of biographies from different perspectives.

Nevertheless, it is difficult to examine the mobile lives of legal and financial advisors without having concrete names to start from. Although for a general account on wealth management, the history of the capitals of finance is indispensable,[26] it will only occasionally provide the names we are interested in, whereas private papers of affluent families combined with government records may provide some crucial hints. During the First World War and again in the Second World War, the governments of the United States and the United Kingdom established enemy property laws allowing the blocking, freezing and vesting of foreign assets. Any state action was based on extensive verbal and written reports containing details on various fortunes, on how they were organised in complicated financial set-ups based on interwoven shell corporations, holdings and foundations, and not least on who was involved.

One of these men thoroughly examined by the Americans and British during the Second World War was Hendrik Jozef Kouwenhoven. Kouwenhoven was born in 1889 in the Netherlands, the youngest of four children of Johanna Katharina and François, who is referred to as a shopkeeper as well as a decorator and upholsterer. Kouwenhoven grew up in Maassluis, an old fishing town in the Rotterdam area, in the province of South Holland, where his parents, who both originated from Delft, had settled in 1885. In 1916, Kouwenhoven and Cornelia van Neuren, who was born 1893 in Hellevoetsluis into a pilot skipper's family and also raised in Maassluis, were married.[27] Kouwenhoven's professional career can be traced back to 1914, when he joined the accounting department of a Dutch Thyssen company in Rotterdam.[28] In 1918, Kouwenhoven moved to the newly-

26 Youssef Cassis: *Capitals of Finance. The Rise and Fall of International Finance Centres, 1780–2009*. Cambridge ^{2}2010.

27 URL: *http://www.genealogieonline.nl/genealogische-databank-maassluis* (6 June 2015).

28 Interrogation of Hendrik J. Kouwenhoven by the Devisenschutzkommando Holland (Foreign Exchange Protection Command), 24 July 1940, National Archives and Records Administration, College Park, Maryland [NARA], RG 466, Entry A1 28, Box 63.

founded Thyssen *Bank voor Handel en Scheepvaart*, where his career took off. By 1921 he had moved up into a management position. Previously he had become acquainted with members of the Thyssen family, who fostered his career and made him one of the most influential advisors for their private fortune for the next twenty years. American and British reports depict Kouwenhoven as a central figure in the wealth management of the Thyssen family in the Netherlands, Germany, the United States of America and Switzerland. One of the most important vehicles for administrating the private assets of the family members was the *Rotterdamsche Trustee Kantoor*, which was housed in the same building as the *Bank voor Handel en Scheepvaart*. It was Kouwenhoven who played a full and active role in creating and shaping the nested structure of his clients' assets on both sides of the Atlantic. He was a leading figure in the creation and expansion of the American Thyssen complex, including a bank, several shell companies as well as real estate, to which end he frequently travelled between Europe and the US.[29] Moreover, Kouwenhoven helped set up family foundations under Swiss law in the 1920s and 1930s that allowed for the inconspicuous transfer of assets to Switzerland. Kouwenhoven was appointed attorney and member of the board.[30] During the 1930s, he was designated executor of the will of Heinrich Thyssen-Bornemisza, one of the most affluent Thyssens. Although he lost Heinrich's trust in 1940 as well as his position as manager, advisor and executor, he could still fulfill his duty as executor to Heinrich's mother Hedwig.[31] In addition, throughout the 1920s and 1930s, Kouwenhoven got involved in the private wealth management of several branches of the Thyssen family as well as in various family matters, e.g. litigation involving siblings and other family members.

In providing details of Kouwenhoven's fields of activity, British and American records give an impression, albeit incomplete, of the scope of his transatlantic and European networking efforts. Although we lack detailed information on his travel schedule, we can say with certainty that the Netherlands remained Kouwenhoven's domicile, as they remained the headquarters of the wealth management of the Thyssen family. In the 1920s, the US became an ever more important venue for the Thyssen assets, and a trustworthy local representative was needed. The

---

29 Vesting Order 248 [Union Banking Corporation], Vesting Order 249 [Seamless Steel Company], Vesting Order 351 [Cedar Swamp Road Corporation], Vesting Order 512 [Domestic Fuel Company], NARA, RG 131, Entry: UD-UP3, Boxes 341, 343, 345 and 415; Vesting Order 8471 [Heirs of August Thyssen junior], NARA, RG 131, Entry A1 247, Box 466.

30 In the matter of the Familienstiftung, see Pelzer, The National Archives, London [TNA], FO 192/220.

31 Wills of Heinrich Thyssen-Bornemisza, 18 Feb. 1936 and 15 Jan. 1937 and Will of Hedwig de Neuter, 21 Feb. 1940, Stiftung zur Industriegeschichte Thyssen, Duisburg [SIT], TB/3 and TB/10.

role fell to Cornelis Lievense. He and his wife Maria moved to New York in 1924. Lievense was a Dutch citizen from Maassluis and a schoolmate of Kouwenhoven's. While there is no clear evidence, it is very likely that Kouwenhoven brought Lievense in as an advisor and proxy of the Thyssen fortune. Before joining the American Thyssen bank *Union Banking Corporation* in New York, Lievense had worked for insurance companies and, for a short time, a Dutch Thyssen company. In the long run, Lievense's activities were not limited to the banking sector. He acquired real estate on behalf of the Thyssen family and founded, in close cooperation with Kouwenhoven, who regularly travelled to the US, several export-import enterprises, probably shell companies.[32] Moreover, Kouwenhoven and Lievense collaborated beyond the boundaries of the Thyssen interest, e.g., jointly publishing and disseminating religious literature. The small publishing company provides evidence of how the structures created for their clients proved useful opportunity structures for the advisors' own purposes, thereby criss-crossing and indeed contradicting their client's interests: For the Thyssens were noted Catholics, while Kouwenhoven and Lievense published Protestant literature.

Lievense's professional career had a strong impact on his private life. In January 1932, Cornelis and Maria Lievense became US citizens. Furthermore, his wife Maria also got involved in the Thyssen finance complex, serving as nominee for American companies. This demonstrates how deeply professional careers affected private lives and how closely they linked up with mobility patterns, both in a social and in a spatial sense. Money moved men – although in ways that are difficult to trace.

Challenges in Studying the Inconspicuous II: Conflicting Images – Rootedness versus Mobility

Depending on the source, we get various, even conflicting images of Kouwenhoven. Studies on the role of Wall Street in the rise of National Socialism, often inspired by conspiracy theories, characterise Kouwenhoven as a "Nazi banker" without giving any details on his life and professional activities.[33] The British steel magnate William Firth, who had to deal with Kouwenhoven on behalf of the British government in 1940, in his report to the Foreign Office depicted Kouwen-

32 Walter C. Gorsuch, Examiner's Report, 5 Oct. 1942, NARA, RG 131, Entry: UD-UP 3, Box 341.

33 Antony C. Sutton: *Wall Street and the Rise of Hitler*. Seal Beach 1976, 107; Fernando Torres Leiva: *El Nuevo Esclavo Negro*. Bloomington 2011, 401; Peter Stuivenberg: *De Boogeyman. Geschiedenis als Complot*. Delft 2012.

hoven as a "first-class crook", a man "of intelligent and pleasing appearance of the Quaker Type – non-smoker, vegetarian, fifteen children", while according to Firth, Kouwenhoven described himself as "a simple block-headed Dutchman with a clear conscience, constantly aware that he must answer to his Maker on Judgment Day."[34] Obituaries published after his death in Ridgewood, New Jersey in 1948, given their conventional character, describe Kouwenhoven as a beloved husband, father, grandfather, son-in-law and brother-in-law.[35] Finally, judging from a website on the local history of Voorburg, where Kouwenhoven lived with his family from 1938 onwards, the expert on finance appears as a good Dutch citizen opposing the German occupation: Ignoring the fact that high officials were living in close proximity, "Mister Kouwenhoven, a director of the Bank voor Handel en Scheepvaart in Rotterdam, refused to work for the Germans in the Second World War, resigned his position and opened his house to people hiding from the Germans."[36] Furthermore, it is said that Kouwenhoven arranged luncheons for children in need, thereby giving the impression of a charitable man.

It is true that additional research on Kouwenhoven could bring to light more reliable information, which could help in assembling the fragmentary and contradictory pieces. The crucial point, however, is that the information we have gives a mixed picture: On the one hand, the visibly charitable life of a firmly rooted Dutchman, on the other hand, a less visible life of transnational networking and mobility. This fits in with concepts and questions brought up by the new mobility paradigm focusing on the connection between deterritorialisation and reterritorialisation, between mobilities and moorings: "Mobilities cannot be described without attention to the necessary spatial, infrastructural and institutional moorings that configure and enable mobilities [...]."[37] Based on the fragmentary insights into Kouwenhoven's life, one may assume that his conspicuous local and national rootedness is closely interlinked with his inconspicuous global networking and businesses. In addition, Kouwenhoven himself was part of the Thyssen system of "spatial, infrastructural and institutional moorings", as were the *Rot-*

---

34 Jebb, Foreign Office, to Cobbold, Bank of England, 20 Mar. 1940 including Annex Report C of Sir William Firth, 16 Mar. 1940, TNA, T 236/6780.

35 Nieuwe Leidsche Courant, 6 Jan. 1948.

36 "De heer Kouwenhoven, mededirecteur van de Bank voor Handel en Scheepvaart te Rotterdam, wilde in de oorlog niet voor de Duitsers werken, nam ontslag en stelde zijn kapitale huis ter beschikking aan diverse onderduikers. En dat ondanks het feit dat op 'Eemwijck' hoge officieren van de SS waren ingekwartierd en op nr. 100 de Duitse Wehrmacht was gevestigd." Entry "Vlietenburgstraat", URL: *https://www.leidschendam-voorburg.nl/Int/Over-Leidschendam-Voorburg-Historie/Straatnamen/Straatnamenboekje-Voorburg/Index-straatnamen-A---Z/Index-straatnamen-A---Z-Straatnamen-met-V.html#10* (6 June 2015).

37 Hannam, Sheller and Urry, Editorial, 3.

terdamsche Trustee Kantoor, Swiss foundations, American real estate and shell companies as well as other legal and financial advisors.

Therefore, insights into the lives of individual experts may exemplify the linkage of rootedness and mobility, of infrastructure and fluidity. In addition, a comparative analysis of the complex transboundary network involved is needed to elaborate the interplay between institutions (under different national laws) and advisors, encompassing their spatial movements as well as their visible engagements at a national, regional or local level. An in-depth analysis of this network will bring to light a rather complex web of social and spatial entanglements throughout the world.

Exemplary investigations of Swiss legal and financial experts would probably be a promising starting point, not only because Switzerland was one of the most attractive places for ultra-affluent people throughout the twentieth century, but also merely because biographical information already exists and is accessible via the *Historisches Lexikon der Schweiz* (HLS) or the database *Elites suisses au XXème siècle*.[38] Yet neither of them will provide extensive details on activities across borders because both databases function within a national framework, thus tending to neglect the spatial movements and border-crossings of their protagonists. Heinrich Blass (1883–1972), for instance, was a central financial advisor to the ultra-affluent clientele, with activities and networks reaching far beyond his post as director of *Crédit Suisse*. As the HLS provides no information on Blass, the *Elites suisses* database contains helpful details on his education and professional positions, indicating that Blass belonged to the Swiss economic elite. In fact, the life-course of Heinrich Blass as far as it is known does not suggest a distinctive transnational dimension. However, his correspondence, parts of which were recently discovered by chance, may modify the picture, for it reveals a large transboundary network of connections. Blass may have been born, lived and worked in Zurich, and there may be little evidence of extensive travels.[39] Yet he managed holdings in Argentina, established contacts in Europe and South America at the highest social level, and arranged for his clients' legal advice in various countries.[40] Against this background, Zurich can be regarded as his local mooring and gateway to the world, allowing him to act globally without moving spatially.

---

38 URL: *http://www.hls-dhs-dss.ch/* (13 July 2015) and URL: *http://www.unil.ch/elitessuisses* (13 July 2015).

39 US Occupation Headquarters, WWII OMGUS Property Control & External Assets Branch, General Records of the US Census Section Chief: Thyssen Interrogation, 1949, NARA, RG 260, Entry A1 427, Box 667.

40 US Embassy, Buenos Aires: Memorandum Relationship Colamina, Oversea Trust and Fritz Thyssen, NARA, RG 59, CDF 1940–1944, Box 2568, Doc. 740.00112; US Political Adviser for Ger-

There is reason to believe that local moorings and visible rootedness were assets or rather resources facilitating transboundary activities and connections. A further example will help clarify this: In the middle of the twentieth century, the lawyer and notary Robert van Aken was, in his own words, legal advisor to one third of the most affluent inhabitants of the canton of Ticino[41] and thus professionally involved in questions of movements of people and money across borders. Van Aken himself often had to travel across Europe. Yet despite this, or perhaps for this very reason, he is not to be found in the biographical reference works mentioned above. Like Blass, Robert van Aken appears to have been closely attached to his home region. He was a former partner of the law firm of Brenno Bertoni, a Ticino-rooted Swiss liberal intellectual and from 1920 to 1935 a member of the Swiss Council of States,[42] as well as a friend of Brenno Galli, head of the finance department of the canton of Ticino in the 1950s and a Swiss politician.[43] Van Aken's clients were "international people" moving to Switzerland in order to save taxes, as well as artists and intellectuals like Hermann Hesse or Edgar Salin.[44] Yet at the same time, one cannot ignore that van Aken's local connections were the prime incentives for his clients to choose him as their legal advisor, thus laying the ground for further responsibilities beyond questions of saving taxes by moving money to Switzerland.

Conclusion

To sum up, even though detailed information is still lacking, biographical insights – albeit fragmentary ones – into legal and financial advisors constitute a rewarding field of research for historians interested in understanding the interconnection between people, money and mobility in the twentieth century. Managing other people's money across borders was a catalyst in mobilising the advisors' lives – spatially and socially –, blurring the boundaries between work

many: Censorship Intercept on Fritz Thyssen, 17 May 1947, NARA, RG 59, CDF 1945–1949, Box 6743, Doc. 862.20235/5-1747; T.W.E. Property Thyssen Gold (1939–1948), TNA, T 236/6780.

41 [Robert van Aken] to Hans Heinrich Thyssen-Bornemisza, 27 Nov. 1958, SIT, TB 02203.

42 Andrea Ghiringhelli: Bertoni, Brenno, in: URL: *http://www.hls-dhs-dss.ch/textes/d/D3487.php* (14 July 2015).

43 Id.: Galli, Brenno, in: URL: *http://www.hls-dhs-dss.ch/textes/d/D6305.php* (14 July 2015); URL: *http://www2.unil.ch/elitessuisses/index.php?page=detailPerso&idIdentite=50358* (14 July 2015).

44 Depository Edgar Salin, Universitätsbibliothek Basel; Correspondence between Robert van Aken and Hermann Hesse, Deutsches Literaturarchiv Marbach.

and private lives. At the same time, being mobile across borders often was interrelated with local rootedness. In fact, local rootedness can be considered an important source for activities across places and borders.

Analysing the hidden helpers, however, requires a heightened awareness of the vital importance of infrastructures and an acknowledgement of the strategic importance of inconspicuous structures and invisible helpers, both not easily accessible to historians. Hence, it becomes clear that historical analyses of the linkages between wealth and mobility should not be limited to wealth, its distribution and its biographical impact on the wealthy, but choose a broader perspective and simultaneously modify the topic. I would suggest calling this approach "infrastructures of wealth", thereby drawing together the personal, spatial and material dimensions of the creation and maintenance of wealth distribution.

Moreover, the focus on the experts on finance and its legal implications can be a starting point for sharpening our understanding of economic globalisation and its impact on the life of anyone involved. A new light will be cast on capitalism and its genealogy, helping us to distinguish its dimensions and significance. A quotation from a highly successful contemporary wealth advisor and strong believer in capitalism underscores the significance of this project:

> What we really invest in is capitalism itself. Capitalism is an engine of prosperity that's bigger than any one company or even one country. The beautiful thing is that we all have access to this wealth-creating force, as entrepreneurs, workers, or investors. When we invest money, we're reflecting our belief in capitalism. We're expressing confidence that it can – and will – lift us into greater prosperity over time.[45]

Finally, enquiries into the history of wealth management can add an economic perspective to the academic debates on "mobility and biography", thus restoring attention to the material in a field that often concentrates on questions of culture. But in the way that cultural aspects shape individuals' sense of belonging and their capacity to move across spatial and social borders, economic aspects do so by motivating, mediating and moulding mobilities.

Acknowledgement

I wish to thank Joanna Holroyd, Joe Kroll and Sarah Panter for their careful editing.

45 Steven D. Lockshin: *Get Wise to Your Advisor. How to Reach Your Investment Goals Without Getting Ripped Off*. Hoboken, NJ 2013, 243–244.

Nico Randeraad

Triggers of Mobility: International Congresses (1840–1914) and their Visitors

Abstract: *This article seeks to assess in which ways tracing mobilities provides new insights into the strategies pertaining to transnational knowledge exchange related to social reform in the second half of the nineteenth and the beginning of the twentieth century. It follows four visitors to international congresses in the period around 1900 to evaluate to what extent their movements were likely to effect change at the international, national or local level. In order to structure the analysis I have identified two "frames", i.e. two pairs of opposing aspirations, which emerged in the transnational social reform debates of the turn of the century: (1) the tension between international and national (sometimes also local) ambitions; (2) the interplay of state intervention and civil society organisations in providing welfare. The four actors occupied different but by no means fixed positions on these axes.*

Introduction

In his famous opening address to the International Peace Congress of 1849 in Paris, Victor Hugo highlighted increasing speed and reduced distances as a leap towards global fraternity: "Thanks to railroads, Europe will soon be no larger than France was in the middle ages. Thanks to steam-ships, we now traverse the mighty ocean more easily than the Mediterranean was formerly crossed". And he completed his speech with the prediction that soon "the electric wire of concord shall encircle the globe and embrace the world".[1] Mobility, in other words, was thought to be the key to universal peace.

This kind of faith in progress was not only widespread among peace activists such as Hugo, but characterised the convictions of visitors to a wide range of international congresses which since the 1840s – with gradually increasing frequency – were organised in European and American cities. The Belgian minister of the interior, Ferdinand Piercot, opening the first international statistical congress of 1853, solemnly declared that "statistics would strengthen the bonds between nations and the sense of brotherhood, and peace, which protects mankind from

1 *Report of the Proceedings of the Second General Peace Congress Held in Paris on the 22nd, 23rd and 24th of August, 1849*. London 1849, 12.

the resurgence of foolhardy national rival, would be deepened everywhere".[2] Half a century later, around 1900, enthusiasm was just as great, if not greater, in joyous expectation of the promises the new century would have in store. At the occasion of the World Exhibition of 1900 held in Paris the French government allowed 127 congresses of that year to bear the title "official", and was widely believed to have thus contributed to intellectual and social development on a global scale, as the Italian Prince of Cassano observed:

> L'oeuvre des congrès internationaux deviendra le facteur le plus puissant du progrès moral et matériel, elle se transformera en une sorte de corps délibérant international chargé d'aider et d'éclairer les législateurs du monde entier.[3]

To dwell on the point, therefore, that the growing numbers of international congresses were nodes of mobility and change, would be superfluous. They almost invariably managed to attract visitors from many different countries. Altogether, the international visitors to 24 selected congresses from the period 1876–1912 travelled over ten million kilometres to reach their destinations.[4] But what do all these movements mean? To what extent did the high hopes of the organisers correspond with the intentions and experiences of the participants? Mobility is rarely a goal or a "deliverable" good in itself. This essay, therefore, seeks to assess in which ways tracing mobilities provides new answers to questions related to transnational knowledge exchange in the second half of the nineteenth and the beginning of the twentieth century. Following the *leitmotif* of this volume, I have taken four biographical snapshots of congress visitors to evaluate to what extent the movements of congress participants were likely to effect change at the international, national or local level.

I have selected my four protagonists from a sample of thousands of participants in 24 international congresses on social reform from the period 1876–1912. This initial sample includes congresses on six themes (each theme represented by

---

2 Quoted in Nico Randeraad: *States and Statistics in the Nineteenth Century. Europe by Numbers*. Manchester 2010, 14.

3 Quoted in Anne Rasmussen: Les Congrès internationaux liés aux Expositions universelles de Paris (1867–1900), in: *Mil neuf cent. Cahiers Georges Sorel* 7 (1989), 34.

4 This is a rough calculation based on data in our Nodegoat-powered database, which includes information on the distances between home and destination cities of congress visitors. See *tic.ugent.be* for a summary of this digital humanities project. The database is described in greater detail in Thomas D'haeninck, Nico Randeraad and Christophe Verbruggen: Visualizing Longitudinal Data. Rooted Cosmopolitans in the Low Countries, 1850–1914, in: *BD2015, Biographical Data in a Digital World 2015. Proceedings of the First Conference on Biographical Data in a Digital World 2015*, Amsterdam (9 Apr. 2015). URL: *http://ceur-ws.org/Vol-1399/* (17 July 2015).

four congresses, spread over the period): poor relief, penitentiary reform, hygiene, global health, statistics and peace.[5] Representativeness with regard to the sample was not my first concern, although the four selected individuals evidently shared an interest in reform issues and were prepared to travel for it. The journeys made in their lifetime are a vivid illustration of an urge to get professionally mobile. My account concentrates on Victor Desguin from Belgium, Louis Guillaume from Switzerland, Henri Monod from France and Wilhelmus Hubertus Nolens from the Netherlands. The four of them participated in one or more congresses of the sample, sometimes in congresses related to different themes, but also in ones that were not included in the original sample. To some extent they belonged to an international congress elite and regularly occupied functions in what at the time was called the "bureau de congrès". It is not unlikely that the four knew each other, or at least met once, but rather than assessing their common profile I intend to explore how they "used" their attendance at international congresses in different ways.

It is safe to say that my protagonists were social reformers, albeit in different ways, and it was certainly not their primary identifier. The realm of social reform is vast. It has been felicitously compared to a "nébuleuse réformatrice", a galaxy without a clearly identifiable core or sharply defined borders.[6] The abovementioned themes of the congress sample reflect this diversity. I understand social reform as the wide variety of attempts to counter the adverse effects of industrialisation and globalisation that emerged in the nineteenth century. In other words, following Topalov, I see social reform as a "reform field", in the Bourdieuian sense, where politics and policies, ideas and practices, instruments and actors, all dealing with reform issues, were located.[7]

In order to structure my analysis I have identified two "frames", i.e. two pairs of opposing aspirations, which emerged in the transnational social reform debates of the turn of the century: 1. the tension between international and national (sometimes also local) ambitions; 2. the interplay of state intervention and civil society organisations in providing welfare. My four actors occupied different

5 The sample includes personal data concerning the transnational participants in 24 international congresses from the period 1876–1912, i.e. the persons travelling to another country to attend a congress. The dataset has been compiled for a larger project on the transnationalisation of social reform. For further insights into the approach, see Chris Leonards and Nico Randeraad: Transnational Experts in Social Reform, 1840–1880, in: *International Review of Social History* 55, no. 2 (2010), 215–239.

6 Christian Topalov (ed.): *Laboratoires du nouveau siècle. La nébuleuse réformatrice et ses réseaux en France, 1880–1914*. Paris 1999.

7 Id.: Le champ réformateur, 1880–1914. Un modèle, in: ibid., 461–474.

positions on these axes but, as I intend to show, their ideas and opinions were by no means fixed and could change over time depending on the broader context. Following insights of the Chicago School on collective behaviour I intend to find out how these actors gave meaning to their presence at international congresses, and how others acknowledged or dismissed their authority. Interventions made during the congresses play a central role in the analysis, but these will be placed against the wider social, political and cultural background of the selected persons.

This article ties in with the boom of research into the history of transnational networks, in particular the scholarship on cross-border transfers and exchanges related to social integration, public health and peace.[8] Mobility is a natural companion of transnational history. I hope to offer a modest contribution to the "new mobilities paradigm" and various new approaches in the genre of biography, not so much by trying to historicise their conceptual innovations (which, particularly in the case of the future-oriented mobility agenda, would be slightly forced and perhaps counterproductive) but rather by showing the value of transnational arenas for historians studying the lives and mobilities of "activists beyond borders".[9]

Internationalism-Nationalism-Local Activism

International congresses were not for internationalists only. Most international congresses dealt with issues that could only be solved at the national level or at least needed national consensus before international steps were possible. Some congresses, such as those of the Red Cross, were more likely to pursue an internationalist agenda, but even there national Red Cross societies lay in wait to appropriate humanitarian ideals for national purposes.[10] Internationalism existed in many guises and was seldom a purpose in itself. By now, numerous studies

8 For a recent overview with numerous references, see Pierre-Yves Saunier: *Transnational History*. Basingstoke 2013.

9 The term is coined by Margaret E. Keck and Kathryn Sikkink: *Activists beyond Borders. Advocacy Networks in International Politics*. Ithaca, NY 1998. See also Sydney Tarrow: *Strangers at the Gates. Movements and States in Contentious Politics*. Cambridge 2012. For some contemporary research stemming from the "new mobilities paradigm", see Weert Canzler, Vincent Kaufmann and Sven Kesselring (eds.): *Tracing Mobilities. Towards a Cosmopolitan Perspective*. Farnham 2009.

10 John F. Hutchinson: *Champions of Charity. War and the Rise of the Red Cross*. Boulder, CO 1996.

have underlined the multifarious, unsteady and sometimes contradictory nature of internationalism.[11]

Scientific universalism was the alleged common denominator of all international congresses, from statistics to welfare and from chemistry to demography. During congress sessions, the appeal to science could often briefly unite opponents, but it could not stop or fundamentally bend the nationalist orientations of scientists.[12] It was no different for politicians and administrators who claimed to have faith in science. They too appropriated scientific truths for their own agendas.

There was not just an intricate nexus between internationalism and nationalism but, as the "transnational turn" in recent historiography has shown, local experiences and interests could also add to the jumble of connections. Bernard Struck and others have justly drawn attention to the multiplicity of scales on which transnational history takes place. This perspective enables the analysis of the different spatial scopes of individual actors' movements ranging from local micro-scale to national and global macro levels.[13] Following this approach I start out from the interconnectedness of local activism, national reform agendas and the transnational circulation of ideas and practices related to welfare and social reform. Despite the increasing salience of national and transnational exchanges of ideas about social reform, the main orientation of the transnational actors continued to be the local (urban) level.

Before the expansion of the municipal governments under the welfare state, the Church and private organisations were the main providers of social assistance and sanitary infrastructure. It was hardly a surprise, therefore, that many representatives of local government and religious and secular welfare institutions found their way to the social welfare (*bienfaisance*) and hygiene congresses. These

---

11 See, for example, Madeleine Herren: *Hintertüren zur Macht. Internationalismus und modernisierungsorientierte Außenpolitik in Belgien, der Schweiz und den USA, 1865–1914*. München 2000; Martin H. Geyer and Johannes Paulmann (eds.): *The Mechanics of Internationalism. Culture, Society, and Politics from the 1840s to the First World War*. Oxford 2001; Mark Mazower: *Governing the World. The History of an Idea*. London 2012; Glenda Sluga: *Internationalism in the Age of Nationalism*. Philadelphia 2013; and Daniel L. Laqua: *The Age of Internationalism and Belgium, 1880–1930. Peace, Progress and Prestige*. Manchester 2013.

12 Elisabeth Crawford: *Nationalism and Internationalism in Science, 1880–1939. Four Studies of the Nobel Population*. Cambridge 1992; Ralph Jessen and Jakob Vogel (eds.): *Wissenschaft und Nation in der europäischen Geschichte*. Frankfurt 2002; Geert Somsen: A History of Universalism. Conceptions of the Internationality of Science from the Enlightenment to the Cold War, in: *Minerva* 46, no. 3 (2008), 361–379.

13 Bernard Struck, Kate Ferris and Jacques Revel: Introduction. Space and Scale in Transnational History, in: *International History Review* 33, no. 4 (2011), 573–584, esp. 577.

were topics that had been put on the agenda of international congresses early on. Brussels had hosted the first international hygiene congress in 1852 and the first international welfare congress in 1856. The ruling liberals in Belgium were particularly keen on displaying their performances in these areas. Not only the standard bearers at the central level, such as Auguste Visschers and Edouard Ducpétiaux, were prominent participants, but also mayors, aldermen, communal councillors and high officials from the larger cities such as Brussels, Liège, Antwerp and Ghent frequently made an appearance.

Victor Desguin (1838–1919), medical doctor and long-term member of the municipal council of Antwerp, made his entrance onto the international scene by becoming a member of the *Association Internationale pour le Progrès des Sciences Sociales* (1862–67) when he was serving in the army as a battalion doctor.[14] Academic recognition was important for the young Desguin. In 1864 he won first prize in a competition on rheumatism held by the *Académie Impériale de Médecine* of Paris.[15] But he had political aspirations as well. In 1876 he was elected as a liberal to the provincial council of Antwerp, followed by his election into the municipal council in 1879, a seat he held until 1918. Between 1892 and 1918 he was also a member of the municipal executive as alderman for education and public health, acting as mayor during three short intervals.[16] Furthermore, he was a member of various local and national learned societies in Belgium. In 1877 he was among the founders of the *Société royale de médecine publique de Belgique*, an organisation that assembled medical and non-medical experts on public health questions.

Desguin's membership of the local masonic lodge *Les Amis du Commerce et la Persévérance Réunis*, his involvement in the *Société de Médecine d'Anvers* and his contacts with doctors in other cities profiling themselves as hygienists fuelled his ambitions to engage himself in aid and assistance to the poor and the destitute in Antwerp.[17] In order to carry out a hygienist agenda he needed access to political

14 Christian Müller: The Politics of Expertise. The Association Internationale pour le Progrès des Sciences Sociales, Democratic Peace Movements and International Law Networks in Europe, 1850–1875, in: Davide Rodogno, Bernard Struck and Jakob Vogel (eds.): *Shaping the Transnational Sphere. Experts, Networks and Issues from the 1840s to the 1930s*. New York 2015, 131–151; Carmen Van Praet and Christophe Verbruggen: "Soldiers for a Joint Cause". A Relational Perspective on Local and International Educational Leagues and Associations in the 1860s, in: *BMGN – Low Countries Historical Review* 130, no. 1 (2015), 4–24.

15 *Bulletin de l'Académie impériale de médecine* 29 (1864–65), Vol. XXX, 178.

16 PPA1 1830–1921 et al., Victor Desguin, in: *ODIS*. Record last modified date: 6 June 2006. URL: *http://www.odis.be/lnk/PS_115* (17 July 2015).

17 Joris Vandendriessche and Kaat Wils: Een traject van onderhandeling. Hygiënisme als wetenschap, Antwerpen 1880–1900, in: *BMGN – Low Countries Historical Review* 128, no. 3 (2013), 3–28.

power, and in order to gain political support he needed a programme that would attract the urban middle classes. Food safety, clean drinking water, medical inspection of schools and prevention against infectious diseases were themes that went well with the electorate. Desguin made sure he supported all these causes.

International congresses played an important role in Desguin's career path. At first he played safe and mixed with his peers at the fourth international medical congress held in Brussels in 1875. He presented a paper on the physiological effects of alcohol.[18] Desguin's next, bolder step was to put the consumption of alcohol in a much wider perspective at the international hygiene congress held in Brussels in 1876. While his paper, based on research in different countries, was as meticulous as his medical contributions, his focus had shifted to the societal consequences of alcoholism. He discussed the tasks of the central state, local government and private initiative in dealing with alcohol problems. For his own country he emphasised the urgency for following the example of the British, Swedish, Americans and French in establishing a national temperance society. Within a short time he had transformed himself from army doctor to champion of hygienism. From then on he was a respected guest at the international hygiene and demography congresses up until the 15th, which took place in Washington, DC in 1912.

Initially, his appearance at international congresses helped him to establish himself as an expert in hygienic measures in his home town. Once he had obtained a safe seat in the municipal council of Antwerp the combination of political authority and medical expertise added weight to his public appearances. It is interesting to note that in the list of participants included in the congress proceedings, Desguin is often also listed as member of the *Académie royale de médecine de Belgique* or the *Société royale de médecine publique de Belgique*. Apparently, such organisations were even better suited to lending authority to speakers than functions in local government. Later in his career, by virtue of his office as alderman, he frequently attended congresses held in Antwerp or Brussels as president, vice-president or honorary member, even if the topics were unrelated to medicine or hygiene. Eventually, seniority and standing came to count at least as much as expertise.

The participation in international congresses also worked the other way round. Congresses not only boosted individual careers, but also conferred prestige on the institutions delegating people to them. At the sixth international hygiene and demography congress held in Vienna in 1887, Desguin commented at length

18 *Congrès periodique international des sciences médicales, 4me session – Bruxelles – 1875*. Brussels 1876, 38–48.

on the medical inspection of public schools, which the city of Antwerp had institutionalised in 1882. The "Antwerp model" of school hygiene thus earned a certain reputation at the international level.[19] Like many other cities that sent representatives to international congresses, the local government of Antwerp expected Desguin to report on his foreign trips. Hence, Desguin frequently elaborated on his congress visits in the municipal council. Sometimes, these reports were separately published, not just to honour the author but no doubt also to highlight the city's successes in organising public health services. The municipal executive ordered 50 copies of Desguin's paper for the Vienna congress to be distributed to local libraries.[20] The international stage, therefore, was not only a platform for a good cause, but could also serve the careers of delegates and was used to promote the interests of local governments and learned societies.

In the period in question, quite a few medical doctors in urban areas reinvented themselves as hygienists. Louis Guillaume (1833–1924) was one of them. When, in 1856, he started a medical practice in Neuchâtel, not far from his home town of Les Verrières, he could not have expected one day to become the author of a much-read book on hygiene, the head of the federal bureau of statistics of Switzerland and the undisputed leader of the international prison congress. In the tense situation in Neuchâtel during the international crisis of 1856–57, when local royalists sought to re-establish old links between the Principality and the Kingdom of Prussia, he stood as a candidate for the local council, a seat he held until 1860. He dedicated his free time to taking long walks in the Jura Mountains and loved teaching the children in local schools about the wonders of nature. He found an outlet for his passion for the study of nature in the *Club Jurassien*, which he helped to found in 1865, soon followed by a (still existing) non-specialist periodical *Le Rameau du Sapin*. Guillaume was also active in the local historical society and was editor of its journal, the *Musée neuchâtelois*. In short, there was very little to suggest that his reputation would ever outgrow his native region.

Like Desguin, Guillaume nourished a strong sense of mission in matters of hygiene, and it was this drive that led him to push the boundaries of his profession. In 1864 he published his lectures on school hygiene.[21] Though not the first book on the topic, it proved to be a great success, not only among the authorities and citizens of Neuchâtel but also throughout Switzerland and even beyond. It

19 Joris Vandendriessche: Medische expertise en politieke strijd. De dienst medisch schooltoezicht in Antwerpen, 1860–1900, in: *Stadsgeschiedenis* 6, no. 2 (2011), 125.

20 Victor Desguin: *L'inspection médicale dans les écoles*. Bruges 1888; see also Vandendriessche, Medische expertise, 126.

21 Louis Guillaume: *Hygiène scolaire. Considérations sur l'état hygiénique des écoles publiques présentées aux autorités scolaires, aux instituteurs et aux parents*. Geneva 1864.

was translated into several languages, and it may well have stimulated Desguin's interest in this field. The seemingly biggest career change came in 1870, when he was appointed director of the new cantonal prison of Neuchâtel. The fact that his brother-in-law, Eugène Borel, was at the time head of the justice department of the cantonal government no doubt contributed to this appointment. Though Guillaume had gained some experience in penitentiary matters as prison doctor and active member of the local sanitary commission, he still had to make a name for himself as a prison governor. He chose the international route to do so.

He had the good fortune that, shortly after his appointment, the international prison congress reconvened after a long interruption of 25 years, although penal reform had been on the agenda of several welfare congresses held in the 1850s. He secured backing from his fellow Swiss governors by drafting a report on the state of the prison system in the country, and joined the international executive committee of the congress, which – unlike similar committees at other congresses – continued to meet at regular intervals, chiefly to prepare the next congress. During the congress, held in London in July 1872, Guillaume showed deep commitment to the various reform causes that were passed in review, and became a symbol of goodwill and reform-mindedness. He was widely believed to uphold the spirit of the international penitentiary reform movement that was taking shape. At the first preparatory meeting of the international penitentiary commission held in Brussels in 1874 he was installed as secretary-general, an office he would hold until the 1910 congress in Washington.

Yet congresses and preliminary meetings were events that interrupted the daily lives of the participants only briefly. Sometimes, delegates stayed on for a few days, for a site visit or a professional encounter, but since they were usually on duty as official representatives they headed home directly after the congress. Their day-to-day work remained largely confined by the routine of ministerial offices, welfare institutions, prisons and the like, and did not become transnationalised in practice. Internationalism was lived by the fireside. Mobility was a long detour homewards and not meant to function as a linear movement from one locality to another one.

This is not to say that mobility was pointless or that internationalism was an illusion. The concepts need to be seen in the context of the means of communication that were available in the nineteenth century. After his visit to London, Guillaume returned to Neuchâtel to resume his duties at the local prison. It was there that Enoch C. Wines of the United States National Prison Association came to visit him on his European tour. Those who came from far away were more likely to stay longer. The two had met in London. Wines was commissioned by the chairman of the National Prison Association to seek cooperation from governments of European states and to visit as many penal and reformatory institutions as possible. He stayed a few days as guest of Guillaume, and was thoroughly introduced to the system adopted at the Neuchâtel prison. From his account it becomes clear that Guillaume personally supervised the around 80 inmates with extraordinary concern, fully committed to their moral improvement. On Sunday mornings, before church, the director would give a lecture on a matter of general interest to the prisoners and the employees, preceded by a few comments on "minor morals".[22] By and large, Guillaume's methods resembled the progressive Crofton system, developed in Ireland and aimed at encouraging good conduct, which was gradually gaining ground in Switzerland and which Wines wanted to promote in the United States.

Guillaume would continue as prison governor until 1889, when he applied to be director of the Federal Statistical Office of Switzerland. This again seemed a radical career change, but already at the penitentiary congress in London he had underlined the importance of statistics "as a guide to prison reformers". He did not expect immediate results, but "in twenty, thirty, or fifty years, they would allow the keystone of the arch to be supplied".[23] For many reformers statistics were the key to accomplishing their goals. It was no coincidence that social reform issues figured so prominently on the agenda of the international statistical congresses. Because of his new function Guillaume also became "membre titulaire" of the International Statistical Institute established in 1885 as successor of the international statistical congress, and regularly attended its meetings. Throughout the rest of his active life he continued to publish about hygiene, penal reform, education, and statistics. A strong belief in the possibility of moral advancement continued to characterise his publications and professional activities.

Perhaps more than any other person selected for this study, Louis Guillaume personified the multifariousness of social reform around 1900. For him, there were no clear boundaries between the "professions" he practised, medical doctor and prison director, educator and statistician. While such cross-overs were not uncommon in the nineteenth century, the more remarkable element of his biography was the transnational scope of his activities. This "transnational agency" was not intentional or exclusive in the sense that Guillaume wanted to transcend national borders in order to create a new space, but rather to initiate or support reform movements where these were most active, at the local and national level.[24]

22 Enoch C. Wines: *Report on the International Penitentiary Congress of London Held July 3–13, 1872*. Washington, DC 1873, 224.

23 *Prisons and Reformatories at Home and Abroad Being the Transactions of the International Penitentiary Congress Held in London July 3–13, 1872*. London 1872, 451.

24 See, Denis Kitzinger: Towards a Model of Transnational Agency. The Case of Dietrich von Hildebrand, in: *International History Review* 33, no. 4 (2011), 669–686.

State and Civil Society

It is tempting to look at the history of social reform in the nineteenth century as a dichotomy between state-led regulation on the one hand and activism emanating from civil society on the other. These apparently incompatible ways of providing care and assistance are also recognisable in the broadly defined state traditions or welfare state models that political scientists so easily embrace.[25] There is, to simplify things, an Anglo-Saxon model emphasising *laissez-faire* and decentralisation of decision-making, and a continental Napoleonic model privileging bureaucracy and hierarchical intervention. Quite a few polemical discussions at international congresses from the last quarter of the nineteenth century seem to confirm this divide. The organisers of one of the biggest events, the international welfare congress held in Paris during the world's fair of 1900, even decided to explicitly refer to the two camps by calling it *Congrès international d'assistance publique et de bienfaisance privée*.

Around 1900, however, the contrasts were less stark than the caricatured antithesis of political beliefs leads us to suspect. At the international congress of public and private welfare in 1900, the vast majority of participants sought a third, middle way, following traditional distinctions between types of indigents (able bodied, disabled, sick, elderly, etc.), which were held to be more conclusive for determining who would have to deal with them, rather than uncompromising ideological stances.[26] In a wider perspective Peter Baldwin has convincingly argued that historians and social scientists should try not to regard state and civil society in isolation from each other, "as two dueling monads", but rather to focus attention on the interaction between the two.[27] Similar functions were often pursued in different ways. To put it differently, we should concentrate on what Michael Mann has called the "polymorphous crystallisation" of the modern state, with considerable differences between and within nation-states in terms of functions and scope of the state in relation to civil society.[28] Also, the political system as such does not predict how well states accomplished particular tasks. For instance, in trying to get a grip on the spread of cholera, liberal systems were often

25 For a critical historical perspective, see Pauli Kettunen and Klaus Petersen (eds.): *Beyond Welfare State Models. Transnational Historical Perspectives on Social Policy*. Cheltenham 2011.

26 Christian Topalov: Langage de la réforme et déni du politique. Le débat entre assistance publique et bienfaisance privée, 1889–1903, in: *Genèses* 23 (1996), 30–52.

27 Peter Baldwin: The Victorian State in Comparative Perspective, in: Peter Mandler (ed.): *Liberty and Authority in Victorian England*. Oxford 2006, 53.

28 Michael Mann: *The Sources of Social Power. Vol. II: The Rise of Classes and Nation-States, 1760–1914*. Cambridge 1993, 75–88.

at least as effective as more authoritarian ones. By comparing ways in which states have dealt with contagious diseases, Baldwin comes to the conclusion that the issue was often not of interventionism versus *laissez-faire*, but rather of different forms of intervention.[29]

This approach lends itself very well to an attempt to characterise the professional activities of Henri Monod (1843–1911), regular participant in the assistance, hygiene and sanitary congresses in the period around 1900. He made a career in the French ministry of the interior, first at a regional level (ultimately as prefect of various departments) and later in the central ministry in Paris. As long-standing director of the section for public welfare and hygiene (1887–1905), where he earned the nickname of "state philanthropist", he was able to campaign energetically for new legislation in these fields. It would be misleading, however, to look upon his mission as purely state-centred. As we shall see, many of his projects hovered between state intervention and placing societal actors in positions of responsibility.[30]

Monod's family background contributed to forming his views on the organisation of welfare and sanitation, and he was first to recognise this. In a genealogical study he prepared for a family reunion he boasted that his ancestors originated from quite a few different countries: France of course, but also Switzerland, Italy, Belgium, the Netherlands, and Denmark.[31] There were many Protestant pastors among his forefathers. Many of them were forced to flee with their families across borders to save their possessions or even their lives. Through his mother Suzanne Smedley, born in Liverpool, he nourished a partiality to all things British and, of course, acquired a second language naturally. A transnational outlook and a caring attitude were part of the family tradition. That there must have been an element of truth in this cross-generational socialisation is proved by the career of his niece, Sarah Monod (whose mother also happened to be British), who would become a prominent prison reformer and feminist leader.

Trained as a lawyer, Henri Monod started his administrative career in the secretarial staff of the 1867 Paris world's fair. After the Franco-Prussian war he entered the civil administration and made an extraordinarily rapid career. At 34 he had already reached the rank of prefect, an office he would hold in various departments, ultimately in Finistère (1885–87), where he was confronted with a severe outbreak of cholera. His transfer to Quimper, the department's capital,

29 Peter Baldwin: *Contagion and the State in Europe, 1830–1930*. Cambridge 2005 [1999], 535.

30 See Pierre Rosanvallon: *Le modèle politique français. La société civile contre le jacobinisme de 1789 à nos jours*. Paris 2004.

31 Henri Monod: *La famille Monod, origines, extension (Réunion de famille, 2 novembre 1908)*. Nancy 1909.

was probably no coincidence. Monod had developed a strong interest in the fight against contagious diseases and was eager to put his ideas to the test. A visit to the international hygiene exhibition in London in the summer of 1884 had been instrumental in fanning the flame. He had made the trip together with his friend Joseph Gibert, a medical doctor based in Le Havre and initiator of the first municipal bureau, and Jules Siegfried, then mayor of the same city and also a regular visitor of international congresses. "Ce voyage", he would later write, "mes conversations avec ces deux hommes généreux, m'ont engagé sur la route que depuis lors j'ai suivi".[32]

The path Monod would take was to return to Paris, accept a slightly lower salary, and fully dedicate himself to the administration of public welfare and hygiene.[33] Trying to learn from foreign experience continued to mark his professional attitude. He was a member of the organising committees of the international congresses on public welfare and on hygiene and demography that took place in Paris in 1889. He was not just looking out from the inside, but would also go abroad to attend congresses within the vast field of his office, such as the hygiene and demography congress of Budapest held in 1894 and the child protection congress of Geneva held in 1896.

Monod tried to frame his stance on welfare and hygiene by making a strong plea to science. Looking back at the fight against cholera in Finistère, he showed that traditional administrative action was not enough, and underlined how important it had been to rely on scientific advice:

> Dans la lutte contre les épidémies, qu'il s'agisse de les prévenir ou de les combattre, et généralement en tout ce qui touche à l'hygiène publique, l'administrateur a un rôle modeste et nécessaire : il doit être et peut seulement être l'auxiliaire de l'homme de science. Ce serait de sa part grande témérité d'entreprendre sur ce qui est le domaine propre du savant.[34]

International congresses were an important supplier of scientific truth. By attending a congress, politicians, officials and scientists could prove they had become companions in impartial knowledge. Being able to refer to statistics reinforced their claims to truth. Authoritative publications could further enhance the stature of an expert. In his monograph on the cholera epidemic in Finistère, Monod made sure he ticked these boxes. International sanitary and hygiene congresses were

---

32 Henri Monod: *La santé publique*. Paris 1904, 87 (quoted in Lion Murard and Patrick Zylberman: *L'hygiène dans la République. La santé publique en France, ou l'utopie contrariée 1870–1918*. Paris 1996, 185).

33 I am zooming in here through a biographical case study of Monod, on an episode in the early phase of the French welfare state more extensively discussed in Topalov, Langage de la réforme.

34 Henri Monod: *Le choléra (histoire d'une épidémie, Finistère 1885–1886)*. Paris 1892, 5.

presented as crucial moments in reaching consensus about the origins and combating of the disease. Statistics provided the necessary numerical backbone. And he could refer to his own publications in the field, such as *Les mesures sanitaires en Angleterre depuis 1875 et leurs résultats*, which he had published as a monograph in 1891 after presenting it to the *Société de médecine publique et hygiène professionelle* and pre-publishing it in the *Revue d'Hygiène*. Monod wanted his authority to be beyond doubt.

Speaking at congresses required special qualities. A certain mastery of languages helped. Native French speakers obviously had an advantage, since their language continued to be the *lingua franca* of the international scene. Monod's bilingualism was an additional asset. But he also needed a degree of versatility, first to be able to act as a mediator between the various camps among the French and second to furnish him with sufficient international prestige. Again the appeal to science and reliance on the outcomes of international congresses proved useful. In a speech at the international hygiene exhibition in Le Havre in 1893 he pointed to recent scientific advances, and tried to follow in the footsteps of resolutions made at the sanitary conference held earlier that year in Dresden. In matters of hygiene it was apparently easier to play the scientific card than to call for welfare provision. At the international welfare congress of 1889, held in his home town, Monod played another trump card: the history of the French state since 1789 and its "sacred obligation to provide relief". Since he was mainly talking to a French audience, he cleverly resorted to the old republican spirit to show which way the state was meant to go: "si l'initiative privée doit garder son rôle, un rôle important, c'est pourtant l'État qui devra fixer et diriger l'organisation générale".[35] His call for efficiency raised a storm of applause, according to the proceedings. There was, however, a clear reservation: "L'assistance publique, à défaut d'autre assistance, est due à l'indigent qui se trouve, temporairement ou définitivement, dans l'impossibilité physique de pourvoir aux nécessités de l'existence".[36] Public welfare, therefore, was only meant for the helpless young, the elderly and the sick.

By the next international welfare congress in Paris (1900) the bifurcation of public and private relief in France had become a fait accompli. In his opening speech, mainly directed towards the French majority in the audience, Monod again went back to the French Revolution and its emphasis on the duties of the state *vis-à-vis* the needy. He was pleased to confirm that the route he had laid out a decade ago had proved to be the right one. It had even been advantageous for private welfare: the number of institutions that had acquired the title "d'utilité

35 *Congrès international d'assistance tenue du 28 juillet au 4 août* 1889. *Vol. I.* Paris 1889, 284.
36 Ibid., 286.

publique" (in the public interest) had markedly increased. New organisations had also emerged, such as marine hospitals, sanatoria, and shelters for pregnant women. His mildly triumphalist speech was clearly geared to the occasion. A year later, in an article for the *Revue philanthropique*, he allowed himself to be more critical, both with regard to the efficiency of the public services and to the mentality of the advocates of the private charities. He found it odd that a Catholic organisation, exclusively providing for people of that confession, could call itself *Office central des œuvres de bienfaisance*.[37] As to his own role as civil servant, he believed he was often falsely attacked or put in the wrong camp. He was wary of people who saw him merely as a defender of public welfare, or solely as an enemy of private relief. The fault-finding between representatives of private charity and welfare functionaries reflected petty personal animosity rather than the relations in real terms, he thought: "L'assistance n'est le plus souvent que de la bienfaisance régularisée, et il arrive que la bienfaisance se réduit à n'être qu'une administration".[38] In the end, despite the numerous misunderstandings, he continued to believe that an enlightened balance between different forms of relief was the best way forward.

Monod was a good example of the "hesitant Jacobinism" that characterised the administrative elite of the Third Republic in France.[39] As prefect he had learned at first hand that the powers of the state were neither all-encompassing nor unidirectional. In the often complex political reality of the departmental administration, inflexible interventionism was bound to fail, or would have marginal effects, without sufficient support of local elites. His "multi-level" fight against the cholera epidemic had amply demonstrated this. In Paris, forcing through one's projects was even more difficult than in the provinces, not least because in the polarised political culture of the Third Republic it was always imperative to be on one's guard against political enemies. Consultation and mediation often yielded better results than showing administrative muscle.

This approach also worked at the international level, where unanimous decisions were extremely hard to arrive at, particularly if they were meant to accom-

37 Henri Monod: Bienfaisance privée et assistance publique (notes), in: *Revue philanthropique* 5, no. 9 (1901), 129–151, esp. 137.

38 Ibid., 146.

39 Sudhir Hazareesingh: Vincent Wright and the Jacobin Legacy in Historical and Theoretical Perspectives, in: id. (ed.): *The Jacobin Legacy in Modern France. Essays in Honour of Vincent Wright*. Oxford 2002, 1–20; Sabine Rudischhauser: Regulierte Selbstregulierung im Frankreich der III. Republik. Zivilgesellschaft und "jakobinischer" Staat, in: Peter Collin et al. (eds.): *Regulierte Selbstregulierung in der westlichen Welt des späten 19. und frühen 20. Jahrhunderts*. Frankfurt 2014, 149–188.

plish meaningful change. For Monod, international congresses were platforms to continue the political struggle at home. It helped that two important welfare congresses were held in Paris (in 1889 and 1900) at crucial moments in the development of new social legislation in France. He did not need to travel far to drive his point about public and private relief home. For other causes, however, he was prepared to leave familiar territory. In 1903, at the international hygiene congress in Brussels, he strongly supported the establishment of an International Office of Public Hygiene, eventually founded in 1908 in Paris. By then, Monod had left public service. It must have been a bitter moment for him that while he was presiding over the international congress of hydrology, climatology, geology and therapy using physical agents, held in October 1905 in Venice, the council of ministers decided that it was time for the "state philanthropist" to resign.[40]

Whereas Monod, motivated by a prudent Jacobin approach, strove for an entente between state and civil society initiatives, the Dutch priest and politician Willem Hubert Nolens (1860–1931) based his conception of state-society relations on Catholic doctrine. The encyclical *Rerum Novarum*, issued by Pope Leo XIII in 1891, coincided with Nolens' own decision to give his life a spin towards politics. He was ordained as a priest in 1887 and had obtained a doctorate in political science and law at the University of Utrecht in 1890. Part of his PhD dissertation addressed the social question and made an appeal to employers to understand that they were connected to the workers by another tie than just the financial.[41] It was this progressive view of labour relations that continued to characterise his ideas and initiatives as a politician, a university professor and an internationalist.

In 1896 he was elected to the Second Chamber for the district of Venlo, a seat he would hold until his death. In 1910 he became leader of the parliamentary party of the Catholics and had an important say in the formations of all new governments throughout the 1910s and 1920s without ever entering a cabinet himself. He was member (1902) and later president (1913) of the Dutch Mine Council. Between 1909 and 1925 he occupied the chair of labour legislation at the University of Amsterdam.

In the conciliatory climate surrounding *Rerum Novarum*, the minds of many Catholic intellectuals in Europe turned to internationally concerted action in favour of workers' protection. In the 1890s Nolens often accompanied the Catholic leader Herman Schaepman to the annual congresses of the German Catholics. In this period the organisers of these events frequently put social reform issues

---

40 Murard and Zylberman, L'hygiène dans la République, 450.

41 Jacobus Petrus Gribling: Nolens, Willem Hubert (1860–1931), in: *Biografisch Woordenboek van Nederland*. URL: *http://resources.huygens.knaw.nl/bwn1880-2000/lemmata/bwn1/nolens* [12-11-2013] (17 July 2015).

on the agenda and invited speakers from other countries. In that way they not only fuelled the programme of the Catholic *Zentrum* party in Germany, but also inspired the Dutch Catholics to follow their path. Both Schaepman and Nolens had an academic background and became advocates of a further democratisation of Dutch politics, hoping that they would be able to bind a large proportion of the working class to Catholic candidates (a fully-fledged Catholic party had yet not been formed). In August 1897 the two Dutch Catholic leaders took off to Fribourg in Switzerland to attend the fourth international scientific congress of Catholics, where one of Nolens' heroes, the *Zentrum* politician and professor Georg Friedrich Freiherr von Hertling, would give a lecture. In 1906 Nolens published a translation of Hertling's *Naturrecht und Socialpolitik* (originally published in 1893). From Fribourg, Nolens and Schaepman travelled to Zurich to participate in the international workers' protection congress.

To some extent the Zurich congress was a sequel to the workers' protection (*Arbeiterschutz*) congress organised by the German Emperor Wilhelm II after his turn towards a more integrationist social policy, but it also followed in the footsteps of earlier Swiss initiatives to come to some sort of international arrangement with regard to workers' protection. A wide variety of politicians, officials, employers and workers' representatives were invited to discuss child and women's labour, the length of the working day, Sunday rest and the establishment of an international bureau for workers' protection. What was often not possible at the national level was realised at this congress: a fruitful exchange of ideas and opinions between liberals, socialists, Catholics and Protestants. It seems that the Dutch representatives did not play a prominent role in the deliberations, but it gave Nolens the opportunity to expand his network.

The Belgian government had planned a similar congress in Brussels in September 1897, on the occasion of the international exhibition, to take stock of the progress made since the Berlin congress of 1890. The Brussels congress had a more official character and was to a greater extent aimed at bureaucrats, university professors and employers than its more "democratic" Swiss counterpart. Nolens presented a rather formalistic paper on Dutch social legislation, mainly consisting of articles from laws and regulations, but otherwise he appears not to have contributed to the debates. The congress also discussed whether it was expedient to create an international labour office. The majority of the participants, however, was not inclined to press ahead on this issue.

During the subsequent international congress for workers' protection held in Paris in 1900 the decision was finally taken to establish an International Association for Labour Legislation (IALL). A fully-fledged organisation proved unfeasible, but the non-governmental association was nevertheless given a permanent office and received subsidies from various national governments and the Vatican.

The seat of the new association was opened in Basel in 1901. The IALL was a mixed transnational community of experts *and* representatives of trade unions, and national employers' and workers' organisations, which thrived on its ability to navigate carefully between labour and capital.[42]

Nolens was present in 1900 at the *Musée Social*, where the founding congress took place, and in 1901 in Basel, when the association started its activities. Given his involvement in the realisation of the international association it was only logical that he would also obtain a seat on the board of the Dutch section established in February 1901. After the death of the first president, A. Kerdijk, in 1905, Nolens was appointed in his place. He would keep this function until the dissolution of the Dutch association in 1926. In this position he would frequently participate in the international gatherings of the association. His prominent role in the early days of Dutch and international bodies dealing with labour legislation made him the obvious person to lead the Dutch delegation to the annual International Labour Conferences after the First World War. He became a close friend of Albert Thomas, the director of the International Labour Office, and was instrumental in furthering relations between the ILO and the Vatican.[43]

Nolens did not limit his international activities to labour legislation issues. He was active in the *Comité permanent international des assurances sociales*, founded in 1889 (renamed *Association internationale des assurances sociales* in 1908), and the *Association internationale pour la lutte contre le chômage*. In these cases Nolens also acted as *trait-d'union* between the international bodies and their Dutch sections. He was involved in the Interparliamentary Conference and in the international peace and arbitration initiatives of the 1900s, which put The Hague on the map as the international capital of peace. From 1900 he also regularly attended the international public and private welfare congresses (in Milan and in Copenhagen, twice in Paris). At the 1910 congress in Copenhagen he acted as president of one of the sections, but otherwise the congress proceedings do not indicate that Nolens was active in the discussions. In the Netherlands he was not known for his oratory skills, and it seems that he did not force himself into the spotlight at the international level either. His strength, however, both nationally and internationally, lay in his ability to connect people and to act as trustworthy mediator.

---

42 Sandrine Kott: From Transnational Reformist Network to International Organization. The International Association for Labour Legislation and the International Labour Organization, 1900–1930s, in: Rodogno, Struck and Vogel, Shaping the Transnational Sphere, 239–258.

43 Jacobus Petrus Gribling: *Willem Hubert Nolens, 1860–1931. Uit het leven van een Priester-Staatsman*. Assen 1978, 267–287.

Nolens was a man of faith and was generally held to be an effective political broker. He was blessed with a rare talent in politics: the art of controlling his personal ambition, which not only helped him in the compromise and consensus seeking political culture of the Netherlands, but also gave him a head start in international contacts. The encyclical *Rerum Novarum* had given him the inspiration and the tools to search for practicable compromises with regard to social security and poor relief. He welcomed a role for the state in these fields whilst trying to assure that all societal parties involved would get a say in the supervision and execution of the arrangements that were offered. In this sense state and society could be brought into relative harmony. This strategy fitted in well with the mainstream ideas circulating within the transnational social reform community in the two decades before the First World War. The Vatican acknowledged his efforts, and appointed him in 1916 to the post of protonotary apostolic, which allowed him to choose a heraldic device. Nolens opted for "*Utrique fidelis*" (faithful to both), thereby expressing his commitment to church and state.

Conclusion

This study has examined the transnational mobility of four social reformers of different national backgrounds and political leanings. Their participation in international congresses received particular attention, since these were stages *par excellence* on which to test to what extent mobility, exchange, and reform were bound up.

The discussion of the relationship between internationalism, nationalism and local activism followed the various spatial orientations of the reform ideas of Victor Desguin of Antwerp and Louis Guillaume of Neuchâtel. Both had degrees in medicine and developed a keen interest in hygienism. The determination to bring about change in their respective environments (the city of Antwerp and the prison of Neuchâtel) led them to orientate themselves internationally. Since in the second half of the nineteenth century the national states provided very little in this field, local reformers often looked across borders. Desguin was a regular visitor to the international hygiene congresses, while Guillaume became the long-standing secretary-general of the international prison congress. Their contributions to the congresses not only helped them to further the cause of hygienist and penal reform across nations, but also – and perhaps more visibly – strengthened their position at home. Whereas sanitary reform in Antwerp remained Desguin's main sphere of action, Guillaume extended his scope to the federal statistics of Switzerland.

Turning to the transnational biographies of Henri Monod from Paris and Willem Hubert Nolens from Venlo, the focus shifted to how they used international platforms to advocate a division of labour between state and civil society in providing elementary social security. Monod, the son of a Protestant pastor, served the French state for almost 40 years and was imbued with a strong sense of administrative mission. This should not, however, be mistaken for a blind urge to centralise welfare and sanitation (his main fields of action) whenever a window of opportunity occurred and to create top-down structures wherever possible. As Monod's activities at the international level highlighted, his principal aim was to develop synergies between public and private arrangements, central and local government, and administrative and scientific expertise. The Catholic priest Willem Hubert Nolens similarly exerted himself to bring parties together in order to find compromises that worked. He did not draw his inspiration from a deep trust in the goodness of the state, but accepted its functionality for practical purposes. Like Monod, he strove for effective interaction between state and societal actors. His conciliatory Catholic background and heightened sense of the realities of the political order, also internationally, made him particularly qualified to act as go-between.

The main advantage of this biographical approach to mobility is that it makes it possible to recognise and to compare the strategies of protagonists at international congresses. They shared a willingness to champion public causes, such as sanitation, poor relief and social security, at a transnational level. Even though they no doubt believed in the expediency of international agreements on these issues, they also regarded the outcomes of the congresses as supporting their struggles at home.

Acknowledgement

I should like to thank the Netherlands Organisation for Scientific Research (NWO) for financial support of the project underlying this contribution.

Lucas Geese, Wolfgang Goldbach and Thomas Saalfeld

Mobility and Representation: Legislators of Non-European Origin in the British House of Commons, 2001–2015

Abstract: *While the share of immigrants as a percentage of the UK population has increased steadily since the 1950s, it was not until the early 2000s that the descriptive representation of such new citizens in the House of Commons became more proportional. Focusing on Members of Parliament with a "Black or Asian Minority Ethnic" background in the three Parliaments between 2001 and 2015, we examine the extent to which these legislators' parliamentary behaviour was influenced by their party membership, legislative experience, "immigrant generation" and constituency demographics. Based conceptually on a sociological "mobilities" framework and Fenno's work on "Home Styles" in the US Congress, we perform a dictionary-based content analysis of over 23,000 parliamentary questions for written answer. Comparing first-generation immigrants and the immediate descendants of such immigrants, we find that the content of questions reflects a relatively strong concern for transnational mobility amongst the former and a stronger focus on questions of social mobility in the UK in the latter group.*

Having been the origin of significant levels of emigration to non-European destinations in previous centuries, European states have become the destinations for large-scale immigration from non-European societies since the Second World War. Great Britain is a case in point: the number of foreign-born residents – so-called "first-generation immigrants" – in England and Wales nearly quadrupled from approximately 1.9 million (4.5 per cent of the "usually resident" population) in 1951, the first census after the Second World War, to around 7.5 million (13 per cent of the population) in the latest census of 2011.[1] While the arrival of a large number of people with transnational biographies is not extraordinary, Great Britain differs from many other European countries in one crucial respect: most of its early post-war immigrants arrived from Commonwealth States and therefore had full citizenship rights on arrival, including voting rights and the right to stand for

1 Office for National Statistics. Non-UK Born Population of England and Wales Quadrupled Between 1951 and 2011 (17 Dec. 2013), in: *Census Analysis, Immigration Patterns of Non-UK Born Populations in England and Wales in 2011.* URL: *http://www.ons.gov.uk/ons/rel/census/2011-census-analysis/immigration-patterns-and-characteristics-of-non-uk-born-population-groups-in-england-and-wales/summary.html* (13 June 2015).

election. Nevertheless, it was not until 1987 that the first four Members of Parliament (MPs) claiming a "Black or Asian Minority Ethnic" (BAME) background were elected to the House of Commons. At the time this "Gang of Four"[2], all members of the Labour Party, constituted approximately 0.6 per cent of all MPs. When the Commons met for the first time after the general election of 2015, this share had increased approximately tenfold to some 6 per cent of all 650 Members (Table 1).

Despite this increase in "descriptive representation" (see below), the political underrepresentation of BAME groups in the United Kingdom continues, as is the case in other liberal democracies. The present study seeks to explore aspects of, and differences among, the behaviour of MPs with a BAME background in the Parliaments elected in 2001, 2005 and 2010 (i.e. between June 2001 and May 2015). Empirically our study is based on the content of parliamentary questions for written answer, which many MPs generate in large numbers. They will serve as indicators of the issues MPs promote in the chamber, or emphasise in their oversight activities *vis-à-vis* the government. Our aim is to highlight variations *within* the group of BAME MPs rather than focusing on similarities and differences between this group and MPs of European descent. Therefore we are not comparing MPs with a BAME background to MPs without such a background. This shifts the analytic focus to some biographical factors such as "immigrant generation" or parliamentary experience on the one hand and elements of the political opportunity structure in which the BAME MPs operate on the other (e.g. MP's party membership or socio-demographic composition of the electoral district).

The emphasis of this study is not on single legislators and their individual life stories but on a few group characteristics that will be used for exploratory statistical analyses. The advantage is greater generalisability, the drawback is a loss in biographical granularity. Our data is far from carefully reconstructing the life-courses especially of the "first generation" of non-European immigrants in the House of Commons.[3] Nevertheless, it carries some key information on the personal experiences, political preferences and structural factors empowering or constraining BAME MPs, which have been found to be significant influences on parliamentary behaviour: This includes the fundamental distinction whether the MPs are immigrants themselves, or whether they are the sons or daughters of immigrants, as the latter often display weaker affective ties to their ancestral "home-

2 These were Diane Abbott, Paul Boateng, Bernie Grant and Keith Vaz.

3 Some data connecting the politicians' biography in their home countries with their career in their countries of residence will become available for the United Kingdom and seven other European countries (Belgium, Germany, Greece, France, Italy, the Netherlands and Spain) in 2017 when "PATHWAYS" (*www.pathways.eu*) a large comparative research project delivers some more finely granulated data on personal backgrounds.

lands" than their parents.[4] We also use information about the party an MP represents. After all, political parties are the primary contexts of political socialisation, provide and constrain opportunities for political careers and select those who represent them in Parliament. Not least, our exogenous variables include the context of electoral competition and the type of demands directed at MPs, which is partially shaped by the socio-demographic makeup of their constituencies.[5]

Compared to other studies in this volume, we find that the institutions in the new country of residence constitute very powerful constraints creating strong incentives for MPs with a BAME background to maintain a clear local or national focus. Although we may discover traces of "rooted cosmopolitanism"[6] in the parliamentary speeches of minority MPs with a BAME background, they clearly constitute a contrast to the artists, bankers and other groups analysed in this volume where ambiguity may, on occasion, have been an asset. Cases where British BAME MPs overtly or covertly represent the interests of ethnically related foreigners or receive foreign donations from such countries are highly exceptional and may be drawn to the attention of the Parliamentary Commissioner for Standards.[7]

Migration, Representation and Mobilities

The present study is in the tradition of work that treats the migratory and ethnic background of MPs as consequential for their behaviour in the legislature, in

4 The importance of the difference especially between immigrants and the "second generation" of their descendants is well documented in sociological and historical research. In sociology, see Richard Alba and Victor Nee (eds.): *Remaking the American Mainstream. Assimilation and Contemporary Immigration*. Cambridge, MA 2005; Alejandro Portes and Rubén G. Rumbaut: *Immigrant America. A Portrait*. Oakland, CA [4]2014. In historical research, see, amongst many others, Eric L. Goldstein: The Great Wave. Eastern European Jewish Immigration to the United States, 1880–1924, in: Marc Lee Raphael (ed.): *The Columbia History of Jews and Judaism in America*. New York 2005, 70–92.

5 Regarding the last two variables, see, for example, Thomas Saalfeld: Parliamentary Questions as Instruments of Substantive Representation. Visible Minorities in the UK House of Commons, 2005–10, in: *Journal of Legislative Studies* 17 (2011), 271–289.

6 Sidney Tarrow: Rooted Cosmopolitans and Transnational Activists, in: id. (ed.): *Strangers at the Gates. Movements and States in Contentious Politics*. Cambridge 2012, 181–199.

7 See, for example, Emily Dugan: Keith Vaz Reported to Parliamentary Standards Commissioner over Lobbying Visa Officials for Controversial Cricketing Tycoon, in: *Independent* (25 July 2015), URL: *http://www.independent.co.uk/news/uk/politics/keith-vaz-reported-to-parliamentary-standards-commissioner-over-lobbying-visa-officials-for-controversial-cricketing-tycoon-10303541.html* (7 Aug. 2015).

their electoral district or *vis-à-vis* the wider attentive public.[8] MPs of immigrant origin bring an element of strong "mobility"[9] to deliberations in the chamber. This experience of mobility – or "motility" as outlined in the introduction to this volume – affects BAME legislators in the House of Commons in at least two ways: First, immigrant MPs have personally experienced "horizontal" trans-border mobility, involving the arrival in a new social, economic and political environment. In this context they often had to overcome "historical political subordination" (e.g. as residents of former British colonies), "low de facto legitimacy"[10] and possibly discrimination – not only in the work place, but also within organisations such as political parties or trade unions.[11]

If their background matters at all to their political attitudes and behaviour, they face a complex task once they stand for elected office: they are only likely to get selected as candidates by their parties and elected by a plurality of the voters in their respective districts, if they can claim to represent *all* residents of their *locally* defined constituencies. This leads to different strategic options for "handling" their ethnicity: at one end of a representational continuum they may have incentives to suppress their own background;[12] at the other end of that spectrum they may define themselves as representatives of minorities throughout the UK reaching beyond their local constituency. For the latter type, representation may even include transnational elements, if they retain links with politics or organisations in their ancestral homeland or concern themselves with global diaspora or faith communities. The House of Commons offers limited institutional opportunities for transnational activity beyond party politics, namely in the so-called "All-Party Parliamentary Groups" that seek to foster exchange with various countries. In 2015, for example, the Conservative MP Rehman Chishti, who was born in Pakistan, served as the chair of the All-Party Parliamentary Group on Pakistan.[13] In short, their horizontal mobility may introduce a trans-constituency

8 Other works especially on the United States Congress or state legislatures in the US have examined the effect the legislators' ethnicity has on constituent attitudes and behaviour – or indeed the patterns of conflict and cooperation in Congress. For a review, see John D. Griffin: When and Why Minority Legislators Matter, in: *Annual Review of Political Science* 17 (2014), 327–336.

9 Kevin Hannam, Mimi Sheller and John Urry: Editorial. Mobilities, Immobilities and Moorings, in: *Mobilities* 1 (2006), 1–22; Mimi Sheller and John Urry: The New Mobilities Paradigm, in: *Environment and Planning* 38 (2006), 207–226.

10 Jane Mansbridge: Should Blacks Represent Blacks and Women Represent Women? A Contingent "Yes", in: *Journal of Politics* 61 (1999), 628–657, esp. 628.

11 Randall Hansen: *Citizenship and Immigration in Postwar Britain*. Oxford 2000.

12 In the US context, this phenomenon is referred to as "deracialization". See Joseph McCormick: The November Elections. The Politics of Deracialization, in: *New Directions* 17 (1990), 22–27.

13 URL: *http://www.publications.parliament.uk/pa/cm/cmallparty/register/pakistan.htm* (6 Aug. 2015).

and transnational element into the process of territorial, district-based representation in the UK.

Secondly, many descendants of immigrants as well as immigrants in politics experienced a spectacular process of upward (vertical) social mobility in the UK. While the descendants of non-European immigrants may (or may not) have encountered as much discrimination on their path to the political elite as "first-generation" immigrants,[14] their transnational links to the politics of their ancestral homelands are often weaker. Nevertheless, family ties and the compression of geographic space through new internet-based media may have compensated for the biographical distance. While technical advances certainly created the conditions for continuous links between the MPs and their ancestral homelands, it remains an empirical question whether there is actually any evidence for attempts to be part of some "imagined community", to borrow Anderson's phrase.[15] In short, the research problem at the heart of this study is the extent to which various – horizontal and vertical – "mobilities" add a new transnational dimension to democratic representation in the United Kingdom (and, by extension, other European countries).

Ethnicity and the opportunity (or the need) to move between different "worlds" open up strategic options.[16] To what extent do differences in the life-courses of MPs with a BAME background shape their behaviour in the chamber – and, not least, towards his or her constituents, whether local, national or even transnational? After all, MPs have choices in the way they perform their roles as legislators.[17] They may find it wise to prioritise tasks assigned to them by their parliamentary parties; they may aspire to ministerial office or to so-called "mega seats"[18] such as committee chairs – and hence do everything to avoid the impression of representing what might be perceived as narrow group interests; or they may see themselves as local constituency representatives. The present study focuses on the legislative behaviour of the 37 MPs of non-European origin who served in the House of Commons between 2001 and 2015 (Appendix 1). In

14 Indications of racism experienced by second-generation immigrants can be found in various autobiographies, including Parmjid Dhanda: *My Political Race*. London 2015.

15 Benedict Anderson: *Imagined Communities. Reflections on the Origin and Spread of Nationalism*. London 2006.

16 Thomas Saalfeld, Karen Bird and Andreas M. Wüst: Epilogue. Towards a Strategic Model of Minority Participation and Representation, in: eid. (eds.): *The Political Representation of Immigrants and Minorities. Voters, Parties and Parliaments in Liberal Democracies*. London 2011, 266–275.

17 Donald Searing: *Westminster's World. Understanding Political Roles*. Cambridge, MA 1994.

18 Royce Carroll, Gary W. Cox and Mónica Pachón: How Parties Create Electoral Democracy. Chapter 2, in: *Legislative Studies Quarterly* 31 (2006), 153–174.

particular, it aims to demonstrate the variability of behaviour *within* this group of MPs. Variability may be induced by factors such as party, pre-parliamentary socialisation (which may depend on the country of birth of ethnic-minority MPs and their continued dedication to "homeland politics"), socialisation in their party and in the chamber (experience) or strategic incentives arising from the demographic composition of the constituency.

Theoretical Framework

Representation is an ambiguous concept spanning several dimensions. In Hanna Pitkin's words "representation means, as the word's etymological origins indicate, *re-presentation*, a making present again. [...] Representation, taken generally, means the making present *in some sense* of something which is nevertheless *not* present literally or in fact."[19] One of the most fundamental further distinctions in this context is the one between "descriptive" and "substantive" representation. Descriptive representation refers to a "shared characteristic linking the governors and the governed".[20] Ethnicity or gender can be such characteristics. Substantive representation, by contrast, refers to "acting in the interest of the represented, in a manner responsive to them" without *necessarily* assuming a link between personal characteristics and policy responsiveness.[21]

Building on this definition, Jane Mansbridge refines the basic distinction between descriptive and substantive representation further. First, her notion of "gyroscopic representation" highlights an important aspect of descriptive representation by describing a mechanism whereby "the representative looks within, as a basis for action, to conceptions of interest, 'common sense,' and principles derived in part from the representative's own background."[22] Second, the notion of substantive representation can be based on three mechanisms: In Mansbridge's terminology, "promissory representation" refers to "the idea that during [electoral] campaigns representatives made promises to constituents, which they then kept or failed to keep." Acting in the interest of the represented can also be based on "anticipatory representation", which "flows directly from

19 Hanna F. Pitkin: *The Concept of Representation*. Berkeley, CA 1967, 8–9. Emphasis in the original.
20 Griffin, When and Why, 328.
21 Pitkin, The Concept, 209.
22 Jane Mansbridge: Rethinking Representation, in: *American Political Science Review* 97 (2003), 515–528, esp. 515.

the idea of retrospective voting: Representatives focus on what they think their constituents will approve at the next election, not on what they promised to do at the last election." In these two mechanisms the candidate's personal characteristics are neither irrelevant nor central. Given comparable electoral incentives, promissory and anticipatory representation may affect the way of ethnic majority and minority MPs in similar ways and electoral competition should establish a more or less close alignment between the voters' preferences and the MPs' behaviour as representatives. "Surrogate representation", by contrast, does depend on the MP's personal traits (like gyroscopic representation): it "occurs when legislators represent constituents outside their own districts"[23], and when this occurs because legislators share some other personal trait with those groups.

The specific *focus* of different types of representation may vary. Richard Fenno conceptualises representation as "a never-ending process whereby the politician works at building and maintaining supportive connections with some proportion of his or her constituents."[24] His empirical studies show that "[a]ll House members are goal seekers. They have ambitions; they want to accomplish things."[25] Thus their representational activities tend to be in line with goals such as "getting reelected, making good public policy, accumulating influence in the House, building a political party locally, performing a civic duty, and helping individuals with their problems."[26] Crucially for our present argument, "reelection subsequently becomes the first-order goal of almost every incumbent House member", although "election is not the only goal that drives the aspirant toward politics in the first place, and reelection is not the only goal that keeps the member in politics afterward."[27] Crucially for the purposes of our study, Fenno assumes

> that each Representative perceives not a single home constituency, but a set of constituencies that nest, like a series of concentric circles, within one another. The largest circle, the district, contains all the residents of the legally prescribed geographical constituency; the next smaller, the reelection constituency, contains all voters who support or might support the member, and the smallest, the primary constituency, consists of their most active and most reliable supporters. African American members [...] perceive a fourth constituency to which they respond, one beyond the district – a national constituency of black citizens who live beyond the borders of any one member's district, but with whom all black members share a set of race-related concerns.[28]

23 All quotes in this paragraph are taken from ibid.
24 Richard F. Fenno: *Going Home. Black Representatives and Their Constituents*. Chicago 2003.
25 Ibid., 6.
26 Ibid.
27 Ibid.
28 Ibid., 7.

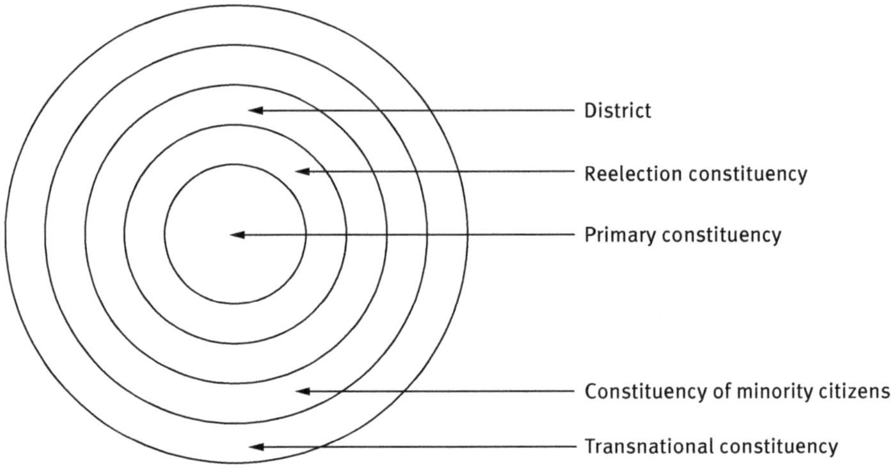

Figure 1: Concentric Circles of Ethnic-Minority Representation (inspired by Fenno)

A modified version of this model of "concentric circles" could be applied to British MPs with a BAME background: The smallest circle, Fenno's "primary constituency", would be the party activists who decide over the MP's reselection and play a crucial role in mobilising the resources for a successful local campaign. Around this core, there would be a second, "reelection constituency" comprising the MP's (and his or her party's) likely voters in the district. The third, "district" circle would include all potential voters – and, indeed, residents – in the MP's territorially defined electoral district. This is appropriate, because a backbencher's reputation depends, amongst other factors, on the visibility of his or her constituency casework on behalf of all residents in the district regardless of their citizenship status or political allegiance. We know from qualitative work that some – but by no means all – BAME MPs may consider themselves as representing a fourth circle, namely the "constituency of minority citizens" beyond their immediate electoral district. For example Bernie Grant, one of the first four BAME MPs elected to the House of Commons after 1945, stated: "I'm an African MP. I'm quite happy working on race issues."[29] Paul Boateng, elected in the same cohort of minority MPs in 1987, took a more differentiated approach: "I am an MP who is black. I am not a black MP. I am an MP with a wide variety of interests and who has had portfolios

29 Bernie Grant MP, quoted in Jaqi Nixon: The Role of Black and Asian MPs at Westminster, in: Shamit Saggar (ed.): *Race and British Electoral Politics*. London 1998, 202–222, esp. 207.

which are not race-specific but who has a commitment and a responsibility to the struggle for racial justice."[30]

Unlike Fenno's Black Congressmen and Congresswomen, some of the British BAME MPs are not only members of a minority, they are immigrants themselves and maintain close links with their ancestral home countries. Such MPs may well be responsive to a fifth, "transnational" constituency that may, however, have close interconnections with their local constituency. One – unusually striking – illustration for the transnational character of political representation in the first immigrant generation is Chaudhry Mohammad Sarwar, who was born in Pakistan in 1952, immigrated to the UK in 1976, made a personal fortune as owner of a successful retail chain and served as Labour MP for Glasgow Govan (later Glasgow Central) between 1997 and 2010. Throughout his tenure as MP, he maintained close personal and business links with organisations in his ancestral homeland. Amongst other activities, he established a Pakistan-UK Forum to promote dialogue between Pakistani and UK parliamentarians. He was critical of the Blair government's foreign policy in relation to Iraq and to aspects of its anti-terrorism legislation. He combined his transnational role with his membership (2004–2010) and chairmanship (2005–2010) of the House of Commons Scottish Affairs Committee. In 2013 he renounced his British citizenship to take up the position of governor of Punjab, initially representing the conservative Pakistan Muslim League. He resigned from this position in 2015.[31] The fact that his son, Anas Sarwar, was able to secure the Labour Party nomination for his father's seat and was subsequently elected as his successor as MP in 2010 suggests that the family had established – and retained – a high level of local political capital in the constituency even after Mohammad Sarwar's retirement in 2010. While Mohammad Sarwar may be an untypical case, his political biography shows some aspects of the "rooted cosmopolitanism" referred to above and in the introduction to this volume.

30 Paul Boateng MP, quoted ibid., 207.

31 Profile of Mohammad Sarwar, URL: *http://www.theyworkforyou.com/mp/10528/mohammad_sarwar/glasgow_central#profile* (13 June 2015); Andrew Buncombe: UK's First Muslim MP Mohammad Sarwar Becomes Governor of Pakistan's Punjab Province, in: *The Independent* (5 Aug. 2013). URL: *http://www.independent.co.uk/news/world/asia/uks-first-muslim-mp-mohammad-sarwar-becomes-governor-of-pakistans-punjab-province-8746743.html* (13 June 2015); Abdul Manan: Governor Punjab Chaudhry Sarwar Resigns after Making Anti-Govt Remarks, in: *The Express Tribune with the International New York Times* (29 Jan. 2015), URL: *http://tribune.com.pk/story/829511/governor-punjab-chaudhry-sarwar-resigns/* (13 June 2015).

Justin Grimmer shows how US Senators actively seek to influence their own visibility and their constituents' evaluations of their activities as legislators.[32] "Representatives strategically use presentational styles to subtly suggest the terms that constituents should use when evaluating their members of Congress."[33] Legislators' speeches in the chamber, activities in the electoral district and press releases are part of this attempt:

> Legislators provide information about work in Washington – selectively highlighting activities to cultivate support with constituents. Legislators also provide explanations – clarifying how and why their work in Washington is valuable. Legislators provide both information and interpretation about work in Washington to build support among constituents.[34]

Grimmer demonstrates that the political make-up of the constituency matters a great deal in this context: Legislators who are ideologically out of step with their constituents (e.g., Democratic legislators representing predominantly Republican districts or *vice versa*) highlight non-ideological activities as advocates of local interests. Legislators who are well-aligned with the political majorities in their districts, by contrast, tend to highlight their involvement in national policy debates.[35]

Works such as Grimmer's show that the socio-demographic and political composition of electoral districts matters for legislative behaviour and the communication between voters and constituents. In the European context there is still a dearth of studies on how ethnic-minority legislators communicate with their constituents. In the context of the UK House of Commons, MPs use parliamentary questions for written answer as a signal to voters and attentive members of the public, to use a term similar to Ralf Dahrendorf's distinction between "active" members of the public who participate in political life, "passive" members who are recipients of political communication and "latent" publics consisting of politically apathetic persons who are disinterested in political signals of any kind.[36] The parliamentary questions asked by UK MPs are reported by internet-based monitoring platforms like TheyWorkForYou (*http://www.theyworkforyou.com*) along with Members' biographies, voting records in the chamber, expenses,

---

32 Justin Grimmer: *Representational Style in Congress. What Legislators Say and Why It Matters.* Cambridge 2013.

33 Ibid., 12.

34 Ibid.

35 Ibid., 164.

36 Ralf Dahrendorf: Aktive und passive Öffentlichkeit. Über Teilnahme und Initiative im politischen Prozeß moderner Gesellschaften, in: Wolfgang R. Langenbucher (ed.): *Politische Kommunikation. Grundlagen, Strukturen, Prozesse*. Wien 1993, 42–51.

speeches and other information.[37] More importantly, MPs actively communicate their questions via their own personal websites. Labour MP Diane Abbott, for example, maintains tabs on her personal website informing visitors about her parliamentary speeches, questions, press releases and other publications.[38] Similarly, the Conservative MP Adam Afriyie prints the text of press releases on his personal website including, for example, a press release about a parliamentary question he tabled in relation to his Windsor constituency: "Adam Afriyie keeps fighting for flood defences [...] The MP for Windsor, Adam Afriyie was behind a recent Parliamentary Question, asking how many homes would be protected by new flooding defences." In the same press release, he reports the response of the Conservative government minister: "The Minister who replied, Dan Rogerson, said that the Government's plans would protect 400 homes in Windsor and Maidenhead and up to 3,000 in total around the Thames Valley."[39]

From a wider comparative-politics perspective one important question in this context is whether candidate-centred electoral systems enhance (a) the descriptive and (b) the substantive representation of ethnic-minority interests, if minorities are concentrated in particular districts. Every candidate who wishes to win a seat in the House has to run in one of the country's 650 territorially-defined single-member districts as his or her party's sole candidate and will attain this seat only if he or she gains a plurality of votes in that district against all other parties and their candidates. As a result, the UK's electoral system for Westminster elections is often seen as a "candidate-centred" system that creates strong incentives to cultivate a personal vote.[40] These incentives, some authors argue, translate directly into their responsiveness towards constituents' demands.[41] At least in marginal seats MPs perceive themselves as being highly accountable to their voters, because voters need to monitor the performance of just one MP (as opposed to many MPs in multi-member districts), and because voters possess the necessary means to punish their representative in the next general elections individually and retro-

37 Similarly, the web portal The Public Whip. URL: *http://www.publicwhip.org.uk* (13 June 2015).

38 See Diane Abbott's personal website. URL: *http://www.dianeabbott.org.uk/* (31 May 2015).

39 Adam Afriyie Keeps Fighting for Flood Defences – Posted by Adam Afriyie – Press Release (25 Mar. 2015), URL: *http://adamafriyie.org/* (31 May 2015).

40 This interpretation of the British first-past-the-post system is not uncontentious. John M. Carey and Matthew S. Shugart (Incentives to Cultivate a Personal Vote. A Rank Ordering of Electoral Formulas, in: *Electoral Studies* 14 (1995), 417–439) do not attribute a strong incentive to cultivate a personal vote to it. Sven-Oliver Proksch and Jonathan B. Slapin (*The Politics of Parliamentary Debate. Parties, Rebels and Representation*. Cambridge 2014), by contrast, do.

41 Richard F. Fenno: *Home Style. House Members in their Districts*. Boston 1978; Bruce E. Cain, John A. Ferejohn and Morris P. Fiorina: *The Personal Vote. Constituency Service and Electoral Independence*. Cambridge, MA 1987; Carey and Shugart, Incentives.

spectively.[42] As a result, there should be favourable conditions for Mansbridge's "anticipatory representation" to operate. Thus, if the assumption holds that MPs are mainly motivated by their desire to seek re-election,[43] MPs will anticipate their electoral vulnerability and align their parliamentary actions with the perceived demands of their constituents. While MPs are seen as "agents" of their electoral "principals" in such models, they simultaneously have incentives to use all means of communication available to them to influence the expectations and perceptions of their constituents, that is, their "reelection constituency" in Fenno's terms. Therefore we would expect higher shares of "non-white" residents in a constituency to increase the likelihood of MPs submitting parliamentary questions that refer to immigrants and ethnic minorities in a supportive manner.

However, this seemingly straightforward effect may be causally very intricate for three main reasons: First, when selecting candidates for the electoral race in a district, parties might take the district's socio-demographic composition into account and nominate BAME candidates to stand in constituencies with a high share of "non-white" voters, or they might select "white" candidates with a reputation of being highly committed to issues of ethnic diversity. Correlations between district demographics and legislative behaviour may therefore be the result of a selection effect rather than incentives and mechanisms that are typically attributed to the first-past-the-post electoral system. Second, MPs will use the parliamentary arena – as any other public forum available to them – to "manage the expectations" of their constituents and shape their perceptions.[44] Thus there may be an element of reverse causality. Finally, there may be situations where the first-past-the-post electoral system actually dampens the incentives to be responsive to constituency demographics. Despite a slowly growing attractiveness of the Conservative Party especially to British Asian voters,[45] Britain's minority voters overall still have a strong preference to cast their vote for the Labour Party.[46] These voters typically reside in urban areas, which are often Labour strongholds, or "safe La-

42 James D. Fearon: Electoral Accountability and the Control of Politicians. Selecting Good Types versus Sanctioning Poor Performances, in: Adam Przeworski, Susan Stokes and Bernard Manin (eds.): *Democracy, Accountability and Representation*. Cambridge 1999, 55–97; Audrey André, Sam Depauw and Matthew S. Shugart: The Effect of Electoral Institutions on Legislative Behaviour, in: Shane Martin, Thomas Saalfeld and Kaare W. Strøm (eds.): *The Oxford Handbook of Legislative Studies*. Oxford 2015, 231–249; Mansbridge, Rethinking Representation, 515–528.

43 David R. Mayhew: *Congress. The Electoral Connection*. New Haven, CT 1974.

44 See Grimmer, Representational Style.

45 Anthony F. Heath et al.: *The Political Integration of Ethnic Minorities in Britain*. Oxford 2013.

46 Thomas Saalfeld: Party Choices in Comparative Perspectives. 3.3. United Kingdom, in: Bird, id. and Wüst, Political Representation, 73–76.

bour seats".[47] Hence, the incentives for BAME MPs to exhibit strong responsiveness to such voter groups might in fact be diminished, thus encouraging "shirking strategies"[48] due to the perception of being elected to a safe seat. In short, because districts with a high share of immigrants and minorities are in many cases "safe" constituencies for BAME MPs, the electoral incentive to be responsive to immigrant and minority demands might be reduced rather than enhanced. In these cases, MPs may have incentives to focus on their careers in parliament, government or other areas of public life.

Research Design and Data

The present study is based on a sample consisting of data on all 37 MPs with a BAME background that belonged to the Parliaments elected in 2001, 2005 and 2010 and submitted at least one parliamentary question for written answer during this period. These MPs were identified using the database of Operation Black Vote,[49] the Parliamentary Candidates UK website[50] and the sources given at the bottom of Table 1.

Table 1 gives the number of MPs with a BAME Background in the UK from the general election of 1987 to the general election of May 2015. It demonstrates that the vast majority of MPs with a BAME background between 1987 and 2010 belonged to the Labour Party. It was not until the general election of 2010 that a larger number of Conservative MPs with an ethnic-minority background were elected to the House of Commons. The Parliaments studied in this contribution are shaded in grey.

Our dependent variable seeks to capture these MPs' legislative communication and oversight activities using the number and content of questions for written answer they submitted. Earlier studies used a variety of alternative indicators (e.g., select-committee membership, voting or texts of personal websites), but revealed that parliamentary questions for written answer are a relatively valid indi-

47 Paul Mitchell: The United Kingdom. Plurality Rule under Siege, in: Michael Gallagher and id. (eds.): *The Politics of Electoral Systems*. Oxford 2005, 157–184.

48 Kaare W. Strøm: Delegation and Accountability in Parliamentary Democracies, in: *European Journal of Political Research* 37 (2000), 261–289.

49 URL: *http://www.obv.org.uk/* (16 June 2015).

50 URL: *http://parliamentarycandidates.org/2015-candidates/bme-mps-elected-at-2015-general-election/* (6 Aug. 2015)

Table 1: Backbenchers with a "Black or Asian Minority Ethnic" Background in the UK, 2001–2015

	1987	1992	1997	2001	2005	2010	2015
Conservative Party	0	1	0	1	2	11	17
Labour Party	4	5	9	12	15	17	23
Liberal Democrats	0	0	0	1	0	0	0
Other parties	0	0	0	0	0	0	1
Total per Parliament	4	6	9	14	17	28	41

Sources: John Wood and Richard Cracknell: *Ethnic Minorities in Politics, Government and Public Life*. London 2013 (House of Commons Library, SN/SG/1156); Tim Carr and Iain Dale: *The Politicos Guide to the New House of Commons 2015. Profiles of the New MPs and Analysis of the 2015 General Election Results*. London 2015 (Google e-book, no page number).

Note: The data for 2001 were corrected to include MPs who retired, died or joined the House of Commons in a by-election during the respective Parliament.

cator available for empirical study in the UK.[51] The first reason is the very nature of parliamentary questions: given some standardised formal requirements laid down in rules of procedure and parliamentary practice they are relatively short, precise and unambiguous pieces of text. Second, as Martin points out, parliamentary questions are an appropriate measure "to verify the role behaviour of legislators more independently"[52] than, for instance, elite interviews that may lack validity and reliability due to profiling tendencies of interviewees. A third reason is that their use is less constrained by parliamentary leaderships than, for example, speeches on the floor of the House or votes. Therefore parliamentary questions form a more informative and reliable indicator of the legislators' priorities than others.[53] Finally, parliamentary questions can be a cost-saving way for an MP to express immediate constituents' concerns and helping him or her to gain a personal reputation, whether in subject-, focus-, or role-specific terms.[54] Therefore, they are used in relatively large numbers, lending themselves to quantitative analysis.

---

51 Thomas Saalfeld and Kalliopi Kyriakopoulou: Presence and Behaviour. Black and Minority Ethnic MPs in the British House of Commons, in: Bird, Saalfeld and Wüst, Political Representation, 230–249.

52 Shane Martin: Using Parliamentary Questions to Measure Constituency Focus. An Application to the Irish Case, in: *Political Studies* 59 (2011), 472–488, esp. 474.

53 Ibid.

54 Stefanie Bailer: People's Voice or Information Pool? The Role of, and Reasons for, Parliamentary Questions in the Swiss Parliament, in: *Journal of Legislative Studies* 17 (2011), 302–314; Federico Russo: The Constituency as a Focus of Representation. Studying the Italian Case through the Analysis of Parliamentary Questions, in: *Journal of Legislative Studies* 17 (2011), 290–301;

First analyses of questions[55] also showed that MPs typically ask two types of questions with slightly different connotations: (a) questions on the problems and rights of ethnic minorities in the UK and (b) questions about immigration and the social and political risks associated with it.

The 23,197 parliamentary questions were extracted via *http://www.theywork foryou.com*. This website is maintained by UK Citizens Online Democracy, a registered charity that takes open data from the House of Commons and presents it in such a user-friendly way on its website that citizens are able to keep track of their MPs' parliamentary activities. Besides its service to UK citizens, the website also provides an Application Programming Interface (API) that can be accessed to retrieve data stored in the website's database.[56] In our case, we were exclusively interested in the parliamentary questions for written answers section, which TheyWorkForYou has recorded for every MP since the early 2000s. However, it is worth mentioning that much more information on MPs can be requested from the API, for instance parliamentary debates or biographical background.

For the web scraping procedure, we used the statistical software R, which also allows many programming operations. In order to perform the operations necessary for data retrieval a first step was to identify all 37 MPs with a BAME background and their TheyWorkForYou IDs. We followed largely the instructions given in Munzert et al.[57] and used the R packages RCurl (to communicate with the web server from *theyworkforyou.com*), jsonlite (to read content in JSON format and convert it to R objects) and stringr (to clean the raw texts from HTML-tags).[58] Based on these steps we were able to compile a dataset containing the texts of *all* 23,197 parliamentary questions for written answer (irrespective of content) submitted by the 37 MPs in our sample between June 2001 and May 2015. Unlike earlier studies,[59] we do not use a contrasting sample of non-BAME MPs. Instead, we seek to highlight variations within the population of MPs with a BAME background. For each question we created a series of dummy variables registering, for example,

---

Shane Martin: Parliamentary Questions, the Behaviour of Legislators, and the Function of Legislatures. An Introduction, in: *Journal of Legislative Studies* 17 (2011), 259–270.

55 Saalfeld, Parliamentary Questions.

56 Yet, it remains important to say that the access to the database is not unlimited and that users should read the "Terms of usage". URL: *http://www.theyworkforyou.com/api/* (13 June 2015).

57 Simon Munzert et al.: *Automated Data Collection with R. A Practical Guide to Web Scraping and Text Mining.* West Sussex 2015.

58 This procedure yielded also the answers of ministers, which were removed during preprocessing.

59 Saalfeld, Parliamentary Questions; id. and Daniel Bischof: Minority-Ethnic MPs and the Substantive Representation of Minority Interests in the House of Commons, 2005–2011, in: *Parliamentary Affairs* 66 (2013), 305–328.

whether the question explicitly referred to ethnic minorities in, or immigration to, the United Kingdom. Further dummy variables record whether the question made explicit reference to the MP's local constituency, national policy, ancestral homeland or problems of social mobility in the UK. These questions were identified by using a series of "dictionaries", which can be found in Appendix 2.

Independent variables are the MP's party, the time of his or her first election to the House of Commons, the percentage of "non-white" residents in the MP's constituency and whether the MP was a non-European immigrant ("first-generation immigrant") or the immediate descendant of at least one non-European immigrant ("second-generation immigrant").[60] Biographical data were extracted from the MPs' personal websites and Wikipedia entries.[61] Each MP has an extensive Wikipedia page. The information was verified using further information that could be retrieved via the platform TheyWorkForYou.[62] The contextual variables about constituency demographics were extracted from the British Census of 2001 and 2011.[63] We used the percentage of "non-white" residents, which is documented by parliamentary constituency.[64] Constituency demographics for the 2001–2005 Parliament were taken from the 2001 Census. We used the results of the 2011 Census for the 2010–2015 Parliament and calculated the arithmetic mean of the 2001 and 2011 Censuses to estimate an approximate measure of ethnic constituency composition for the 2005–2010 Parliament.

---

60 One MP was the granddaughter of immigrants from the Caribbean.

61 URL: *http://en.wikipedia.org.*

62 URL: *http://www.theyworkforyou.com.*

63 Data on constituency composition ("non-white ethnicities, per cent of the population") extracted from Census 2001 and 2011. URL: *http://www.ons.gov.uk/ons/index.html* (13 June 2015); *Census 2001 – Report for Parliamentary Constituencies. National Statistics Publication, Crown Copyright*. London 2003.

64 The census data for 2001 and 2011 are not perfectly aligned. In the 2001 Census we used data on "all ethnic groups except all sub-categories of White and Irish Traveller (Northern Ireland only)". Source: Census 2001 – Report, 34 (footnote 2). In the 2011 Census the format of the question on ethnic groups in England and Wales was more detailed than in 2001, mainly to reflect changing needs and the dynamic profile of different ethnic groups. Consequently, new response categories for "Gypsy or Irish Traveller" and "Arab" were introduced (footnote 13). URL: *http://www.ons.gov.uk/ons/guide-method/census/2011/how-our-census-works/how-we-planned-the-2011-census/questionnaire-development/finalising-the-2011-questionnaire/index.html* (13 June 2015). We used the information from the "final recommended questions 2011 – Ethnic group". URL: *http://www.ons.gov.uk/ons/guide-method/census/2011/the-2011-census/2011-census-questionnaire-content/final-recommended-questions-2011---ethnic-group.pdf* (13 June 2015).

Data Analysis

In the following sections, we investigate whether parliamentary questions for written answer, which can be seen as a signal MPs send to the "active" public, are firstly used to highlight the MP's position in partisan national policy debates as compared to, secondly, local matters relating to the MP's electoral district in the UK. In addition we examine the extent to which MPs engage, thirdly, in "surrogate representation" in Mansbridge's terms and appear as representatives of ethnic minorities in the UK as a whole. Finally, we assess whether, and to what extent, MPs in our sample appear as representatives of their ancestral countries or countries that are the ancestral homeland of many of their constituents.

An illustration of the first type of general policy question would be the question tabled by Labour MP Chuka Umunna as Shadow Secretary of State for Business, Innovation and Skills to the Minister he shadowed on 23 March 2015: "To ask the Secretary of State for Business, Innovation and Skills, what recent discussions he has had on the EU Accounting and Transparency Directives; and what steps he is taking to ensure compliance with those Directives."[65] An example of a narrower constituency matter raised in a parliamentary question would be a question asked by Jonathan Sayeed, Conservative MP for Mid Bedfordshire on 5 April 2005: "To ask the Secretary of State for Defence which soldiers who have served and been injured in the recent Iraqi conflict live in the constituency of Mid Bedfordshire."[66] On occasion, MPs use parliamentary questions to ask about particular constituents, like Labour MP Keith Vaz on 1 September 2003: "To ask the Secretary of State for the Home Department when he expects to reply to the letter of 13 January 2003 from the hon. Member for Leicester, East to the Minister for State, Citizenship and Immigration, P1048812, concerning his constituent, Mrs. Patel."[67] An example of the third representational focus, which Mansbridge termed "surrogate representation" would be the question by Labour MP Ashok Kumar, tabled on 17 December 2008: "To ask the Secretary of State for Health (1) whether his Department has commissioned research into mental health problems amongst Asian women in England; (2) what steps his Department is taking to address the stigma attached

---

65 House of Commons Debates, 23 Mar. 2015. URL: *http://www.parliament.uk/business/publications/written-questions-answers-statements/written-question/Commons/2015-03-23/228761* (13 June 2015).

66 House of Commons Debates, 5 Apr. 2005. URL: *http://www.publications.parliament.uk/pa/cm200405/cmhansrd/vo050405/text/50405w17.htm#50405w17.html_wqn11* (13 June 2015).

67 House of Commons Debates, 1 Sept. 2003. URL: *http://www.publications.parliament.uk/pa/cm200203/cmhansrd/vo030901/text/30901w71.htm#30901w71.html_wqn3* (13 June 2015).

to mental health problems in the Asian community."[68] Finally, an example of the fourth representational focus, a transnational focus on the MP's ancestral homeland, would be the question tabled by Pakistani-born Mohammad Sarwar, MP for Glasgow Central on 24 June 2003: "To ask the Minister of State, Department for International Development what progress has been made with the Department's support for tuberculosis (a) vaccination and (b) treatment in Pakistan."[69]

Policy Area and Party

Our first strategy of identifying the representational focus of our questions is to examine the policy areas covered by the parliamentary questions. These are relatively easy to establish as each question is addressed to a particular minister. Rather than formulating strict hypotheses, we will rely on "observable implications" or theoretical expectations. In other words, if MPs saw their role in predominantly contributing to national or partisan policy debates, we would expect a large number of their parliamentary questions addressed to those secretaries of state responsible for broad national policy issues such as finance, business, foreign affairs, defence or justice. If MPs sought to act predominantly as "appropriators" of government funds for their local constituents, or for wider minority constituencies, we would expect the bulk of their questions to relate to social affairs, health, education, agriculture, transport and other departments responsible for welfare issues and targeted local or group-oriented benefits. If they wished to demonstrate concern for developments in their own ancestral homeland, or the homelands of their constituents, we would expect an emphasis on questions about overseas development and, crucially for immigration issues, home affairs. At this exploratory stage, our analyses will be univariate and bivariate only.

Figure 2 plots the number parliamentary questions for written answer asked by MPs with a BAME background in the three Parliaments between 2001 and 2015. The horizontal bars provide a breakdown by government department. These data do not provide a very clear picture in the sense of the observable implications referred to above. The largest number of questions was addressed to the ministers of health, the interior, justice and business. Education and foreign affairs were also frequent matters covered in such questions. Some of these policy areas cover larger questions of national policy (such as justice or foreign affairs), others might

68 House of Commons Debates, 17 Dec. 2008. URL: *http://www.publications.parliament.uk/pa/cm200809/cmhansrd/cm081217/text/81217w0034.htm#081217112001751* (13 June 2015).
69 House of Commons Debates, 24 June 2003. URL: *http://www.publications.parliament.uk/pa/cm200203/cmhansrd/vo030624/text/30624w10.htm#30624w10.html_wqn6* (13 June 2015).

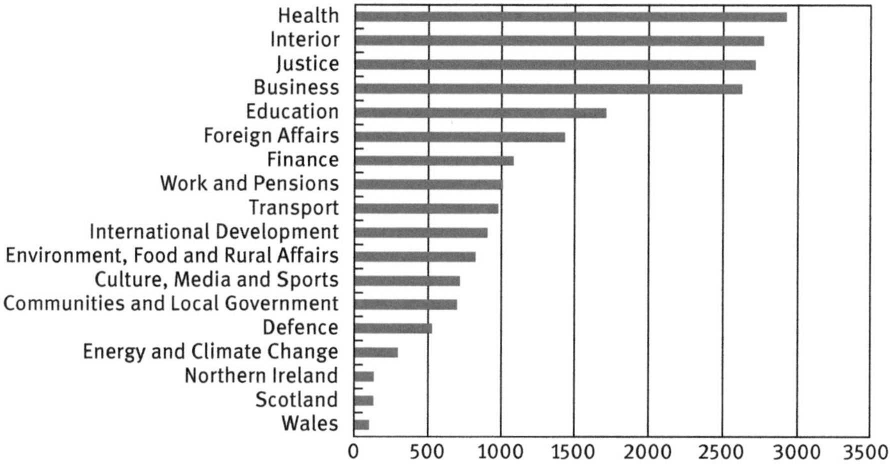

Figure 2: Number of Parliamentary Questions for Written Answer Submitted by BAME MPs in the UK 2001–2015 by Department (N = 23,197)

Source: Extracted by the authors from *http://www.theyworkforyou.com*.

be conceived of as dealing with welfare issues relevant to immigrants and ethnic minorities as well as other groups in UK society (such as health, education or work and pensions). Yet another category might be seen as being particularly relevant to immigrants (interior) or homeland politics (overseas development).

A clearer picture emerges, if we break the data down not only by policy areas but also by political party of the questioner. Figure 3 is based on the distribution of parliamentary questions across the main government departments. This distribution is calculated separately for both main parties and represented by a bar for each party. This is necessary, because the number of MPs with a BAME background is strongly skewed towards the Labour Party. As in Figure 2, Figure 3 includes all questions for written answer submitted by all 37 Members of Parliament with a BAME background who tabled such questions during the 2001–2005, 2005–2010 and 2010–2015 Parliaments. For example, the diagram shows that just under 14 per cent of all (17,966) questions tabled by relevant Labour MPs were addressed to the Health Secretary. By contrast, only 7.44 per cent of all (5,096) questions submitted by Conservative MPs with a BAME background were addressed to this minister. In other words, Labour MPs with a BAME background were almost twice as likely to address parliamentary questions for written answers to health ministers as their Conservative counterparts. A comparatively stronger focus by relevant Labour MPs can also be observed for home affairs ("interior"), business, education, foreign affairs and international development. With the exception of

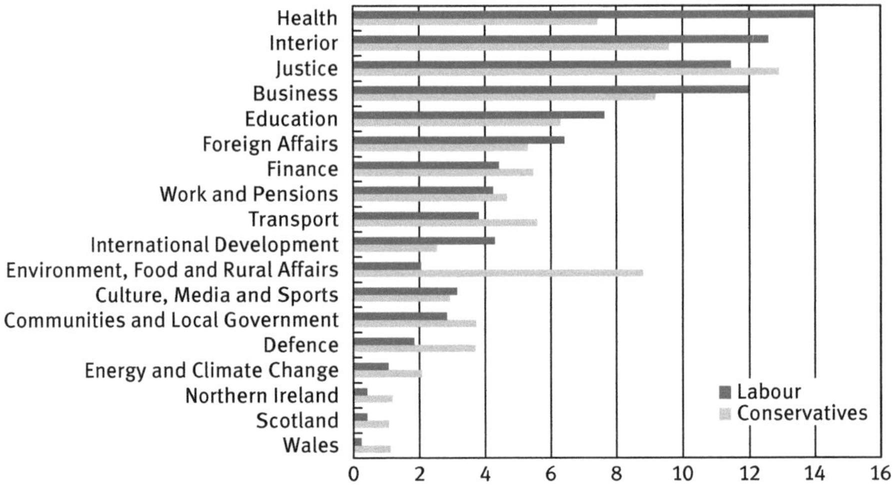

Figure 3: Distribution of Parliamentary Questions for Written Answer Submitted by BAME MPs in the UK 2001–2015 by Department for Each Main Party (percentages, N = 23,197)

Source: Extracted by the authors from *http://www.theyworkforyou.com*.

the relatively higher propensity of Labour MPs to submit questions to the ministers dealing with business and foreign affairs, this pattern is largely consistent with the general ideological profile of the Labour Party as a welfarist party. Conservative MPs with a BAME background, by contrast, were considerably more likely to submit questions on the responsibilities of the secretaries of state in charge of environment, food and rural affairs; for energy and climate change; for defence, for Scotland, Wales and Northern Ireland and for transport. These patterns are more consistent with an interpretation where MPs with a BAME background behave largely in line with their parties' general policy profiles and are therefore more participants in national partisan policy debates than engaging in sending legislative signals to their local constituencies or to the wider ethnic-minority constituency in the country.[70]

70 For a study of this type (without reference to MPs' ethnic background), see Kira Killermann and Sven-Oliver Proksch: *Dynamic Political Rhetoric. Electoral, Economic, and Partisan Determinants of Speech-Making in the UK Parliament*. Paper Presented at the 7th ECPR General Conference in Bordeaux, 4–7 Sept. 2013.

Representational Focus

Our key interest lies in variations in the representational focus of UK MPs with a BAME background along the lines of Fenno's (above) argument. In order to establish this focus all questions were searched automatically using the lists of search words in Appendix 2. We identified all questions submitted by the 37 MPs with a BAME background relating to problems of ethnic minorities in the United Kingdom on the one hand and current immigration to the United Kingdom on the other. This distinction has proved to be useful in earlier publications and should help to capture different dimensions of Fenno's fourth circle relating to the interests of ethnic minorities in the country as a whole.[71] In other words, it should capture questioning patterns where MPs with a BAME background engage in "surrogate representation" in Mansbridge's sense. In addition, we sought to capture questions that explicitly referred to the MP's local constituency, national policymaking, the MP's ancestral homeland, and issues of social mobility in the United Kingdom as a problem that migrants face when arriving in a new society. The following tables are based on the number of questions that can be identified as addressing one of the six representational foci named above. The raw counts were crosstabulated by the MP's political party, immigrant "generation", constituency demographics (percentage of "non-whites" in the district) and career stage. The tables report column percentages and allow a first exploration of this new dataset.[72]

Variations by Political Party

Table 2 demonstrates that Labour MPs with a BAME background clearly have a stronger propensity than their Conservative counterparts to address questions relating to the problems of ethnic minorities in the UK: 3.41 per cent of the 17,966 questions submitted by Labour MPs with a BAME background explicitly referred to issues relating to ethnic minorities in the UK, whereas the corresponding value for the 5,096 questions submitted by Conservative MPs with a similar background was 0.84 per cent. By contrast, the inter-party differences in the percentage of questions dealing with current immigration are statistically significant but minor in terms of magnitude. Whereas the questions of MPs from both parties overwhelmingly had explicit references to national policy making, Labour MPs with a BAME background were slightly less likely to do so than their Conservative counterparts; instead, they were slightly more likely to focus on

71 Saalfeld and Bischof, Minority-Ethnic MPs.

72 Multivariate analyses using appropriate statistical controls will follow in subsequent work.

Table 2: Representational Focus of BAME MPs by Party, 2001–2015 (column percentages)

Explicit focus of the question on ... (%)	Party			
	Conservative Party	Labour Party	Liberal Democrats	Total
Ethnic minorities	0.84	3.41	2.96	2.84
Immigration	5.67	5.46	0.74	5.48
Local constituency	9.05	10.29	18.52	10.07
National policy	27.86	24.75	8.15	25.34
Ancestral homeland	0.86	2.87	2.96	2.43
Social mobility in the UK	5.69	8.24	10.37	7.69
Total N	*5,096*	*17,966*	*135*	*23,197*

Source: Extracted from *http://www.theyworkforyou.com*.

Note: All χ^2 tests are statistically significant at least at the five-percent level.

their local constituencies and clearly more likely to submit questions relating to their ancestral homelands. Not least, they were more concerned with problems relating to vertical mobility in the United Kingdom.

Variations by "Immigrant Generation"

Table 3 follows a similar logic and distinguishes between the 9,586 questions submitted by "first-generation" immigrants (that is, persons who were immigrants themselves) and the 13,611 questions submitted by descendants of immigrants ("second" or, in one case, "third" generation). These data are aggregated across parties. The table shows that MPs who are immigrants themselves are clearly more likely to raise matters relating to the problems of ethnic minorities and current immigration to the United Kingdom in their questions than MPs with a BAME background with at least one immigrant among their parents or grandparents. Immigrants are more likely to highlight issues relating to their own local constituency, to national policy debates and, above all, to their ancestral homeland than minority MPs who are the descendants of at least one immigrant. By contrast, MPs with a BAME background whose parents or grandparents were immigrants are clearly more likely to demonstrate concern for questions of social mobility in the United Kingdom. In other words, the concern for transnational mobility is gradually superseded by a concern with questions of equal opportunity.

Table 3: Representational Focus of BAME MPs by Immigrant "Generation", 2001–2015 (column percentages)

Explicit focus of the question on ... (%)	Immigrant "generation"		
	First generation	Second generation	Total
Ethnic minorities	4.14	1.92	2.84
Immigration	7.14	4.31	5.48
Local constituency	10.98	9.42	10.07
National policy	27.93	23.51	25.34
Ancestral homeland	4.45	1.00	2.43
Social mobility in the UK	6.07	8.83	7.69
Total N	*9,586*	*13,611*	*23,197*

Source: Extracted from *http://www.theyworkforyou.com.*

Note: All χ^2 tests are statistically significant at least at the five-percent level.

Variations by Constituency Demographics

Table 4 performs a similar analysis distinguishing the questions asked by MPs with a BAME background representing different shares of "non-white" residents. Although we have not identified "majority-minority districts" in this table, it seeks to capture differences in the socio-demographic context of representation: 2,147 questions were submitted by MPs with a BAME background representing dis-

Table 4: Representational Focus of BAME MPs by Constituency Demographics, 2001–2015 (column percentages)

Explicit focus of the question on ... (%)	Percentage of "non-white" population in the constituency				
	Less than 2.50 %	2.50–9.99 %	10.00–24.99 %	At least 25.00 %	Total
Ethnic minorities	2.65	0.68	1.32	3.92	2.84
Immigration	1.72	5.94	2.55	6.36	5.48
Local constituency	22.87	8.59	22.73	6.58	10.07
National policy	23.61	27.53	27.36	24.46	25.34
Ancestral homeland	1.44	0.55	2.09	3.34	2.43
Social mobility in the UK	7.50	7.17	6.41	8.12	7.69
Total N	*2,147*	*5,132*	*2,200*	*13,718*	*23,197*

Source: Extracted from *http://www.theyworkforyou.com.*

Note: All χ^2 tests are statistically significant at least at the five-percent level.

tricts with less than 2.50 per cent "non-whites" (based on the UK Census of 2001 and 2011); 5,132 questions by MPs with districts having a share of "non-white" residents between 2.50 and 9.99 per cent; 2,200 questions by MPs representing districts with at least 10 but less than 25 per cent "non-whites" and 13,718 questions by MPs representing at least 25 per cent "non-white" residents. The data shows that MPs representing more than 25 per cent "non-whites" are clearly more likely than other MPs to refer to ethnic minorities or problems of current immigration to the United Kingdom. Other than that, these bivariate data does not provide very clear patterns except that MPs representing constituencies with more than 25 per cent "non-whites" are much less likely to submit questions directly relating to their local constituencies, whereas they are slightly more likely to refer to their ancestral homeland or to problems of social mobility in the UK in general.

Variations by Career Stage

Table 5 examines the representational focus of questions asked by MPs with a parliamentary career of up to five years (12,009 questions), i.e. members mostly in their first term. It compares the distribution of questions asked by experienced legislators with a legislative service of at least two complete parliaments (more than 10 years, 8,514 questions) and an intermediate category of MPs who served more than one and less than two full terms as MPs (2,674 questions). The theoretical reason is that Fenno's studies on the detected career-cycle patterns in the

Table 5: Representational Focus of BAME MPs by Career Stage, 2001–2015 (column percentages)

Explicit focus of the question on … (%)	**Length of parliamentary service at the time of submitting the question**			
	Up to 5 years	**6–10 years**	**More than 10 years**	**Total**
Ethnic minorities	1.54	2.99	4.63	2.84
Immigration	4.58	3.70	7.31	5.48
Local constituency	10.25	8.08	10.43	10.07
National policy	26.84	17.02	25.83	25.34
Ancestral homeland	1.36	1.53	4.22	2.43
Social mobility in the UK	9.24	5.12	6.31	7.69
Total N	*12,009*	*2,674*	*8,514*	*23,197*

Source: Extracted from *http://www.theyworkforyou.com*.

Note: All χ^2 tests are statistically significant at least at the five-percent level.

US Congress with Members displaying a stronger local constituency focus in their early years and an increasing tendency to adopt a national policy focus as they get re-elected and are safer in their seats. Questions in the House of Commons do not display such a pattern. This may largely be the result of confounding factors (here: age of the MP), which will be controlled in future multi-variate analyses. In the House of Commons, questions submitted by experienced MPs tend to disproportionately refer to ethnic minorities and immigrants. They are as likely to refer to their local constituencies and to national policy making in their questions as first-term members. There are, again, two differences: Experienced MPs are more likely to refer to their ancestral homelands in their questions; and questions submitted by parliamentary freshers show a stronger concern for problems of social mobility in the UK.

Conclusions

The horizontal and vertical mobility caused by immigration to the United Kingdom has begun to affect democratic representation in the House of Commons. Whereas the country experienced a strong expansion of non-European immigration between 1945 and 1987, there were no elected MPs who self-identified as having a BAME background on the seat rows of the House of Commons. The 1987 general election witnessed the election of four Labour MPs with a BAME background. The number of MPs with a BAME background increased, first predominantly on the Labour benches; from 2010 we can also observe an acceleration of "descriptive" representation on the Conservative benches. For researchers of democratic representation one of the questions is whether this increase in descriptive representation has also affected patterns of "substantive" representation, be it in policy making or "gyroscopic" as well as "surrogate" representation. Based on content analyses of over 23,000 parliamentary questions for written answer tabled by MPs with a BAME background between 2001 and 2015, we find complex patterns within this group of MPs that require further, multi-variate investigation in quasi-experimental designs with a control group. First and most importantly, UK MPs with a BAME background generally do not operate as policy advocates with a single-minded mission of promoting the interests of ethnic minorities and immigrants. On the whole, they participate in national policy debates as representatives of their parties. Self-selection to and socialisation in their parties is *the* key factor shaping their behaviour. These differences are demonstrable when we compare MPs with a BAME background across different parties. Nevertheless, there are further differences: experienced (usually older) Labour MPs, especially those who are immigrants themselves and represent urban districts with a high share of "non-white" residents are clearly more likely to refer to the problems of ethnic minorities and immigrants in their parliamentary questions for written answer than their colleagues. They also maintain transnational links with their ancestral homelands, which clearly show up in their questions. By contrast, Conservative and less experienced MPs representing districts with less than one-quarter of "non-whites" have a stronger focus on social mobility in the UK. They seem less concerned with people "arriving" and more concerned with their constituents "getting on".

Acknowledgements

The authors gratefully acknowledge the financial support for this work given by the German Research Foundation (DFG, grant no. SA 2160/3-1). This grant is part of the larger ORA+ project "Pathways to Power: The Political Representation of Citizens of Immigrant Origin in Seven European Democracies (PATHWAYS)", co-funded by the Agence nationale de la recherche (ANR, principal investigator: Manlio Cinalli), the Deutsche Forschungsgemeinschaft (DFG, principal investigator: Thomas Saalfeld) the Economic and Social Research Council (ESRC, principal investigator: Laura Morales) and the Nederlandse Organisatie voor Wetenschappelijk (NWO, principal investigator: Jean Tillie).

Appendix 1: List of MPs with a BAME Background

Abbott, Diane; Afriyie, Adam; Ali, Rushanara; Boateng, Paul; Butler, Dawn; Chishti, Rehman; Dhanda, Parmjit; Gill, Parmjit; Grant, Helen; Gyimah, Sam; Hendrick, Mark; Javid, Sajid; Khabra, Piara S.; Khan, Sadiq; King, Oona; Kumar, Ashok; Kwarteng, Kwasi; Lammy, David; Mahmood, Khalid; Mahmood, Shabana; Malhotra, Seema; Malik, Shahid; Nandy, Lisa; Onwurah, Chi; Patel, Priti; Qureshi, Yasmin; Sarwar, Anas; Sarwar, Mohammad; Sayeed, Jonathan; Sharma, Alok; Sharma, Virendra; Singh, Marsha; Umunna, Chuka; Uppal, Paul; Vara, Shailesh; Vaz, Keith; Vaz, Valerie; Zahawi, Nadhim

Appendix 2: Keywords Used for the Analysis of Parliamentary Questions

Problems of ethnic minorities	Immigration	Local constituency	National policy	Ancestral homeland	Social mobility in the UK
community	freedom of movement	<names of relevant	the government	Jamaica*	social mobility
cohesion	free movement of people	constituencies>	the previous	Ghana*	upwardly mobile
Black and Asian	language test	my constituen*	government	Bangladesh*	discriminat*
ethnic minorit*	points of entry	my surgery	this country	Pakistan*	employ*
Asian, asian	UK border	where I was born	this nation	Nigeria*	entrepreneur*
Black, black	asylum	where I live	British nation	Kenya*	educat*
racial, race	immigra*, migra*	where I grew up	British interest	Somali*	aspiration*
Islam., islam.	traffick*	local	United Kingdom	Guyana*	career*
Muslim., muslim.	naturalis*	constituent	UK national	India*	equal opportunit*
Hindu	refugee	constituency	British	Uganda*	
Sikh	foreigner*		Britain*	Yemen*	
temple	alien*		government,	Iraq*	
mosque	EU citizen		Government		
Urdu	work permit				
Arabic	Schengen				
priest*	single entry				
imam*	multiple entry				
integrat*	worker registration				
terror*	entered the UK				
	Romanian and Bulgarian				
	migrant workers				
	visa*				
	nationals				
	Gypsy and Traveller				
	foreign national				

Note: An asterisk (*) indicates that the search word was truncated.

Gesa zur Nieden

Mobile Musicians: Paths of Migration in Early Modern Europe

Abstract: *In recent years, the cultural history of music has been challenging cultural notions of style and political representation by studying migrating musicians as actors in early modern court, urban and musical life. Following the aesthetic concept of authenticity, this article examines the construction and use of cultural characterisations of mobility and migration in Glückstadt, a "city of exiles" founded by Christian IV in 1616, and in the biography of Johann Jakob Froberger, who throughout his life travelled in the service of the Viennese court. While first manifestations of a concept of authenticity can be studied very effectively by looking at the example of mobile musicians and their music, their cases also reveal immobilities, the aspiration to rise in social status and the desire to settle securely. Since these elements affected the concept of musical works at the time, they may be fruitfully connected to hybrid music editions.*

Due to the action and network-oriented approach that has been shaping musicological research for several years, the wide definition of mobility within the recently proclaimed "mobility turn"[1] does not seem to add much to a music history that has constantly reflected on the distribution of musical compositions and treatises, the availability of instruments and – last but not least – the gathering of musicians and listeners within early modern court or city life.[2] Indeed, the relatedness of music to sound has always fostered the study of musical performances as encounters of people and objects, and the mobility of people was even more central for the existence of music during the sixteenth to eighteenth centuries when musical notation and practice were constantly developed[3] and when patrons moved their courts frequently for dynastic, diplomatic or educa-

1 Kevin Hannam, Mimi Sheller and John Urry: Editorial. Mobilities, Immobilities and Moorings, in: *Mobilities* 1 (2006), 1–22; Mimi Sheller and John Urry: The New Mobilities Paradigm, in: *Environment and Planning 38* (2006), 207–226.

2 For an emblematic overview of the cultural history of music at early modern courts, see Samantha Owens, Barbara M. Reul and Janice Stockigt (eds.): *Music at German Courts, 1715–1760*. Woodbridge 2011, 11–12.

3 Sylvie Bouissou: Entre sources et œuvre, à la quête d'une authenticité, in: Monique Desroches and Ghyslaine Guertin (eds.): *Construire le savoir musical. Enjeux épistémologiques, esthétiques et sociaux*. Paris 2003, 79–97.

tional reasons (e.g. the Grand Tour).[4] While the reconstruction of individual mobile or migratory musicians' biographies is often difficult due to the dispersion of sources, the way music exists seems nevertheless constantly to provoke biographically relevant research questions on collegiality, rivalry and cooperation between musicians, even in studies of musical institutions.[5]

Besides a local or even intra-institutional mobility, music historians have also studied migratory music and musicians who moved individually or systematically on supra-regional levels throughout Europe and beyond.[6] Related to early modern history, beyond court movements or individual journeys of scholars or exiles, two consecutive systematic movements have been central to musicological research: First the broad presence of French-Flemish, mostly cleric musicians in fifteenth- and sixteenth-century Europe that went along with the distribution of composed vocal polyphony in the context of a new ideal of piety,[7] and second the so-called "diaspora" of Italian musicians during the seventeenth and eighteenth centuries that responded to the resounding secular success of the new genres of opera and solo concertos that had started out on the Italian peninsula since 1600 and spread to the whole of Europe by the 1650s.[8] From then on, courtly and also public demand corresponded to the economic needs of Italian musicians who mostly fled their saturated home markets.[9]

4 For the current state of research on the Grand Tour, see Margret Scharrer: Kavalierstouren und Musiktransfer am Beispiel ausgesuchter Prinzenreisen, in: Sabine Ehrmann-Herfort and Silke Leopold (eds.): *Migration und Identität. Wanderbewegungen und Kulturkontakte in der Musikgeschichte*. Kassel 2013, 151–170. Music migrations within dynastic court movements are currently examined by Berthold Over, research fellow of the HERA MusMig-project. URL: *http://heranet.info/musmig/index* (26 Aug. 2015).

5 Christian Ahrens: *"Zu Gotha ist eine gute Kapelle ...". Aus dem Innenleben einer thüringischen Hofkapelle des 18. Jahrhunderts*. Stuttgart 2009.

6 See, for example, Arne Spohr: *"How chances it they travel?". Englische Musiker in Dänemark und Norddeutschland 1579–1630*. Wiesbaden 2009.

7 Klaus Hortschansky: Frankoflämische Musik, in: *MGG*^{2}, Sachteil 3. Kassel 1995, 673–688.

8 Giorgio Pestelli: Il melodramma italiano all'estero fino alla metà del Settecento, in: Alberto Basso (ed.), *Musica in scena. Storia dello spettacolo musicale*. Turin 1996, 3–93; Anna Laura Bellina (ed.): *Il teatro dei due mondi. L'opera italiana nei paesi di lingua iberica*. Treviso 2000; Reinhard Strohm (ed.): *The Eigthteenth-Century Diaspora of Italian Music and Musicians*. Turnhout 2001; Norbert Dubowy, Corinna Herr and Alina Zórawska-Witkowska (eds.): *Italian Opera in Central Europe 1614–1780. Vol. 3: Opera Subjects and European Relationships*. Berlin 2007; Melania Bucciarelli, Norbert Dubowy and Reinhard Strohm (eds.): *Italian Opera in Central Europe. Vol. 1: Institutions and Ceremonies*. Berlin 2008; Corinna Herr et al. (eds.): *Italian Opera in Central Europe 1614–1780. Vol. 2: Italianità. Image and Practice*. Berlin 2008; Damien Colas and Alessandro Di Profio (eds.): *D'une scène à l'autre. L'opéra italien en Europe, 2 vols*. Wavre 2009.

9 Strohm, Eighteenth-Century Diaspora. More recently, a research group studied the reverse movement of European musicians, who travelled or migrated to Venice, Rome and Naples

The study of this last systematic movement shows a historiographical change that has encouraged the examination of mobile musicians for the last 15 years: Probably due to the accentuation of cultural mediators within the concepts of cultural transfer and *histoire croisée*, there has been a shift in perspective from migratory music and musicians as parts of symbolic representation centred around a prince and his territory in terms of conspicuous consumption and a cultural history of politics[10] to the examination of the reasons, intentions and consequences of the musicians' mobility.[11] These can be reconstructed mainly on the basis of biographical elements like economic or artistic conditions, supra-regional career paths or the gain of social status. In this context, they have been examined via collective biographies in relation to groups of musicians who shared an institutional affiliation, a linguistic origin or a musical education,[12] as well as in relation to biographies in order to explain developments of individual style and performance practice.[13]

Since collective and individual biographies on music mediators have deepened knowledge of the cultural hybridity of European musical practices and networks of musical life, traditional stylistic classifications on the basis of geographical or national cultural and stylistic entities have been challenged in at least two ways: On the one side, socio-cultural contexts of musical composition and performance have been examined on the basis of networks and actions in everyday life and at special feasts, ranging from performances in single palaces or theatres

between 1650 and 1750: Anne-Madeleine Goulet and Gesa zur Nieden (eds.): *Europäische Musiker in Venedig, Rom und Neapel (1650–1750)*. Kassel 2015.

10 For an emblematic overview, see *Händel-Jahrbuch* 58 (2012) that contains a collection of papers held at the conference "Händel und Dresden. Musik als europäisches Kulturphänomen" in Halle 2011.

11 Goulet and zur Nieden, Europäische Musiker.

12 See the collective biography in Britta Kägler: Von "Geschücklichkeiten", Pfauenfedern und einem "Phonascus". Kollektivbiographische Studien zu deutschsprachigen Musikern in den italienischen Musikzentren Venedig und Rom (1650–1750), in: Goulet and zur Nieden, Europäische Musiker, 236–268; Denise Launay: Les musiciens français itinérants au XVIIe siècle, in: *Colloques internationaux du Centre de la Recherche Scientifique. La découverte de la France au XVIIe siècle, neuvième colloque de Marseille organisé par le Centre Méridional des Rencontres sur le XVIIe siècle*. Paris 1980, 621–633; Christian Meyer (ed.): *Le musicien et ses voyages. Pratiques, réseaux et representations*. Berlin 2003.

13 For an overview on Handel, see Juliane Riepe: *Händel vor dem Fernrohr. Die Italienreise*. Beeskow 2013; Panja Mücke: Transferwege und Blockaden. Zu Händels Borrowings im frühneuzeitlichen Kommunikationssystem, in: *Händel-Jahrbuch* 58 (2012), 185–203; Silke Leopold: Was hat Händel in Italien gelernt?, in: Alberto Colzani et al. (eds.): *Relazioni musicali tra Italia e Germania nell'età barocca. Atti del VI Convegno internazionale sulla musica italiana nei secoli XVII–XVIII, Loveno di Menaggio (Como), 11–13 luglio 1995*. Como 1997, 387–408.

up to the musical reputation of entire cities and courts via agents or so-called brokers.[14] From this perspective, categorical descriptions like "Italian" or "French music" can be seen as instruments to facilitate the integration or exclusion of musicians on a local level, a process linked to not always entirely aesthetic concerns, but also to social or economic contexts as well as to the knowledge of languages.[15] During the late eighteenth century, first-hand experience of "Italian" performances and performers was often claimed as a qualification by musicians from the German-speaking lands in search for employment as chapel masters.[16] Concerning musical genres, their categorical notions often served as a point of orientation for musical interaction between musicians unknown to each other instead of representing a "national" culture and its social and aesthetic characteristics.[17] In this regard, the socio-cultural study of the musicians' practices in everyday life also puts into perspective the many cultural definitions deployed by music consumers that served to deal with foreign languages and to interpret music within a specific political context.

On the other side, biographies have been linked to politico-symbolical representation with the effect of articulating individual approaches to the artistic symbolisation of political power.[18] This historiographical evolution includes an attention to personal relations between musicians and their patrons, which are studied in an interdisciplinary manner on the basis of a wide range of musical, pictorial, cameralistic and diplomatic sources,[19] but also a re-evaluation of musical documents like scores or treatises as proof of the rising importance of a person-centred

---

14 This term is used by Arnaldo Morelli: Marenzio, the Courtier. Some Thoughts on Patronage in the Court of Rome, in: Mauro Calcagno (ed.): *"Compositor moderno et vago". Perspectives on Luca Marenzio's Secular and Devotional Music*. Turnhout 2012, 229–236. See also Melanie Traversier: Costruire la fama musicale. La diplomazia napoletana al servizio della musica durante il regno di Carlo di Borbone, in: Goulet and zur Nieden, Europäische Musiker, 171–189.

15 Jerôme de la Gorce: La résistance à l'opéra italien en France au XVIIe siècle, in: Herr et al., Italian Opera in Central Europe, 209–218.

16 Juliane Riepe: Rom als Station deutscher Musiker des 17. und 18. Jahrhunderts auf Italienreise. Aspekte eines biographischen Modells im Wandel, in: Goulet and zur Nieden, Europäische Musiker, 227–228.

17 See Thierry Favier's part in Jean Boutier: Tavola rotonda. Incroci tra storia cultural e storia della musica a livello europeo. Metodi e problematiche per il XVII e il XVIII secolo, in: Goulet and zur Nieden, Europäische Musiker, 626–632.

18 Klaus Pietschmann: Repräsentationsformen in der frankoflämischen Musikkultur des 15. und 16. Jahrhunderts. Transfer, Austausch, Akkulturation, in: *Musiktheorie* 25 (2010), 99–115.

19 For diplomatic studies on music and music migrations, see the collected volume Rebekah Ahrendt, Mark Ferraguto and Damien Mahiet (eds.): *Music* and *Diplomacy from the Early Modern Era to the Present*. New York 2014.

authorship and authority.[20] As mentioned before, early modern musicians from German-speaking lands strove to document diverse musical and linguistic skills that were often improved by their travels. Such a concentration on individuals and their various skills objects but also enriches the fluid concept of early modern musical works that has been accounted for in recently developed hybrid digital editions.[21] This historiographical and methodological constellation poses the question whether the impossible task of defining a document of reference for the authentic transmission of a historical work and its musical execution can be substituted by an idea of a biographically reconstructed authority and sociality within the starting development of modern authenticity.[22] More precisely this is a matter of balancing a too-strong notion of geographic-cultural entities against a total cultural hybridisation of musical practices and styles or a complete atomisation of performance practices and reception models on the basis of single performances. Such a view does not only allow for a description of an early modern "fragmentary individualisation" but also for an understanding of the diversity and complexity of early modern types of mobility.[23]

Recent philosophical and aesthetic definitions of authenticity have opened the possibility of applying the concept to historical periods before the late eighteenth century. On the basis of these new reflections, it is now possible to connect authenticity to personal behaviour as well as to objects and situations in the biographies of early modern mobile musicians that constantly oscillated between different social and aesthetic norms: First of all authenticity is a concept of testimony that is linked to the authority of the message or document and the sociality of the mediator.[24] Even personal authenticity is now seen as less influential in

---

20 Kordula Knaus: Italian Courts and their Musicians in the Early Modern Period. Authority, Authorship and Gender, in: ead. and Susanne Kogler (eds.): *Autorschaft – Genie – Geschlecht. Musikalische Schaffensprozesse von der Frühen Neuzeit bis zur Gegenwart*. Köln 2013, 67–84.

21 Janine Droese et al.: Musik – Theater – Text. Grundfragen der Musiktheaterphilologie im Spiegel der OPERA-Hybridausgaben, in: *Editio. Internationales Jahrbuch für Editionswissenschaft* 27 (2013), 72–95.

22 For the development of a modern authenticity in relation to the composers' authorship and authority, see Michele Calella: *Musikalische Autorschaft. Der Komponist zwischen Mittelalter und Neuzeit*. Kassel 2014.

23 Wolfgang Bonß and Sven Kesselring: Mobilität am Übergang von der Ersten zur Zweiten Moderne, in: Ulrich Beck and Wolfgang Bonß (eds.): *Die Modernisierung der Moderne*. Frankfurt 2001, 187 and 189.

24 Sybille Krämer: Zum Paradoxon von Zeugenschaft im Spannungsfeld von Personalität und Depersonalisierung, in: Michael Rössner and Heidemarie Uhl (eds.): *Renaissance der Authentizität? Über die neue Sehnsucht nach dem Ursprünglichen*. Bielefeld 2012, 15–26.

the creation of social fragmentation out of individuality and subjectivity[25] and has been linked to social rules and norms as well as to barely definable "forces". These norms and "forces" relativise and counterbalance the importance of liberty as a central condition for authenticity and constitute the framework in which authentic persons or objects can emerge.[26] As for early modern music history, the artistic and social norms were strongly influenced by established musical genres and their conventions, by the last traces of climate theory and its cultural characterisations, and by the incipient connection of language and political statehood.[27] Early modern musical authenticity is thus about managing one's musicianship within this framework.

As far as musicology is concerned, the concept of authenticity is strongly linked to historically informed practices of performance and music editing that seek to follow the intentions of the composer and the sound and practice of his time. Within this realm, Peter Kivy argues that the intentions even of early modern composers can be reconstructed by work on historical and cultural contexts as well as by the analysis of the music itself.[28] In summary, Kivy's "historical authenticity" is linked to the beginning of an authenticity defined as authority and authorship that are thought to persist unaffected by cultural and temporal differences and can therefore be studied particularly well in the instance of mobile musicians and their experiences.

On the basis of this state of research, in the following I will trace some of the forces driving mobile musicians' paths by comparing cultural characterisations of the musical life of particular cities with those that result from individual professional careers: First, I will concentrate on the construction of a cultural characterisation of Glückstadt, a so-called "city of exiles"[29] in the duchy of Holstein founded by Christian IV of Denmark in 1616. During the seventeenth and

---

25 Charles Taylor: *The Malaise of Modernity*. Ontario 1991.

26 Christoph Menke: Was ist eine "Ethik der Authentizität"?, in: Michael Kühnlein and Matthias Lutz-Bachmann (eds.): *Unerfüllte Moderne? Neue Perspektiven auf das Werk von Charles Taylor*. Berlin 2011, 217–238.

27 For climate theories in music, see John T. Scott: Climate, Causation, and the Power of Music in Montesquieu and Rousseau, in: Claude Dauphin (ed.): *Musique et langage chez Rousseau*. Oxford 2004, 51–61.

28 Peter Kivy: *Authenticities. Philosophical Reflections on Musical Performances*. Ithaca, NY 1995, 26–28.

29 "City of exiles" (*Exulantenstadt*) is a term used in urban history to describe cities that were built up by – mostly religious – exiles. Heinz Stoob: Über frühneuzeitliche Städtetypen, in: id. (ed.): *Räume, Formen und Schichten der mitteleuropäischen Städte. Eine Aufsatzfolge*. Köln 1970, 246–284; Raingard Esser: Art. "Exulantenstadt", in: Friedrich Jaeger (ed.): *Enzyklopädie der Neuzeit. Vol. 3: Dynastie-Freundschaftslinien*. Stuttgart 2006, 732–733.

eighteenth centuries, the active musicians in that town constantly referred to the words *Glück* (luck) or *Fortuna* (fortune) in different artistic and/or personal ways, as aiding or impeding mobility. Second, I will turn to Johann Jakob Froberger's (1616–1667) biography and musical career. Froberger was a harpsichord player, organist and composer in the service of Holy Roman Emperor Ferdinand III and left many clues to his individual solutions to the problem of symbolic representation but also to his own biography in his music. My contention is that the conditions of musical life were often reflected in musical compositions and that this habit served to establish cultural categories that were manageable by musicians who had to cope with the frequent re-formation of court chapels and the constant need to gain permission for new musical performances to be able to earn one's living. Such conditions facilitated efforts to improve financial income as well as social status in different ways. At the same time, they form a substantial basis for the study of historical authenticity in its development towards a "personal authenticity" between everyday mobility, systematic movements, cultural notions and biography.

The City of Fortune

The city of Glückstadt is particularly interesting for the study of mobile musicians since it was established by Christian IV, king of Denmark and Norway, as a so-called "city of exiles". During the whole seventeenth and eighteenth centuries the king tried to promote settlement in the newly founded town situated on the river Elbe, a few kilometres downstream from Hamburg, by inviting different religious groups like Sephardic Jews originally from Spain and Portugal, who arrived in Glückstadt from the Netherlands, or French Huguenots.[30] Moreover, Dutch merchants and sailors were attracted by the king's plan to surpass the city of Hamburg in trade by benefiting from its more favourite geographical position for shipping.[31] Beyond a maximum of religious freedom, new citizens could also benefit from the fact that in 1649, Frederick III of Denmark made Glückstadt the administrative capital of Holstein. Already in 1630, his father Christian IV had concluded an agreement with Spain that confirmed Glückstadt as the place to issue passes for shipping to Spain and Portugal. This led to the settlement of at least a few Spanish

30 See the announcement of privileges in Walter Wilkes: *Der Glückstadt Lust-, Leid- und Freudenspiegel*. München 1964, 9–10.

31 Gerhard Köhn: *Die Bevölkerung der Residenz, Festung und Exulantenstadt Glückstadt von der Gründung 1616 bis zum Endausbau 1652*. Neumünster 1974, 22–26.

Catholics and increased the number of Dutch sailors, since the passes protected their ships from attacks by privateers.[32]

Throughout the seventeenth century, Glückstadt struggled to become a major city of trade.[33] The geographical position turned out to be extremely unfavourable for this plan, because the city was surrounded by unhealthy marshland and a sandbank soon blocked the port entrance. While in 1643 the marshland protected Glückstadt almost more than its fortress from invasion by Swedish forces,[34] city life was strongly influenced by the presence of local troops and their musicians. Besides a town musician, musical life developed in parallel to the settlement of several religious communities. Until 1708 Glückstadt had two main Christian churches, the town church and the castle church. Cantors also had the duty to instruct the pupils at the local school.[35] At the latest by 1668 the Portuguese state contributed to the salary of the town musician.[36] The position of the town musician seems to have been sold by the owner or passed over to family members since family ties can be traced between most of the town musicians of Glückstadt from the 1630s to 1841.[37] Nevertheless it seems as if various families of musicians were present in Glückstadt, since in 1673 a musician named Bertram is noted in juridical documents for having participated in a brawl.[38] In 1696, one Georg Baltzer Bertram replaced his father-in-law Mathias Höpner, who had served as a town musician from 1684 till his death in 1694.[39] During his activity as a town musician, Bertram constantly tried to increase his privileges by asking for an assistant but first of all by complaining about musicians who restricted his rights and duties. This concerned all types of local musicians from the organist up to

32 Ibid., 52–54.

33 Karl Asmussen: Das Wirtschaftsleben und die Bevölkerung Glückstadts von der Gründung bis 1869, in: *Glückstadt im Wandel der Zeiten. Vol. 2.* Glückstadt 1966, 161–236.

34 Paul Douglas Lockhart: *Denmark in the Thirty Year's War, 1618–1648. King Christian IV and the Decline of the Oldenburg-State.* London 1996, 261.

35 Royal Decree, 23 Feb. 1646 (State Archives Schleswig-Holstein, Dep. 133, № 88.5); Arnfried Edler: *Der nordelbische Organist. Studien zu Sozialstatus, Funktion und kompositorischer Produktion eines Musikerberufes von der Reformation bis zum 20. Jahrhundert.* Kassel 1982, 83.

36 Letter by the Secretary Jacobus Jacobi, 23 Nov. 1668 (State Archives Schleswig-Holstein, Dep. 133, № 141). See also Decree by the City Assembly of Glückstadt, 14 Apr. 1730 (Municipal Archives Glückstadt, 1015, № 9).

37 Mirko Soll: *Verrechtlichte Musik. Die Stadtmusikanten der Herzogtümer Schleswig und Holstein. Eine Untersuchung aufgrund archivalischer Quellen.* Münster 2006, 462.

38 Glückstädtische Pfandbrüche 1673–1674 (Municipal Archives Glückstadt, Mf1 LVI).

39 Letter by the Town Government, 1 June 1696 (State Archives Schleswig-Holstein, Dep. 133, № 141).

military musicians and a second town musician.[40] The main source of all these conflicts seems to be Bertram's attempt to rule the musical life of Glückstadt on his own, a concern that he hid behind the effort to guarantee a functioning and qualitatively satisfactory musical ensemble. This argument was often linked with the fear of losing skilled or merely trained musicians who seemed to flee the town of Glückstadt as soon as possible. Thus Bertram accused the second town musician, Hans König, of playing music with non-professionals at weddings or feasts and his son and assistant to have secretly left the city.[41]

That Bertram was simultaneously open to performing with military or church musicians can be seen by the example of a Christmas cantata that he composed in 1712. The libretto of this cantata specifies that it was to be performed at the town and garrison church and that it had to be played by one soloist (singer or instrumentalist), two bassoons and three oboes.[42] Because of this large number of woodwinds it is most likely that Bertram asked the military oboists to join the ensemble.[43] The text of this cantata is likely to reflect the atmosphere that characterised the cultural life of Glückstadt during the seventeenth and eighteenth centuries and which might have been the reason why many musicians left the town. The cantata describes the stormy sea and ends with the evocation of celestial salvation supported by a choir of angels, which "hebt unser ewigs Glück hervor". After the sermon, an ode restarts with the verse: "Schmeißt ihr hohen Unglücks-Wogen! Schmeißt mein Schifflein hin und her. Rase, weites Trübsals-Meer! Mich bestrahlt ein Himmels-Bogen."[44]

Since the foundation of the city, metaphors of the rough sea contrasted with the fortunate name of Glückstadt were very common. They are present throughout the seventeenth and eighteenth centuries in poetry by local writers like Johann Rist and Christoph Woltereck and thus seem to reflect the changeful story of the town that never managed to come even close to attaining the goal of surpassing Hamburg in trade and settlement. While in 1643 Rist connected the name of

40 State Archives Schleswig-Holstein, Dep. 133, № 141 and Dep. 65.2, № 3411–IV.

41 Letter by the Royal Chancellery von Hagen, 24 Oct. 1722 (Municipal Archives Glückstadt, 1015); Soll, Verrechtlichte Musik, 316.

42 Weihnachts-Freude in der Stadt- und Garnisons-Gemeinde zu Glückstadt. Vormittags musicalisch vorgestellet durch Georg Baltzer Bertram, gedruckt im Jahre Christi 1712, in: *Digitale Sammlungen der Staatsbibliothek Berlin*. URL: *http://digital.staatsbibliothek-berlin.de/werkansicht/?PPN=PPN663930138&PHYSID=PHYS_0001&USE=800* (20 June 2015).

43 The State and Municipal Archives contain documentation on several differences between town musicians and military musicians, especially oboists, for the years 1732 (Bertram) and 1742 (Palschau): State Archives Schleswig-Holstein, Dep. 65.2: Deutsche Kanzlei zu Kopenhagen, № 3411–IV.

44 Weihnachts-Freude.

Glückstadt to a positive future of the city that was going to enrich the royal family tree,[45] in 1712 Woltereck used it in poems and madrigals about drunkards and bankruptcy, too.[46] In one poem the writer abandons hope that the tree of fortune will ever bear fruit and places it under an ideal of beauty characterised by a Nordic wind.[47]

That a northern orientation at the Danish court was intended by both Bertram and Woltereck can be shown by the fact that Bertram applied for a position in Copenhagen and that Woltereck dedicated his *Holsteinische Musen* to the Danish king. In compliance with the absolutism that had been established by Frederick III, both compared the King to a celestial light, in contrast to the changing river of fortune.[48] While in 1643 Johann Rist still related the metaphor of the sky to the foundation of Glückstadt, in 1712, Bertram's "Himmels-Bogen" seemed to allude to a violin bow and might thus have explicitly backed Bertram's candidature for Copenhagen.[49]

Beyond this merging of music and the image of Glückstadt the musical activity of local musicians like Bertram but also of the local nobility seems to have fostered quite a diverse musical life. During their stays in Glückstadt the Danish Kings mostly refrained from organising impressive musical performances, but they seemed to encourage local musical activities:[50] In 1632 Christian IV sent the printer Andreas Koch from Copenhagen to become the royal printer of Glückstadt.

45 In 1643 Rist wrote the following verses about the new castle of Glückstadt on the occasion of the wedding of Frederic III with Sophia Amalia of Brunswick-Lüneburg: "Unmöglich wird es sein ein solches Schloß zu zeigen,/ Daß solche Helden itzt in Fröhlichkeit besteigen/ als Dir, Du Burg des Glücks, weit über allen Werth/ Und Gut zu schätzen, itzt so gnädig wiederfährt./ Schau den Regenten-Baum mit seinen edlen Zweigen,/ Den Baum, vor welchem sich in tieffer Demuth neigen/ Die Königreiche, so gehorchen Deiner Macht/ [...] Du Burg des Glücks, der Cimbren höchste Zier,/ [...] Dich soll gar nicht verletzen/ Feur, Wasser, Wetter Krieg und was sonst pflegt zu setzen/ Die Schlösser in Verderb. Du Glücks-Burg sollst allein/ Ein unvergleichlichs Haus und Schmuck der Elbe sein." Johanni Risten G.P. Lobrede .... Hamburg 1643, quoted after *Neues Staatsbürgerliches Magazin* 1, no. 1 (1932), 303.

46 *Christoph Wolterecks Holsteinische Musen, worinnen enthalten Ehren-Gedichte/ Briefe/ Cantaten/ Oden/ Sonette/ Madrigalen/ Sinngedichte und Grabschriften, Glückstadt. Bey Gotthilff Lehmann Königlich privilegierter Buchhändler (1712)*, 289 and 291.

47 Ibid., 246.

48 "Denn ob ihr Wohlfahrts-Strom gleich nach und nach versieget; Ihr Morgenstern des Glücks noch immer schläfrig steiget: So lebt ihr König hoch/ ihr Trost und Sonnen-Licht." Wolterecks Holsteinische Musen, "Zuschrift".

49 Soll, Verrechtlichte Musik, 462.

50 Aubéry du Maurier reports the following on Christian's IV journey to Glückstadt in 1637: "Il venoit de Copenhague en un Calèche à deux chevaux, accompagné seulement de quatre ou cinq Cavaliers, ce qui nous fit admirer à tous le mépris que se sage Prince faisoit du faste et du pompe

In 1664 his son Melchior Koch printed a wedding song for two singers and three instrumentalists (basso continuo, violin, flute) that contains a musical riddle consisting of a rectangle of four staves that can be sung from the inside or from the outside of the rectangle. The centre is occupied by a picture showing the couple sleeping in their bed and the last stave finishes with the announcement of another son or singer.[51] Most notably, in these publications, the instruments and performance indications are given in various languages from Italian ("lento piano", "forte"), French ("violon") and Low German ("Fleute"). This has various reasons: First, the printer most probably brought material from the musically Italianised court of Copenhagen and used it to print local music in Glückstadt.[52] Second, since the 1640s a strong interest in French culture can be documented. In 1648 the tax collector Søren Terkelsen, who was born in Glückstadt, translated Honoré d'Urfé's *Astrée* into German using melodies by Johann Rist and the Danish court trumpeter Gabriel Voigtländer.[53] In 1705 Lehmann printed a treatise on French dances with *courantes, minuets* and *bourrées*.[54] Third, the local town musicians were keen to attract a big audience and to play at as many private feasts as possible, including those of the Dutch community.

Indeed, the amount and size of musical performances were also an interest of the city council, which wished to regain a functioning musical ensemble around the town musician after the departure of Hans König.[55] Finally, probably following the Portuguese, who underscored their citizens' rights by contributing to the town musician's salary, in 1718 the king published a new royal privilege "für die/ der

---

des Rois." Aubéry du Maurier: *Memoires de Hambourg de Lubeck et de Holstein, de Dannemark, de Suède et de Pologne, 1735*, 9–10.

51 *Gespräch des himlischen Bräutigambs mit seiner Braut aus dem hohen Liede Salomonis/ Auff den hochzeitlichen Ehren- und Freuden-Tag/ Des Wol Edlen/ Besten und Hochgelahrten Herrn Friderici Helms* [...] *In Glückstadt celebriret am 24. Novembris dieses 1664 Jahres. In die Sing- und Spiel-Kunst verfasset à Philomuso*. Glückstadt/ Drucks Melchior Koch.

52 Christoph Reske: *Die Buchdrucker des 16. und 17. Jahrhunderts im deutschen Sprachgebiet*. Wiesbaden 2007, 297.

53 Steffen Arndal: Übersetzung, Parodie, Kontrafaktur. Zur Rezeption des deutschen Barockliedes in Dänemark, in: Gudrun Busch (ed.): *Studien zum deutschen weltlichen Kunstlied des 17. und 18. Jahrhunderts*. Amsterdam 1992, 88.

54 I.H.P. (ed.): *Maître de Danse, oder Tanz-Meister/ Welcher lehret/ wie ein Tänzer so die Fundamenta gefasset/ ohne Hüllfe/ sich selbsten die gebräuchlichsten Französischen Tänze beybringen könne, Glückstadt und Leipzig/ bey Gotthilff Lehmann/ Königlichen Privilegirten Buchhändler*. Glückstadt/ Gedruckt bey Johann Friederich Schwendimann Königl. Buchdrucker. Anno M.DCCV. See also Stephanie Schroedter, Marie-Thérèse Mourey and Giles Bennett (eds.): *Barocktanz im Zeichen französisch-deutschen Kulturtransfers. Quellen zur Tanzkultur um 1700*. Hildesheim 2008.

55 Royal Order to the Municipal Authorities, 28 Sept. 1723 (State Archives Schleswig, Dep. 133 № 141).

Reformirten Religion zu-gethane/ so wol Deutsch- und Französischer/ als auch Engell- und Holländischer Nationen, welche sich etwa alhie in Glückstadt zu setzen und häuslich nieder zulassen resolviren möchten". The initial of the text is decorated by an emblem showing a lute and a score that entwine around a tree, replacing the winds and gales that kept Wolterecks "tree of fortune" from bearing fruit.[56] In summary, by 1718 the culturally diverse music of Glückstadt had become an important element symbolising urban development. Probably because of this in the 1760s some French Huguenots from Hamburg and Berlin tried to establish a French colony in Glückstadt, bringing their own cantors and organists with them, who were also to instruct their children in French.[57] In this case, the image of Glückstadt as a home to the arts served more to attract new citizens from outside the city than enabling local musicians to build up a reputation as a basis for obtaining a post as a court musician in Copenhagen.

Nevertheless, most of the musicians working in Glückstadt were disappointed by Fortuna. Throughout the eighteenth century, they continued to use the term "fortune" in relation to their decision to continue their careers and biographies abroad. In 1792 Heinrich Conrad Wille announced his departure after three years of service as a town musician with the following words: "Lange schon war der Wunsch in mir rege/: da ich nie glücklich in Glückstadt war, und auch nie sein kann/: mich auf Reisen zu begeben, um zu sehen, ob Mad[ame] Fortuna nicht in ihrem Glückstöpfchen noch ein gutes Loos für mich aufgehoben."[58]

A musician who obviously enjoyed living in Glückstadt was the organist Johann Conrad Rosenbusch, who is noted for his unconventional behaviour towards the municipal authorities. Rosenbusch had been educated and worked in Erfurt, Stuttgart, Gotha, Itzehoe and Hamburg before settling in Glückstadt in 1713 at the age of forty. The Hamburg music writer Johann Mattheson said of him in his biographical compendium *Grundlage einer Ehrenpforte* that "er lebt bisher vergnügt an solchem Orte".[59] According to Mattheson, one of the first music biographers, the organist of Glückstadt also appreciated the idea of his biographical enterprise.

---

56 *Königlich allergnädigstes PRIVILEGIUM für die/ der Reformierten Religion zu-gethane/ so wol Deutsch- und Französischer/ als auch Engell- und Holländischer Nationen, welche sich etwa allhie in Glückstadt zu setzen und häuslich nieder zulassen resolviren möchten*. Glückstadt, gedruckt in der Königl. privil. Buchdr. 1718 (Municipal Archives Glückstadt, № 1248–1249).

57 State Archives Schleswig-Holstein, Dep. 65.2: Deutsche Kanzlei zu Kopenhagen, № 3390: Französisch-reformierte Gemeinde in Glückstadt.

58 Municipal Archives Glückstadt Nr. 1015; Letter by the town musician Heinrich Conrad Wille, 8 Aug. 1792, cited in: Soll, Verrechtlichte Musik, 208.

59 Johann Mattheson: *Grundlage einer Ehrenpforte*. Hamburg 1740, 295.

At the end of his entry on Rosenbusch, Mattheson copies a letter by him dated 9 December 1739:

> Es ist mir eine Freude, daß Ew. Hochedl. die in vielen Jahren mühsam errichtete Ehrenpforte endlich wollen ans Licht treten lassen: der Herr seegne solches Werck zu seiner Ehre, und lasse die es lesen dadurch zur Erkenntniß seiner Wege auf Erden (**welche gemeiniglich bey den Musicis wunderbar sind**) gelangen ....[60]

By comparing musicians' biographies to a celestial marvelousness, a theme that other musicians of Glückstadt used for the Danish court and their own ambitions to become court musicians, it seems as if Rosenbusch saw his path of terrestrial life in the town of Glückstadt, where he served for more than 20 years in the town church, as already perfect or felicitous. It is interesting to notice that Rosenbusch did not try to enlarge his privileges or to become noticed by printed musical compositions. In contrast he stuck to an unconventional assertion of his privileges by putting forward his own social and musical authority.[61] Mattheson sees Rosenbusch's authority in the fact that he instructed a blind musician, who later became the organist in Itzehoe and he describes this success as Rosenbusch's most important, quasi divine "work".[62] In this way the metaphor of fortune and celestial light was used not only for professional advancement at court through mobility or to gain local authority among the audiences. It also served as a biographical milestone of self-determined settlement and stability that found its way into Mattheson's biographies in the atmosphere of the early enlightenment, where the divine forces were translated into earthly musical or educational "works". In relation to their initiators, those works made their own biographical paths marvellous.[63]

A Life Journey in Music

How authority emerges out of supra-regional mobility and how it can lead to a stable position or settlement can be shown by the example of Johann Jakob Froberger. He is one among the group of early modern musicians whose music

60 Ibid., 296. Emphasis in the original.

61 Edler, Der nordelbische Organist, 110, 113–114 and 190–191.

62 Mattheson, Grundlage einer Ehrenpforte, 295.

63 For the combination of religion and enlightenment in the work of Johann Rist, see Anne-Charlott Trepp: *Von der Glückseligkeit alles zu wissen. Die Erforschung der Natur als religiöse Praxis in der Frühen Neuzeit*. Frankfurt 2009, 78–277.

incorporates the most diverse elements of political representation and individual biography. Moreover, Froberger's life can be characterised as a path of professional stabilisation and social advancement. In 1637, still at the beginning of his career, Froberger converted to Catholicism to earn a scholarship from Ferdinand III to study in Rome.[64] This journey was organised by the Holy Roman Emperor's confessor, the Jesuit Joseph Gans, who found Froberger a temporary home at the Palazzo de Cupis, where the Habsburg ambassador resided. Probably through Gans, Froberger came into contact with the celebrated polymath Athanasius Kircher, with whom he started to work on the *arca musarithmica*, a machine for musical composing. At the end of his stay in Rome, Kircher asked Froberger to convey the machine to the emperor. Since Kircher did not ask the King's confessor Gans, who tried to transmit the machine to Ferdinand himself, Froberger got an audience of several hours with the Holy Roman Emperor.[65] Froberger afterwards intensified his contact with Ferdinand by the composition of music that contained imperial symbols and riddles: In 1649 after a second journey to Italy, Froberger dedicated a manuscript of new toccatas, fantasias and *canzone* to the Emperor. This manuscript contained also his *Fantasia sopra Ut Re Mi Fa Sol La*, which Kircher published a year later in his *Musurgia Universalis*, dedicated to Archduke Leopold Wilhelm of Austria.[66] Beyond the decoration of the manuscript with the symbols of the sun, the sceptre, the orb and the sword, Froberger introduced a musical symbolic value into his compositions by means of solmisation. Indeed, the Kircher-inspired *Fantasia sopra Sollare* ("shining") consists of the recurrent line "lascia fare mi" ("let me do"). This line can be interpreted in at least three ways: First it strengthens Froberger's capacity to contribute to the power and radiation ("let me do the shining"). Second, Froberger seems to allude to the power of music as an instrument for political representing but also for aristocratic pleasure ("let the Fa Re Mi do the shining"). Third, the line "lascia fare mi" can be read as a tribute to the Emperor ("let F*e*rdin*a*ndo *Re* de' Ro*mani* do the shining").[67] In

64 Herwig Knaus: *Die Musiker im Archivbestand des Kaiserlichen Obersthofmeisteramtes (1637–1705)*. Wien 1967, 90–91; Rudolf Rasch: Johann Jacob Froberger's Travels 1649–1653, in: Christopher Hogwood (ed.): *The Keyboard in Baroque Europe*. Cambridge 2003, 20–21.

65 Claudio Annibaldi: Froberger in Rome. From Frescobaldi's Craftsmanship to Kircher's Compositional Secrets, in: *Current Musicology* 58 (1998), 14–18; Ulf Scharlau: Neue Quellenfunde zur Biographie Johann Jakob Frobergers, in: *Die Musikforschung* 22 (1969), 47–52.

66 Libro Secondo. Di Toccate, Fantasie, Canzone, Allemande, Courante, Sarabande, Gigue et altre partite. Alla Sac.a Caes.a M.ta. Devotissim.te dedicato in Vienna lì 29 Settembre 1649 da Gio. Giacomo Froberger, see the facsimile in: Siegbert Rampe (ed.): *Neue Ausgabe sämtlicher Clavier- und Orgelwerke. Vol. 1: Libro Secondo (1649)*. Kassel 1993.

67 In 1647 the Emperor had already received a treatise on the solmisation of his latin name "Ferdinandus Tertius" *FER-DI-NAN-DUS TER-TI-US sive Sanctae-Crucis musicae errorem totius*

Johann Jakob Froberger: Fantasia sopra Sollare, in: *Libro Secondo*. Wien 1649.

summary, with his compositions dedicated to Ferdinand III Froberger established a politico-symbolical but also a personal relationship with the Emperor for which his individual capacities could not be neglected.[68]

Probably because of such a combination, in 1649, Ferdinand III sent his court organist Froberger on a journey to Brussels and France. On this journey Froberger stopped in Dresden where he handed over a letter from Ferdinand to the elector of Saxony.[69] According to Mattheson, Johann Georg I asked Froberger to compete against the organist Matthias Weckmann. After Weckmann's improvisation on one of Froberger's themes, the Viennese court organist honoured his colleague by exclaiming "[d]ieser ist wahrhafftig ein rechter Virtuos".[70] Even beyond this expression it is obvious that Mattheson's biographical narrative stresses the personal

orbis terrarum corrigentis novi canone. Wien 1647. See Steven Saunders: New Discoveries Concerning Ferdinand III's Musical Compositions, in: *Studien zur Musikwissenschaft* 45 (1996), 8.

68 For the favourable climate at the Viennese court for such a combination, see Ferdinand Zehentreiter: Der Fürst als Künstlerkollege und Volkspädagoge. Die Musik-Patronage im Habsburgerreich und ihre Bedeutung für die Autonomisierung des Komponierens, in: Ulrich Oevermann, Johannes Süßmann and Christine Tauber (eds.): *Die Kunst der Mächtigen und die Macht der Kunst. Untersuchungen zu Mäzenatentum und Kulturpatronage*. Berlin 2007, 201–221.

69 Siegbert Rampe: Das "Hinze-Manuskript" – Ein Dokument zu Biographie und Werk von Matthias Weckmann und Johann Jacob Froberger, in: *Schütz-Jahrbuch* 19 (1997), 88–103.

70 Mattheson, Grundlage einer Ehrenpforte, 396.

relationship between the elector of Saxony and his musician as well as between the two musicians, who served different courts. Furthermore, the cooperative interaction between the two musicians may have been motivated by the general court protocol like the Viennese one that demanded that musicians "mantenghino buona, sincera e cordiale amicizia con tutti li musici, onorando e rispettando ognuno".[71] That music was an important instrument to foster peace and friendship between politically or dynastically related courts reflects itself, for example, in the intention of Leopold Wilhelm to organise an opera performance at the next Reichstag where the archduke planned to bring his musicians.[72]

When Froberger travelled to Paris in the service of Archduke Leopold Wilhelm, who awarded him 240 guilders in Brussels between 1649 and 1652, the atmosphere for his music was less receptive. In his volume *La muze historique* Jean Loret qualifies Froberger as a "piffre [glutton] d'allemand" and a "très médiocre personage" after a concert with a great ensemble and a large audience in Paris on 29 September 1652.[73] While Loret's rejection of the Viennese governor of Brussels who had received Mazarin as a refugee during the *fronde* seems quite natural, this rejection stands in contrast to Froberger's individual networks which he tied during his stay in Paris. First of all his compositions are evidence of friendships that Froberger built up with French musicians like the organist Louis Couperin and the lutenist Charles de Fleury, sieur de Blanrocher.[74] For the latter he even wrote a *memento mori* that reflects on Blanrocher's death after he had rushed down the stairs.[75] Beyond the strong ties to his colleagues, Froberger was in contact with French nobles who supported Mazarin's suspension, as Jean Loret probably did. In 1652 Froberger composed a Suite with a Gigue "nommée la ruse Mazarinique. [...] NB Lament et à discrétion, comme le retour de Mons. Le Cardinal Mazarin

---

71 Jakob Wührer and Martin Scheutz: *Zu Diensten Ihrer Majestät. Hofordnungen und Instruktionsbücher am frühneuzeitlichen Wiener Hof.* Wien 2011, 709.

72 Renate Schreiber: *Ein Galleria nach meinem Humor. Erzherzog Leopold Wilhelm*. Wien 2004, 31.

73 Jean Loret: *La muze historique, ou Recueil des lettres en vers contenant les nouvelles tu temps. Vol. 1: 1650–1654*, ed. Ravenel and La Pelouze. Paris 1857, 291–292. For Froberger's sojourns in Paris in 1650 and 1652, see also Catherine Massip: Froberger et la France, in: *J.J. Froberger Musicien Européen. Colloque organisé par la ville et l'École Nationale de Musique de Montbéliard*. Paris 1998, 67–75.

74 Ibid.

75 Philippe Vendrix: Froberger et la mort, in: J.J. Froberger, 77–85; Matthias Schneider: Con discrezione. Stationen und Widerhall des "Europäers" Johann Jacob Froberger, in: Harald Schwaetzer and Henrieke Stahl-Schwaetzer (eds.): *Der Traum Europas. Kultur und Sozialität als Aufgabe. Ein interdisziplinäres Symposion*. Regensburg 2000, 226–231.

à Paris" – a striking contrast to Froberger's own Paris debut with a big concert.[76] In summary, during his travels in the service of Ferdinand III and his brother Leopold Wilhelm, Froberger assumed a personally more important role that he also reflected upon ironically in his compositions.

On the basis of the current state of research it is probable that Froberger returned to the German lands in the company of the count of Thurn, another supporter of the *frondeurs*, but also of Leopold Wilhelm, who on his way to the imperial diet in Regensburg, where the emperor had already taken his whole court orchestra, passed through many of the archducal and archiepiscopal residences.[77] The archbishop of Mainz in particular assumed an important role between the princes and "commoners" among the representatives of the estates of the empire. In this atmosphere and on the basis of his individual role as a musician with representative tasks, Froberger might have felt encouraged to make use of an own emblem as a seal of a letter.[78]

Shortly after the imperial diet, Froberger retired from service at the Viennese court for which he had served three stints as an organist: from 1 to 30 October 1637, from April 1641 to October 1645 and from April 1653 to 30 June 1657, providing for himself by travelling to Rome, Paris, Brussels, London and the Spanish Netherlands in the service of the Holy Roman Empire and of Leopold Wilhelm in between these periods.[79] Froberger spent his last years (ca. 1664–1667) at the residence of Duchess Sibylla von Württemberg in Héricourt where he kept his title of a Viennese court organist and where he lived in a close artistic and friendly contact with the duchess. He held on to his Catholic faith and made his own works available only to a harpsichord-player whom he had personally instructed.[80] His effective but also very personal musical and social practice probably had made him incompatible with the representative demands of the new court of Leopold III, who had been elected as the new Emperor after the extinction of Ferdinand's III direct line with the death of his son Ferdinand IV.[81] Froberger's personal loyalty to Ferdinand III is reflected in a *Lamentation faite sur la très douloreuse mort de*

76 David Schulenberg: Crossing the Rhine with Froberger. Suites, Symbols and Seventeenth-Century Musical Autobiography, in: Claire Fontijn (ed.): *Fiori musicali. Liber amicorum Alexander Silbiger.* Sterling Heights 2010, 296.

77 Rampe, "Hinze-Manuskript", 98.

78 Annibaldi, Froberger in Rome, 25–27.

79 Rasch, Johann Jacob Froberger's Travels, 19–35.

80 Yves Ruggeri: Froberger à Montbéliard, in: J.J. Froberger musicien européen, 23–37.

81 See Bob van Asperen: Frobergiana. Neue Erkenntnisse über die "Allemande, faite en passant le Rhin", in: *Concerto* 21, no. 192 (2004), 27.

Sa Majesté Impériale Ferdinand le Troisième, et se joue lentement avec discretion, which ends with a triple f" and which he already wrote in 1657.[82]

Music Mobilities

The retraced paths and mobilities of early modern musicians, which have been shown here from an urban and a biographical perspective, converge in two main points: First, the study of supra-regional mobilities also reveals local mobilities or even immobilities. Most of these mobilities can be connected to professional paths and incomes that were assured by the nobility or by the urban authorities, but they may be even more effectively grouped under the concept of personal or documental authenticity and thus anticipate the modern concept of motility.[83] Within the framework of the beginnings of a biographical music historiography by Johann Mattheson and a certain autonomy that was allowed town and court musicians for the symbolic representation of their cities and courts, many musicians created their own concept of musical works. These concepts could be religiously or biographically motivated, as in the case of Rosenbusch at Glückstadt, or they could reflect the authentic proportions of a musical career, as in Froberger's compositions. A common predilection for musical riddles may have provided a fertile ground for the development of musical works with personal biographical reflections and serving personal intentions. Second, many biographical paths seem to end with a stable settlement on an equal, satisfactory social footing. This settlement seems justified by and to profit from supra-regional experiences, but its target and orientation was probably the recognition of a newly-gained social status. This advancement often resulted from a close relationship with nobles and princes, but it could be fostered as well by a personally independent interpretation of judicial norms and the appropriate concept of musical works, which at the time still oscillated between a divine and a personal characterisation.[84] The sed-

82 Minoriten-Kodex 743, Wien, um 1708/1709 (Minoritenkonvent, Klosterbibliothek und Archiv Wien, Ms. XIV 743).

83 Weert Canzler, Vincent Kaufmann and Sven Kesselring: Tracing Mobilities – An Introduction, in: iid. (eds.), *Tracing Mobilities. Towards a Cosmopolitan Perspective*. Aldershot 2008, 3–4. See also Sarah Panter, Johannes Paulmann and Margit Szöllösi-Janze: Mobility and Biography. Methodological Challenges and Perspectives, in: *European History Yearbook* 16 (2015), 1–14.

84 As to the early modern period, Canzler's, Kaufmann's and Keselring's claim that "motility can be used towards objectives other than social mobility" can be differentiated according to social hierarchy between patrons and the musicians. Canzler, Kaufmann and Kesselring, Tracing Mobilities, 5. In the context of the demonstrated communicational permeability of the boundary

iments of such a personal authenticity in musical compositions and/or practices may be good orientation points not only for the relationship between early modern mobilities and the existence of music but also for the preparation of hybrid music editions.

between patrons and musicians through musical works, court musicians may constitute an interesting object for the study of early "rooted" transregional or even global lives in the sense of an understanding of the early modern period as a "laboratory of modernity".

Alix Heiniger and Thomas David

Mobility and Social Control: French Immigration in Geneva during the Belle Époque

Abstract: *Following recent research that invites historians to take into account immigrant communities to understand migration control policies before the First World War, this article examines the activities of French philanthropists in Geneva during the Belle Époque. It aims to show how these actors belonging to the French elite of Geneva drew the line between poor people who could stay in the canton and the ones who had to leave, and how they exercised social control within the community. The authorities of Geneva, in particular the police, expelled people with no means of support. The article thus argues that social rights were at the core of migration policies. In so doing, it examines three different groups of immigrants: the French elite, who took care of the community, the people they supported by their philanthropic activities and the people who were expelled from Geneva by the police.*

> With the Chamber of Commerce, which devotes itself especially to the study and defence of commercial and industrial interests, with the *groupement des Sociétés de bienfaisance* [Association of Charities], which provides assistance to those whom fate has disadvantaged compared to their happier compatriots, the *Cercle français* [French Circle] constitutes the firm tripod which the Consulate-General needs to accomplish its mission [...].[1]

In a commemorative brochure on the *Cercle français*, a society dedicated to providing a meeting place for French residents of Geneva, its committee stressed the division of roles between French organisations. It put forward a tripod which included a venue for social gatherings (the *Cercle français*), an association to defend French economic interests in Geneva (the Chamber of Commerce) and the promotion of philanthropic activities (the Association of Charities). In evoking the latter, the author stressed the complex character of migration, which covered a diversity of social situations, and the involvement of more affluent French citizens in helping their compatriots whose financial situation was less fortunate. This observation invites us to grasp the phenomenon of migration in all its complexity by bringing the category of national affiliation together with other factors in order to understand what transnational mobility really meant in the course of the lives of individuals and the manner in which it has contributed to shaping modern

1 *Cercle Français de Genève*. Geneva 1939, 15.

society. On a conceptual level, this aim calls for a merger of the two approaches which have dominated the history of migration: on the one hand, transnational experiences of immigrants (focusing on the integration of migrants into their new environment and their connections to their country of origin) and, on the other, approaches focusing on migration policies aimed at immigrants.[2]

This article intends to navigate between these two poles in order to demonstrate the functioning of the mechanisms of inclusion and exclusion that permit people to remain in the host society or that would instead disqualify them, obliging them to leave. The migrants themselves were present both among the actors who established and reproduced these mechanisms and among those affected by the policies. Foreign communities constituted complex worlds characterised by strong internal social differences.[3] At their core, the philanthropic organisations allowed the most vulnerable to maintain a standard of living that kept them safe from expulsion. They were fully involved in regulatory policies affecting migration, notably through drawing (or reinforcing) the boundaries between migrants who could remain and those who had to leave. They exercised social control over their most disadvantaged compatriots while, at the same time, providing the assistance necessary to their survival or their integration into the host society.[4] Furthermore, the study of charities benefiting foreigners makes it possible to highlight different kinds of transnational life courses that otherwise would remain hidden, those of the people supported by the charities and those of their leaders. By taking into account different kinds of social groups involved in the migration process, we can tackle the idea of "motility", related to opportunity structures, capacities and agency of individuals.[5] By doing so, we aim to focus on the cultural and social aspects of boundary-crossings, as the requirement for integration differed depending on the social group the migrants belonged to. Moreover, charities and other French organisations in Geneva linked their supporters to both French and Genevan contexts, as they were keen on promoting French interests in the city and developing relationships with their Genevan counterparts. The concept of

---

2 Paul-André Rosental: Historiographical Challenges of Emigration Policy, in: *Annuaire suisse d'histoire économique et sociale. La Suisse ailleurs. Les Suisses de l'étranger – Les Suisses à l'étranger* 29 (2015), 39–52.

3 See, for example, Nancy L. Green: *The Other Americans in Paris. Businessmen, Countesses, Wayward Youth, 1880–1941.* Chicago 2014.

4 Nancy Green shows how Jewish charitable organisations in Paris exercised social control over the community, favouring the integration of newcomers but at the same time restricting their freedom. See Nancy L. Green: To Give and to Receive. Philanthropy and Collective Responsibility among Jews in Paris, in: Peter Mandler (ed.): *The Use of Charity. The Poor on Relief in the Nineteenth-Century Metropolis.* Philadelphia 1990, 197–226.

5 See the introduction to this volume.

"rooted cosmopolitanism" presented in the introduction to this volume is eminently suited to describing these people connected both to their country of origin and to their host society.

In a more global context, French charities in Geneva took part in a process that went far beyond Switzerland. Their activities occurred at a time when most European states had measures on their statute books enabling them to expel foreigners who failed to provide sufficient guarantees concerning their capacity to provide for their own needs. Such policies were reaffirmed at the turn of the century with the advent of social welfare systems, in which the question of the link between citizenship and social rights was omnipresent.[6] Historiography has shown that even when systems governing the circulation of individuals before the First World War appeared to reflect a liberal policy, the living conditions and rights of foreigners were much less favourable than today, and expulsion was a flexible tool for managing migration and maintaining public order.[7]

Geneva is ideal for studying these phenomena since, at the turn of the century, it was home to a very high proportion of foreigners. Amongst these, the French constituted the largest population and had created several charitable organisations for mutual aid, led by French expatriates who collaborated with local private and public institutions. In the first section, we will analyse the specific situation of Geneva, which explains the strong presence of foreigners on its territory. Then, we will focus on the elite of the "French colony" – a term used by the members of the elite themselves – and how its members intended to represent the community and help the most disadvantaged. In the third section, the elite are the subjects of a typology which seeks to understand how social control operated. The final section deals with those who were excluded, who were not integrated into Genevan society and subject to expulsion. Ultimately, our objective is to show that in examining the social hierarchies within the French community, it is possible to reestablish more precisely the complexity of migration phenomena and to comprehend the

6 For France, see Paul-André Rosental: Migrations, souveraineté, droits sociaux. Protéger et expulser les étrangers en Europe du XIXe siècle à nos jours, in: *Annales. Histoire, Sciences Sociales* 2 (2011), 335–373. For Switzerland, see Silvia Arlettaz and Gérald Arlettaz: L'État social national et le problème de l'intégration des étrangers 1890–1925, in: *Études et Sources. L'histoire des assurances sociales* 31 (2006), 191–217.

7 Rosental, Migrations, 335–373; and David Feldman: Was the Nineteenth Century a Golden Age for Immigrants? The Changing Articulation of National, Local and Voluntary Controls, in: Andreas Fahrmeir, Olivier Faron and Patrick Weil (eds.): *Migration Control in the North Atlantic World. The Evolution of State Practices in Europe and the United States from the French Revolution to the Inter-War Period.* New York 2005, 167–177; and Frank Caestecker: The Transformation of Nineteenth-Century West European Expulsion Policy, 1880–1914, in: ibid., 120–137, esp. 121.

process by which foreigners who would be excluded from the territory and those who would be integrated into the host society were selected.

Our analysis is based on both a rich corpus of archives of French charitable organisations active in Geneva at the turn of the century, and the systematic and detailed analysis of the 1,121 files created following the expulsion of individuals from the canton of Geneva in 1902. Combining these two types of data is an original aspect of our approach. It aims to gain insight into the line drawn between individuals integrated into Genevan society and those who were excluded from it, while also showing that philanthropic organisations participated in selecting individuals and, subsequently, in the migration policies devised by public and private institutions. Such an approach brings together "structure" and "agency", showing under what conditions it was possible to remain in Geneva or, on the contrary, why some should leave. Furthermore, those sources reveal biographies of mobility, showing how, when and possibly why migration was considered by individuals to be the right (or the only) choice in their lives.

Foreigners in Switzerland and in Geneva: the Construction of a "Problem"

The turn of the century witnessed an intensification of migratory movements across the globe, due to economic development and progress in communication. This circulation of individuals was particularly striking in Switzerland, where the proportion of foreigners in the resident population was much greater than in other European countries.

Table 1: Proportion of Foreigners in the Population of European Countries (in %)[8]

	1880	1910
Switzerland	7.4	14.7
France	2.7	2.9
Germany	0.6	1.9
United Kingdom	0.8	2.1
Belgium	2.6	3.4

8 Source: Paul Bairoch: La Suisse dans le contexte international aux XIXe et XXe siècles, in: id. and Martin Körner (eds.): *La Suisse dans l'économie mondiale – Die Schweiz in der Weltwirtschaft*. Zurich 1990, 103–140, esp. 119.

These differences, notably in comparison to France, were probably due in part to the application of the principles *jus sanguinis* or *jus solis*, the latter allowing for an almost automatic assimilation from the second generation on. Nonetheless, at this time, most states of the German Empire also applied *jus sanguinis*, without, however, having as large a proportion of foreigners as in Switzerland.

Yet significant disparities also existed within Switzerland. Certain cantons, such as Appenzell Innerrhoden, with only 2.4 per cent aliens, had smaller proportions of foreigners while others had more than 15 per cent. Geneva came out on top with the most foreigners (39.7 per cent), followed by Basel (38.1 per cent) and Ticino (22.0 per cent).[9] These three cantons all share more borders with a third country than with the Confederation. In this respect, Geneva is an extreme case, very well described by the statistician of the canton, Emmanuel Kuhne: "For a long time, the canton of Geneva, almost surrounded by France, was the natural centre of emigration of the Savoy and Gex zones. Being the economic capital of a region of which it is not the political capital explains our city's unusual situation […]."[10]

As Table 2 reveals, for 60 years, the French constituted the most significant portion of Geneva's foreign population. Like others, the statistician associated this situation with a problem: "The danger for Genevan nationality is obvious and it has long worried the far-sighted among us."[11] For him, the naturalisation of those born in the territory constituted a solution. Nevertheless, there were still "an

Table 2: Foreign Population in the Canton of Geneva (1860–1920)[12]

	Foreigners (in %)	French (in %)	Total Population (in absolute numbers)
1860	34.7	29.3	82,876
1870	38.2	31.5	93,239
1880	37.3	29.5	101,595
1900	38.9	25.9	132,389
1910	41.5	21.5	165,986
1920	30.2	15.6	171,000

9 Calculations are based on *Statistiques historiques de la Suisse*. URL: *http://www.fsw.uzh.ch/histstat/main.php* (18 May 2015), "population" Tables B 23 and B 44.

10 Emmanuel Kuhne: *Les étrangers dans le canton de Genève*. Geneva 1898, esp. 3.

11 Ibid.

12 Sources: Genève, in: *Dictionnaire historique de la Suisse*. URL: *http://www.hls-dhs-dss.ch/textes/f/F7398.php* (22 June 2015); Paul Bairoch and Jean-Paul Bovee: *Annuaire statistique rétrospectif de Genève*. Geneva 1986, esp. 15–16.

enormous number of residents who enlarge our population without having either our habits or our traditions and who have, thanks to treaties of establishment, the same rights as nationals, except in terms of voting."[13] Still, the contribution of the foreign population was required for the economic development of the canton since, according to Kuhne's research, Genevans had abandoned certain professions and left them to foreigners: "In the country, the workers, servants and labourers are almost all French and the Genevans tend to form a sort of aristocracy which owns and cultivates the land, but leaves the hard work to others."[14] Foreigners were overrepresented in less qualified jobs and a great many of them worked as day labourers or domestic servants. In the industrial sector, they represented more than 45 per cent of those in the clothing and grooming industry, and they constituted 50 per cent of those working in construction. They were also active in the development and maintenance of roads. However, they were largely absent from watchmaking, one historic industry of Geneva.[15]

An analysis of residence permit registers from the year 1900, which includes the foreigners who arrived in the canton but not those who were already established, shows that most of the migrants were young adults. The author of this analysis concluded that they were attracted by the economic opportunities of the canton. He formed the hypothesis of a dichotomous structure related to the nature of the migration. On the one hand, migrants settled for the long term and were likely to make a home and start a family in Geneva and, on the other hand, transmigrants (mostly men) intended to work a few months and then leave.[16] While many French residents of Geneva fit these profiles, others were experiencing wholly different economic and social situations. The study of French philanthropic organisations reveals two other types of social profiles, of people who benefitted from their help and of their considerably more affluent leaders.

---

13 Kuhne, Les étrangers, 13.

14 Ibid., 10.

15 See Emmanuel Kuhne: *Recensement professionnel de 1902*. Geneva 1904, esp. 34.

16 Luc Morisseau: *Les immigrés à Genève en 1900. Une analyse du registre des permis de séjour étrangers* (Master's thesis, University of Geneva, 2008), 24. These seasonal and cross-border migratory shifts were not unique to the canton of Geneva. In France, for example, the same type of circulation existed in the regions of the North and of the Midi, where seasonal workers did agricultural labour starting in the springtime and then left after the harvest. Furthermore, the construction sector also employed a foreign labour force which compensated for a lack of local workers. See Gérard Noiriel: *Immigration, antisémitisme et racisme en France (XIXe – XXe siècle. Discours publics, humiliations privées)*. Paris 2007, esp. 136–137. On the question of internal immigration in the rural environment, see Claire Lemercier and Paul-André Rosental: Pays ruraux et découpage de l'espace. Les réseaux migratoires dans la région lilloise au milieu du XIXe siècle, in: *Population* 4–5 (2000), 691–725.

An Elite Which Looks after the "Colony"

The French colony in Geneva ran four philanthropic organisations, in addition to another dozen which played a less central role in the organisation and distribution of assistance.[17] The oldest of the four charitable organisations was the *Société française mutuelle et philanthropique* (SFMP – The French Mutual and Philanthropic Society), founded in 1842. In 1900, it concluded an agreement with its junior counterpart, created in 1870, the *Société Française Philanthropique* (SFP – the French Philanthropic Society), to rationalise assistance to French citizens and avoid "duplication or worse." Following this accord, the consulate decided to delegate to the SFP the help it was giving to "French destitutes" and provided it with a subsidy, thereby making it the central body within the colony for the distribution of assistance.[18] Two other charitable organisations were founded later to assist specific groups: children and the elderly. In 1899, a review committee chaired by the consul general of France created the *Œuvre de l'Enfance française abandonnée* (The French Charity for Abandoned Children).[19] The last of the four to be established, the *Œuvre des Vieillards et Incurables Français* (The French Charity for the Elderly and Incurably), was created in 1903 and ran the *Asile de Feuillasse*, a home for the elderly.[20] The latter two included a member of three other societies within their respective committees. From 1904 on, an administrator managed the SFP and the two more recent charitable organisations devoted to elderly and to children, which also shared their offices. He was responsible for the distribution of assistance and investigations into the situation of those requesting help.[21] Thus, at the start of the century, the French philanthropic milieu's

---

17 They were also not as close to the consulate. In particular, we have identified the *Cercle ouvrier*, the *Cercle savoisien*, the *Union savoisienne*, the *Société savoisienne*, the *Vétérans des armées de terre et de mer*, the *Anciens combattants de 1870*, the *Union des anciens militaires*, the *Union musicale française*, the *Vallées du Mont Blanc*, the *Électeurs de la Haute-Savoie*, the *Souvenir français*, the *Jeune République* and the *Mont Blanc*.

18 Committee Report for the Year 1900, Société Française Philanthropique de Genève (Private Archives). See also Irma Gadient: Fürsorge(-kriterien) für Französinnen und Franzosen. Französische philanthropische Vereine in Genf und die Zusammenarbeit mit lokalen wohltätigen Institutionen um 1900, in: *Österreichische Zeitschrift für Geschichtswissenschaften* 26, no. 3 (2015), forthcoming.

19 *Journal Français*, 13 Dec. 1907. The committee was composed of nine representatives from the French Chamber of Commerce of Geneva, six from the *Cercle français*, six from the SFP, two from the SFMP and one from each of the bodies mentioned in footnote 17.

20 Report of the Committee on Operations and the Situation of the Society during the Year 1907, Société de l'Œuvre des Vieillards et Incurables Français de Genève (Private Archives).

21 Gadient, Fürsorge(-kriterien), 11.

charitable work became more specialised, rationalised and professionalised, a tendency not unique to foreign organisations and which could also be observed in the practice of private Genevan charities.[22] French philanthropic organisations acted with the support of the French consulate in Geneva. Indeed, in addition to subsidies distributed through its intermediary (the total of which amounted to 3,000 francs[23]), the consul participated in charitable organisations as honorary chairman. The SFP appeared as the core of these developments since its members had initiated these projects of rationalisation and of mutualisation. These efforts allowed them to monopolise the resources of French aid and their distribution to disadvantaged members of the community. This situation was not unique to Geneva. In other cities, organisations representing a foreign colony also provided relief in favour of their compatriots.[24] What seems, however, remarkable in the Genevan case of French relief is how early the system emerged (starting in the middle of the nineteenth century) and the degree of coordination with the French consulary authorities it had reached by the turn of the century. But it is difficult to confirm this hypothesis considering the lack of studies related to other foreign relief organisations.

The representatives of philanthropic organisations were simultaneously involved in other societies connected to the French colony, as well as in Genevan organisations. Alexandre Schwob was a prime example of this multi-positionality. As a member of the committee of the SFP, he played an important role at the heart of the community, being not only behind the establishment of the *Cercle français* but also acting as chief medical officer to the home for French senior citizens, for which he was awarded the Legion of Honour. In addition, his involvement with patients in his neighbourhood earned him the nickname of "the good Lord of Pâquis". He was also a member of local organisations such as the medical society of Geneva, and presided over the Jewish community of the canton. His wife was no less active, founding and presiding over the *Societé des dames françaises de Genève* (Society of French Ladies of Geneva).[25]

---

22 Stéphane Baciocchi et al.: Les mondes de la charité se décrivent eux-mêmes. Une étude des répertoires charitables au XIXe et au début du XXe siècle, in: *Revue d'histoire moderne et contemporaine* 61, no. 3 (2014), 28–66, esp. 33–37.

23 2,000 francs from the Ministry of Foreign Affairs and 1,000 francs from the consulate, for receipts totalling 14,730.60 francs. See Report of the Committee for the Year 1904. Société Française Philanthropique de Genève (Private Archives), esp. 5.

24 See, for instance, Nancy Green's recent book: Other Americans, 196–202.

25 Another example (among many) would be Tony Laval, president of the SFP (1900–1902), who was also head of the new *Société des tramways* in Geneva. See Gadient, Fürsorge(-kriterien), esp. 8. Portrait of A. Schwob in the *Journal Français*, 11 Aug. 1906.

Even if these actors were well integrated into Genevan society, they created and facilitated places which perpetuated the idea of a French community in organising events on national holidays and cultivating distinctive national characteristics. The *Journal Français*, which claimed to be the "voice of French colonies in Switzerland,"[26] was part of this dynamic, in publicising eminent figures and events in the life of this community, to which it referred as "the Colony". The principal places for social encounters between these actors were the *Cercle français*, the French Chamber of Commerce and the philanthropic organisations. Founded in 1896, the *Cercle français* united the "elite of the Colony"[27]. When asked their occupation, the most commonly named were merchant (27), annuitant (11), landlord (10), physician and director of French firms such as *Crédit Lyonnais*, *Moët et Chandon* or *Peugeot*. The annual membership fee rose to 50 francs, well beyond that of local philanthropic societies, which asked for approximately five francs. The *Cercle* also admitted Genevans whose social profile was close to that of other members. From 1916 on, the members' list also shows that less than half saw military action, and that those who "fell gloriously on the field of honour for France" were mostly officers.[28] This reflects two tendencies: On one hand, it indicates that they were somewhat older; on the other hand, in the context of war, publicising the military involvement of members amounts to affirming the contribution of the French citizens established in Geneva to the defence of their homeland. Such demonstrations of patriotism also appeared in other social contexts and environments where the French community made itself known, notably the French Chamber of Commerce and the *Journal Français*. The *Cercle* offered a place where members could meet and socialise during the week, much like a club, and at times dinners were sponsored by a member. It served a dual function, which may appear contradictory, but which, in fact, constituted a particular resource: it allowed its members to cultivate national cohesion while also integrating them into local society by creating links with Genevan members.

The French Chamber of Commerce in Geneva, which initiated the *Cercle*, was established two years earlier and brought together people with similar social profiles (merchants, industrialists or bankers). Aside from being a place for social encounters, the Chamber defended its members' economic interests before Genevan and Swiss authorities, closely monitoring negotiations with regard to the train lines or the volume of French exports to Switzerland.[29]

---

26 This was the caption inscribed on the front page.

27 *Journal Français*, 11 Nov. 1910.

28 List of members, as of 1 July 1916, Cercle Français de Genève (Bibliothèque de Genève).

29 Founded in 1894, it had 850 members in 1906. *Journal Français*, 19 May 1906.

Thus, the *Cercle* and the Chamber pursued the triple objective of serving as a place for social encounters for the French elite, cultivating distinctive national characteristics amongst French citizens, and encouraging integration through contacts with the Genevan elite. In addition to these activities, one may add philanthropy, which in some ways constituted the third component of the tripod: sociability, economic promotion and elites' social responsibility. This last aspect was the means to link individuals situated at the extremes of the community's social hierarchy, since the most affluent assumed the responsibility for helping the neediest. The SFP, which occupied a central place in the philanthropic activities of the French community, was directed by a committee composed exclusively of men, whose terms of involvement varied from relatively short periods of two or three years to remarkably long commitments, such as that of the outgoing president in 1900 who served in this position for more than 25 years. These two types of mandates demonstrate the degree to which these officeholders were settled in Geneva: some for the long term, while others for only a short period. While the committee was exclusively male, women also contributed to philanthropic activities, particularly by organising social and cultural fund-raising events.

Membership of the *Cercle* and the SFP frequently overlapped.[30] Business and banking were well represented by employees of such companies as *Crédit Lyonnais*. The proximity of the two societies was further reinforced by the fact that the SFP held its annual assemblies in the salons of the *Cercle*.[31] Léon Niepce personified the links between the two societies. This French industrialist, born in Isère in 1855 and elected president of the Chamber in 1906, was deeply involved in French charitable organisations. He was active in the *Fondation de l'Enfance française abandonnée* and in the *Asile des vieillards français*, over which he presided from 1905 on. In addition, he was on the committee of the SFP.[32] The latter also cultivated direct links with France, on the one hand by receiving donations from eminent philanthropists, such as Baron de Rothschild or Madame d'Haussonville[33]

30 Unfortunately, these are the only two lists available to us. List of members as of 1 July 1916, Cercle français de Genève (Bibliothèque de Genève); Report of the Committee for the Year 1903. Société Française Philanthropique de Genève (Private Archives).

31 Report of the Committee for the Year 1900. Société Française Philanthropique de Genève (Private Archives).

32 Portrait de Léon Niepce, *Journal Français*, 9 June 1906.

33 The Baron de Rothschild came from a family of Parisian bankers and philanthropists notable for the establishment of the eponymous hospital. About the Rothschild family, see Rainer Liedtke's contribution in this volume. Madame d'Haussonville is probably the wife of the politician and lawyer Paul-Gabriel d'Haussonville. He was also known for his reform activities and wrote essays about several social issues (prison, child protection and workers' life conditions in Paris).

and, on the other, by coming to the aid of compatriots in neighbouring French territories during extraordinary events such as at St. Gervais in 1892.[34] Yet the SFP's activity concentrated primarily on the French population of Geneva. Its actions demonstrated the boundaries of the colony for, in deciding on the granting of aid, it had the power to decide on whether to include or exclude the most disadvantaged. Those excluded, who failed to meet the criteria that allowed foreigners to remain in the canton, were simply expelled from its territory, and then banned from the French community of Geneva.

Vulnerable Populations in the Community: The Beneficiaries of Charitable Organisations

In principle, the fate of French citizens asking for help in the territory of Geneva was determined by the 1882 Treaty of Establishment between France and Switzerland.[35] As with all bilateral texts, it provided for reciprocity in the treatment of the expatriates of the other country. Furthermore, in matters of assistance it rested on the assumption of responsibility for the care of individuals, up to and including the possibility of their safe return, the rest being left to the judgment of the cantons. This task fell back on private organisations who had the responsibility to provide assistance. Yet, at the same time, this also underscored their importance in foreign communities.[36] This was the situation in Geneva, where the police was responsible for financing the care and repatriation of foreigners without means, and the charitable organisations supported French families in economic difficulties, thus allowing them to stay in the canton. This division of labour between the police and charitable organisations overlaps with the question of inclusion in and exclusion from the French community, since aid from the police contributed to departure from Geneva, and that from charities to staying on.

The assistance practices of French charitable organisations, the SFP, the *Œuvre des Vieillards* and *Enfance française abandonnée*, are analysed in this article, based on archival holdings common to the three organisations, which

34 The overflowing of a stream destroyed a large part of the bathing establishment and left more than 200 victims. See URL: *http://sciences.gloubik.info/spip.php?article1017* (18 May 2015).

35 See Stéphanie Leu: *Les petits et les grands arrangements. L'État bilatéral. Une réponse au défi quotidien de l'échange de populations. Une histoire diplomatique de la migration et du droit des migrants entre France et Suisse. Organisation, acteurs et enjeux (inter)nationaux. Milieu XIXe–1939* (Doctoral thesis, Institut d'Études Politiques de Paris and Université de Berne 2012), 12.

36 Ibid., 142.

contain minutes of meetings, annual reports and accounts for the period between 1886 and 1914. Between 1886 and 1900, the committee of the SFP discussed the allocation of aid in meetings or outside of meetings, and subsequently validated them. Then, from the arrival of the administrator and the establishment of the agreement with the *Enfance Française abandonnée* and the *Œuvre des Vieillards français*, the decisions no longer appeared in the minutes, probably because they now fell to the administrator.[37]

The SFP came to the assistance of three types of groups: the recipients of regular or occasional assistance; those who went to food distribution which operated twice weekly during the winter; and those whose received vouchers for the *Asile de nuit* (night shelter) and were repatriated (at least partly) by the SFP.

The first group includes those installed in Geneva who received either regular or occasional support in the form of a pension. They were usually the children of workers, widows with or without children, senior citizens or those with disabilities. The pensions were quite modest, ranging between three and 15 francs a month, and the one-off payments were of the same amount. The *Societé Française* was concerned with the lifestyles of those seeking its aid. It investigated those who were unknown to them, but most often the requests were presented by members or by another charitable organisation. The latter always received a favourable response, enjoying a form of guarantee in being made by people known to the organisation and whom the committee trusted. Moreover, the other charitable organisations were often involved in helping those they presented to the committee. The Ladies of Charity[38] for example, appeared regularly in the committee's minutes, which sometimes recorded that they were delegated to follow-up on certain individuals. Thus, when the hospital asked the *Societé* to pay for a wooden leg for an elderly French widower, it agreed and pledged additional help, which the Ladies of Charity had to assess, but still did not consider financing the entire cost.[39] This shows that its contribution was part of a programme of assistance, too costly to be assumed in its entirety. In the same way, the SFP granted its aid to individuals already helped and put forward by the *Bureau central de bienfaisance* (Central Charity Bureau), one of the private Genevan institutions which

37 Comité, 1886–1923. Société Française Philanthropique de Genève (Private Archives).

38 These were female philanthropists who worked with the Catholic Church in helping disadvantaged people.

39 Comité, Meeting of 13 Feb. 1894. Société Française Philanthropique de Genève (Private Archives).

played a central role in matters of assistance.[40] The latter notably agreed with other Genevan and foreign charities to divide up those seeking assistance on the basis of their nationality. The goal of this agreement was to rationalise assistance practices and avoid "duplication of efforts and abuses."[41] This document bears witness to the efforts of coordination and rationalisation amongst philanthropic bodies at this time. In general, the sources do not offer any examples of a situation where the SFP refused to contribute to helping a family when another charitable organisation was already involved.

Finally, while this group of French citizens, helped occasionally or regularly by the SFP, often appeared in the committee's minutes, they were not the principal cost factor, at least from 1901 on. Pensions always accounted for less than a third of charitable expenses (1907) and financial help was only a small part of that. These resources were allocated to 286 families in 1900 and 344 in 1901. The two other societies helped a smaller number of people: in 1910, the *Œuvre des Vieillards* maintained on average 25 pensioners in a specially constructed shelter for French senior citizens. To these were added another 16 people receiving outdoor relief, and the *Enfance Française abandonnée* supported 72 children.[42]

The most important item was that of providing food relief (more than half of expenditures of this nature in 1907), which was distributed twice weekly in winter. Its beneficiaries formed the second group according to the type of aid that the SFP provided. To have access to it, they had to demonstrate that they were French nationals. The people who appeared there were not regularly quoted in the minutes of the committee, with the exception of a young girl who was followed up on because she had come looking for bread in 1890. We learn that "her father was a drunken widower" and that she spent her days "alone when her father was working or at the tavern with him." So, it was a matter of collaborating with the Ladies of Charity to place this child in the boarding school which her sister was already attending.[43] This example shows that the process of distributing charity also allowed philanthropists to observe claimants and to participate in the measures selected when they considered it appropriate. In this case, it was a matter of

---

40 See Flavio Baumann: *La pauvreté apprivoisée ou l'assistance comme gestion de la détresse. Etude sur une société de bienfaisance genevoise à la fin du XIXe s. Le Bureau Central de Bienfaisance, 1867–1900* (Master's thesis, University of Geneva, 1983).

41 Accord amongst the Charitable Societies and Administrations (1880), quoted by Frank Lombard: *Annuaire philanthropique genevois*. Geneva 1903, 7.

42 *Journal Français*, 22 Apr. 1910.

43 Comité, meeting of 6 Feb. 1890. Société Française Philanthropique de Genève (Private Archives).

removing the child from its "deplorable situation"[44], in other words, of correcting what was considered a morally unacceptable way of raising a child. Charitable distribution was thus an instrument of social control, presenting an opportunity to gather and observe a marginalised part of the community and to focus on certain subjects. Furthermore, the distribution of essentials doubtless sprang from a form of collective responsibility on the part of the community, expressed by the French charitable organisations. The latter thus showed that they took care of vulnerable French citizens in Geneva.[45]

Finally, the third group of people in whom the SFP was interested in comprised those who received vouchers for the night shelter or soup kitchens or who were repatriated. In the SFP's archives, they were regularly designated "transients" (*passagers*), probably because they were not meant to stay in the city. At least part of them were probably transmigrants. They seemed to constitute the most problematic population for SFP's representatives. Indeed, in 1888, the treasurer explained that it was impossible for him to continue to receive people sent by the consulate and other philanthropic organisations in his home since "[...] many of these people, especially those transients who are generally not very interesting cheaters (*rouleurs*) [sic] turn up filthy, sometimes grey [drunk], one of them even followed by the police right up to the [treasurer's] door, which was far from agreeable."[46] The treasurer clearly distinguished between "transients" and others since the former, as the designation indicates, were not supposed to remain, while the others were established in Geneva, a distinction which the SFP contributed to maintaining through its activities.

This group of French migrants, not settled in Geneva, was sent by the SFP to the night shelter where they could sleep. Similar institutions existed in a number of European cities, notably in Paris, where they contributed to the maintenance of public order through the standards of hygiene and salubrity on their premises, and especially by offering an alternative to the street.[47] The promoters of the Genevan night shelter were convinced that they were playing a socially important role in not refusing entry to their establishment (except in the case of inebriation). In 1904, they wrote: "Would it be wise to be very severe? We do not believe so; our city, which receives so many refugees from surrounding countries,

44 Ibid.

45 The notion of collective responsibility in this context is developed by Nancy Green with respect to the Jewish community of Paris, see Green, Give and Receive, 197–226.

46 Comité, Meeting of 19 Oct. 1888. Société Française Philanthropique de Genève (Private Archives).

47 For Paris, see Lucia Katz: Habiter dans les asiles de nuit parisiens. Le cas de l'Œuvre de l'Hospitalité de Nuit à la fin du XIXe siècle, in: *Hypothèses* 6 (2013), 59–71.

is still one of the safest; if no one begs in the streets and if nighttime attacks are practically unheard of, we firmly believe we can take credit for that."[48]

The night shelters' role was to serve as transit points or transitional housing, since they limited access to a certain number of nights (seven in Geneva, three or four in Paris). Foreigners could sleep there before leaving Geneva. They also served as an alternative to their planned imprisonment, intended as a measure to work against "vagrants". In Geneva, between 1876 and 1903, foreigners constituted between 40 and 50 per cent of the population sleeping in the night shelter; 16 to 23 per cent were French.[49]

Vouchers, provided mostly by the police, with a small number provided by the SFP, gave access to the shelter. The importance of the police in a charitable endeavour, one of the goals of which was to contribute to the maintenance of public order, shows that the individuals concerned were highly marginalised. The shelter presented itself as a temporary place of respite, which would allow the authorities to avoid having to lock up the nationals and instead enable them to find a better situation, permitting the foreigners to rest a few nights before continuing their journey. The commitment of the police was part of their work in maintaining public order.[50] The collaboration of philanthropic institutions shows that they were active participants in this program. Philanthropic institutions therefore played an important role by allowing people to stay off the streets. However, by not helping everyone, they established limits: they assisted in the removal of some foreigners by contributing financially to their repatriation and by leaving them in the hands of the police. The latter identified them in the public arena and served them with an expulsion order signed by the canton's minister of justice who "demanded" that these individuals "withdraw from the canton immediately".[51]

---

48 *XXVIIIth Report of the Committee, Asile de nuit. Geneva 1904*, esp. 6.

49 *XXVIth, XXVIIth, XXVIIIth Reports of the Committee, Asile de nuit*. Geneva 1901–1904.

50 The Genevan penal code offers the following definition: "Vagrants are those with no fixed abode, and no means of support, and who do not regularly practice a trade or a profession." It also provides for a penalty varying between a day and a month for "anyone found begging" (Penal code of the Canton of Geneva, 21 Oct. 1874, Section V, Articles 242 and 243).

51 See the expulsion orders conserved in the series 1985 va 22 Étrangers J, Department of Justice and Police (Archives d'État de Genève, Geneva, Switzerland).

Those Expelled from the Canton

At the turn of the century, administrative expulsions from the canton of Geneva increased substantially.[52] In 1902, the Department of Justice and Police issued 1,121 expulsion orders against individuals and their families.[53] In that year, Geneva experienced a general strike, which was the occasion for renewed police activity against foreigners suspected of involvement in "anarchist" activities or of belonging to groups with such tendencies. The Department of Justice and Police expelled by order or sometimes as a simple "public security measure" 78 persons, of whom 50 were Italians and 20 French,[54] that is barely seven per cent of those expelled in 1902. The general strike had only a limited impact on the number of expulsions, since in 1902 there were fewer expulsions than in 1901 and in 1903. The strikes, which multiplied during the period from 1888 to 1914, were thus not the principal reason for the increased number of expulsions at the turn of the century. Instead, the explanation lies in the work of the police, to which the law granted relative autonomy in managing the canton's foreign population. The minister responsible for the Department of Justice and Police, with the authority delegated by the Genevan government, had the power to expel with an administrative measure – and hence, without going through a judicial process – any foreigner whose "conduct was bad", who was not "in a condition to provide for his own maintenance or that of his family" or "whose stay could harm the interests of the country or the security of the state".[55] The range of behaviours which could fall under this law was extremely vast, thus making expulsion arbitrary.

It is interesting to note that the months with the most expulsions were November, December and January, when there was the least activity in the sectors of agriculture and construction. One might wonder whether the expulsions were not a manner of handling the labour market, by expelling those who failed to find work.

52 The figures available in the Rapports administratifs du Conseil d'État (1888–1914) were compiled by Anne Varidel: *Les étrangers à Genève de 1888 à 1914* (Master's thesis, University of Geneva, 1988), 109.

53 Series 1985 va 22, Étrangers J, boxes 187–196, Department of Justice and Police.

54 On the general strike of 1902, see Charles Philipona: Le Courrier de Genève et la grève générale de 1902, in: Jean Batou, Mauro Cerutti and Charles Heimberg (eds.): *Pour une histoire des gens sans Histoire. Ouvriers, exclues et rebelles en Suisse 19e–20e siècles*. Lausanne 1995, 233–244. On the surveillance work of the political police of Geneva, see Ignace Cuttat: *Les plus basses & les plus louches actions contre la liberté du citoyen? Organisation et méthodes de la police politique à Genève, 1889–1914*. (Master's thesis, University of Geneva, 2013).

55 *Recueil des lois et actes du gouvernement. Loi sur la police des étrangers du 9 février 1844, art. 27 and 28*. Geneva 1844, 69–70.

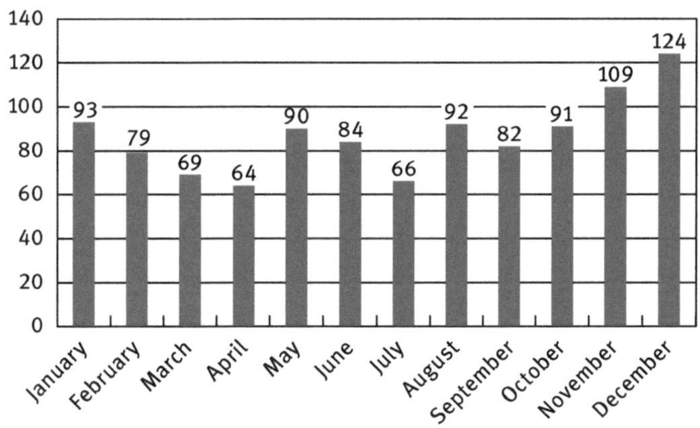

Graph 1: Seasonal Evolution of Expulsions in 1902 (without those expelled due to the strike, therefore "–78 individuals" in the month of October).

Table 3: Individuals Expelled in 1902 by Nationality[56]

Nationality	Individuals expelled in connection with the strike	Individuals expelled (total)	In %[57]
Switzerland (outside of Geneva)	0	90	8.0
German States	6	110	9.8
France	20	550	49.1
Italy	50	307	27.4
Other	2	64	5.7
Total	78	1121	100.0

In terms of social profile, the typical French national expelled from Geneva was a relatively young unmarried man whom the Genevan police declared to be "without proper documentation, with no fixed address and with no means of support."[58] Indeed, out of 550 expulsions, 468 concerned single men, 60 single women and only 18 families; more than three quarters of the files related to unmarried people (77.1 per cent).[59] Women constituted barely 11 per cent of this

56 Series 1985 va 22, Étrangers J, boxes 187–196.

57 The people expelled in connection with the strike are included in this calculation.

58 See files in series 1985 va 22, Étrangers J, boxes 187–196.

59 424 single people, four divorced, 79 married, twelve widowed and 14 for whom the information is missing.

population, a fairly astounding finding since they were more numerous than men amongst foreigners living in the canton.[60] This may be explained by the fact that the majority of female foreigners arriving in Geneva were employed as servants,[61] a sector of activity where there was always high demand.[62]

Half of those expelled were born after 1876; they were less than 26 years old in 1902. Those under 30 constituted more than 66 per cent of the total. Most came to the canton shortly before their expulsions, often on the same day. Rarely do those who had been there for a long time appear amongst the expelled, even if some indicated residence in Geneva "since birth." In most cases, the expulsion order was based on a combination of factors. "Vagrancy" appeared in 255 files out of 550, the explanation "with no visible means of support" in 266, and the absence of a fixed residence in 435.[63] Social and economic vulnerability was, therefore, clearly an important factor in the practice of expulsion. Thus, the work of the police consisted of clearing the public space of foreigners deemed undesirable, due to their itinerant and unstable lifestyle. This process stemmed both from a set of attitudes which proscribed "vagrants"[64] and their lifestyle, and from measures aiming to maintain security and public order *vis-à-vis* those considered a threat.[65]

Most of those expelled came from neighbouring French departments. The Haute-Savoie came first with 107 expelled. The departments near Geneva (Doubs 11, Jura 10, Ain 26, Rhône 53, Isère 22, Savoie 11, and Saône-et-Loire 16) totaled another 149 expelled, with Haute-Savoie accounting for almost 47 per cent of this population. Yet some came from farther afield, such as the 34 Parisians in the group. Most of these people claimed to be active in the secondary and tertiary sectors or in agriculture: we do not find representatives of the liberal professions. The most commonly named occupations declared by those who were expelled were those of farmer (34), day laborer (31), unskilled worker (32), mechanic (18)

60 Varidel, Les étrangers à Genève, 44.

61 According to Morisseau, 58.5 per cent of female arrivals who requested a residence permit in 1901 were employed in this sector. Morisseau, Les immigrés, 19. Moreover, in 1910, foreigners constituted 50.3 per cent of the servants in Geneva. Varidel, Les étrangers à Genève, 77–78.

62 Anne-Lise Head-König: Les apports d'une immigration féminine traditionnelle à la croissance des villes de la Suisse. Le personnel de maison féminin (XVIIIe–début du XXe siècle), in: *Revue Suisse d'Histoire* 49 (1999), 47–63, esp. 52–53.

63 "Theft" appeared in 63 files, "fraud" in 16, and "assault and battery" in 23.

64 On the social image of the vagrant, see Dominique Kalifa: *Les bas-fonds. Histoire d'un imaginaire*. Paris 2013.

65 Vagrants, objects of suspicion because unknown and from elsewhere, were associated with laziness, idleness, and a kind of industry of begging and crime. See the analysis for France by André Gueslin: *D'ailleurs et de nulle part. Mendiants vagrants, clochards, SDF en France depuis le Moyen Âge*. Paris 2013, 201–228.

and servant (twelve, of whom ten were women).[66] Our results correspond to those of a study on the same population between 1905 and 1911.[67]

The hypothesis of expulsion sanctioning social failure,[68] which affected the individuals who came seeking employment and, finding none, were left without means, seems wholly convincing in the light of these data. For the authorities dealing with a young population, newly arrived in the canton, expulsion was a means to prevent these individuals from living on the streets while they waited for work. The French charitable organisations only marginally concerned themselves with these persons. These were probably the ones designated "transients" in the organisations' archives and who constituted, as we have seen, a problematic population in the view of French philanthropists. Once the police encountered them, they were immediately expelled from the canton by an administrative measure.

This practice, part of the tendency of the time to prevent people from living on the street, was reflected in laws concerning the police and the measures taken against "vagrancy" and "begging". The experiences of those expelled are, in this regard, very revealing. François B., aged 29 and originally from a small village on the shores of lac d'Annecy (Haute-Savoie), came to try his luck in Geneva in March 1902. He had recently completed his apprenticeship as a cook for the Christian Brothers in Annecy, after having finished his military service with the mountain infantry. He seemed, therefore, in good health and well-trained. Yet when the police arrested him for creating a "scandal" in the street, they discovered that he had no "means of support" and served him with an expulsion order.[69] In many cases, expulsion reflected the work of the police, who controlled the situation of people found in the street and, with an expulsion order, sanctioned those who declared that they had no "means" or who were treated as "vagrants". Thus, the police could expel more than ten people a day. In this way, they played the role of a filtering body to avoid allowing foreigners with no employment or income to remain on the streets of the canton. This also permitted them to remove the most vulnerable, in accordance with the key concerns of Genevan philanthropists who feared that the foreigners would swell the ranks of those asking for help.[70] Consequently, a number of aspects of police activity coincided with the preoccupations of philanthropists: their work allowed them to expel people likely to ask for help from

---

66 Series 1985 va 22, Étrangers J, boxes 187–196.

67 Pierre Bungener: *Les indésirables à Genève 1905–1911. Mémoire exemplaire basé sur l'étude des files d'expulsions administratives du Département de Justice et Police genevois* (Master's thesis, University of Geneva, 1990).

68 Rosental, Migrations, 335–373.

69 Series 1985 va 22, Étrangers J, file 234, box 188.

70 *Bureau central de bienfaisance. XXIXe Rapport annuel.* Geneva 1896, 12.

the canton, it encouraged their departure in assisting repatriation and it contributed to charitable organisations such as the night shelter by offering vouchers to users. Their action was also in line with that of French philanthropists who, in the minutes of their committee meetings, regularly referred to the services the police performed for them.[71] The police were always mentioned in the context of collaboration and never because they had come into conflict with the philanthropists.

Nonetheless, the police were no less severe in their treatment of people long established in Geneva whose conduct "gave rise to complaints." Another François B., aged 23, born and raised by his French parents in Geneva, was questioned by the police because he "frequented public gardens in the company of shifty individuals, must be one of them and never works".[72] The reasons cited for his expulsion order related to his conduct and the irregularity of his residence permit, but it was certainly because the police suspected him of behaving in a morally objectionable manner and of being idle that they inspected him and finally expelled him from the canton, although his parents remained there.

Factors related to morality were cited even more emphatically in the cases of women. When the expulsion order mentioned that a woman "gives rise to complaints", this often meant, that the woman was suspected of selling herself outside of brothels or that she was indeed discovered "soliciting" in public space. In general, the reasons recorded for expulsion orders against women differed from those of their male counterparts. For men, we most often find "vagrancy" (246/468), and "no visible means of support" (261/468), while for women, these were only mentioned in 7/60 and 12/60 files respectively. The dominant reason for women's expulsion orders was that their conduct "gave rise to complaints" (34/60), while this was much less common for men (104/468). Moreover, for a man, this reason also referred to political activities; in particular, it was invoked in expulsion orders related to the strike. Even in the declared motivations, expulsion seemed largely arbitrary, a fact denounced by political representatives at the turn of the twentieth century.[73] They seemed to be a flexible instrument for the police in their mission to maintain public order.

71 See Comité, 1886–1914. Société Française Philanthropique de Genève (Private Archives).

72 Series 1985 va 22, Étrangers J, file 467, box 190.

73 See Varidel, Les étrangers à Genève, 111–112.

Conclusions

The position of the migrant in the majority society was largely determined by his place in the social hierarchy. The most affluent members of the colony could meet to cultivate their specific national traits and to celebrate their patriotic holidays. They were well integrated into the majority society and, through their charitable organisations, collaborated with Genevan philanthropists and with the police. They put themselves forward as representatives of their community and took responsibility for helping the most disadvantaged. At the other extreme of the social hierarchy, vulnerable foreigners could either be helped by French and/or local charitable organisations and the police, or be ordered to be expelled from the canton. The management of migrants was the result of the combination of efforts of these local and French charitable organisations and the work of the police. The affluent French who represented the colony collaborated with this policy, while their compatriots who were completely destitute were subjected to this practice and had to leave the canton.

This distinction can be found in the very construction of the "problem". The discourse establishing the foreigners as a "problem" or a "danger" for Geneva did not choose productive or affluent individuals, such as members of the French organisations analysed earlier, as targets, but those who risked becoming "vagrants" or "beggars".[74] The distinction between the foreigners considered desirable and those labeled undesirable reflected the economic and social developments of this period. On the one hand, industry, agriculture and even Genevan homes needed this foreign manpower, which was indispensable to the canton's economic development. Industrialists and merchants involved in French philanthropic societies, the *Cercle* and the French Chamber of Commerce in Geneva, who were part of the economic engine, showed themselves to be solidly integrated into the local fabric, even if they were meeting to cultivate a particular link with their homeland. Yet on the other hand, social changes entailed their share of inequalities, which were seen in the public space in the form of people who had fallen into great insecurity. Public and private institutions offering social protection gave themselves the mission of rescuing them through assistance, combined with re-

74 This situation would change during the First World War. In 1918, the Swiss government promoted a law against economic "Überfremdung" ("overforeignisation", the feeling of being swamped by foreigners) in order to preserve the national character of Swiss companies. The ordinance promoted by the Swiss government provided that the majority of firm's board members should have the Swiss nationality. See Thomas David et al.: *De la "Forteresse des Alpes" à la valeur actionnariale. Histoire de la gouvernance d'entreprise suisse (1880–2010)*. Zurich 2015, esp. 59–60.

covery measures, such as the night shelter. They considered aid to their fellow citizens legitimate, but refused to extend this right to foreigners. Some of the latter, fitting specific social profiles, were supported by a combination of French and Genevan philanthropic societies' efforts, which allowed them to maintain a roof over their heads and to remain invisible in the street. It was actual visibility in the public space which posed a problem.

Moreover, the management of the French national group by various bodies, the police, and the Genevan and French charitable organisations, demonstrates how the urgent questions of the time, the right to assistance and the nationalisation of Swiss society, were intertwined.[75] Indeed, the Confederates, a term which designates the non-Genevan Swiss, who in 1900 constituted 25.9 per cent of the population, were the largest group to use the night shelter between 1876 and 1903, with rates oscillating around 35–36 per cent from 1901 on. They also comprised a third of new families assisted by the Central Charity Bureau in 1902, far ahead of the Genevans and the French who each constituted approximately a quarter of this population.[76] Nonetheless, even if the Confederates appeared to be the most significant beneficiaries of these two charitable organisations, they were not discussed in terms of the danger they might represent for the "Genevan nationality", to return to the terms used by the statistician Emmanuel Kuhne. In fact, they did not constitute a threat to the public funds since, in principle, their municipality of origin had to provide for their maintenance. The contrasting treatment of the Confederate and foreign populations is a revealing reflection of a paradigm shift: it was no longer a matter of distinguishing Genevans from non-Genevans, but rather of differentiating between Swiss (Genevans and Confederates) and others. The dividing line was determined very clearly by the right to assistance and the financial questions which flowed from this.[77]

75 Arlettaz and Arlettaz, L'État social national, 191–217.

76 Bureau central de bienfaisance. XXXVIe Rapport annuel. Geneva 1902, 11–12.

77 Brigitte Studer, Gérald Arlettaz and Regula Argast: *Le droit d'être suisse. Acquisition, perte et retrait de la nationalité de 1848 à nos jours*. Lausanne 2013.

Forum

Robert Brier

Beyond the Quest for a "Breakthrough": Reflections on the Recent Historiography on Human Rights

Abstract: *Human rights have become a central object of international and global history, with research focusing on the question where the origins of the central position of human rights language in our own time lie. The aim of this article is to take stock of this debate and discuss possible future avenues of research. The existing literature has shown, the article argues, that the 1970s were a crucial time for the rise of human rights, but it also warns against declaring this decade or any other time the definite breakthrough for human rights. Underlining how human rights have always been influenced by their past, discussing how tenuous the international position of human rights remains well into our own time and exposing different meanings human rights acquired historically, the article concludes that the identification of multiple chronologies of post-war human rights history and a focus on the great variety of human rights vernaculars provide more promising avenues along which to push this project ahead than the quest for an elusive human rights breakthrough.*

"Human rights are the *doxa* of our time", Stefan-Ludwig Hoffmann observes, "belonging among those convictions of our society that are tacitly presumed to be self-evident truths and that define the space of the conceivable and utterable".[1] How and when did human rights acquire this position? In response to this question, an exceptionally dynamic field of historical research has emerged. "Once at the margins, human rights and its historiography are at the intellectual vanguard of international and diplomatic history", as Mark Bradley writes.[2]

This emergent literature on human rights differs from previous accounts in its consistently historical approach, a point which no one has made more forcefully than Samuel Moyn in his marvellously iconoclastic book *The Last Utopia*. Most existing accounts of the history of human rights, he argued, are beholden to what Marc Bloch famously called the "idol of origins": the false assumption that historical explanation consists in identifying the origins of a historical phenomenon in order to then record its journey through time. Proponents of this approach, Bloch

1 Stefan-Ludwig Hoffmann: Introduction. Genealogies of Human Rights, in: id. (ed.): *Human Rights in the Twentieth Century*. Cambridge 2011, 1–28, esp. 1.

2 Mark Philip Bradley: American Vernaculars. The United States and the Global Human Rights Imagination, in: *Diplomatic History* 38, no. 1 (2014), 1–21, esp. 3.

noted, do not see "that, to the great despair of historians, men fail to change their vocabulary every time they change their customs". Medieval society may have used the Roman term "beneficium" and the Germanic term "fief", but this does not mean that the origins of feudalism lie in Roman or Germanic times, for the people of the middle ages gave these terms a wholly new significance. A "historical phenomenon can", therefore, "never be understood apart from its moment in time".[3]

In seeking to explain why human rights have become such a prominent idea in our own times, the new historiography of human rights thus does not look for deep origins, but asks instead why more recent historical actors have found this idea useful for their political purposes, desires or problems and how its meanings may have changed in the process.[4] Whereas some historians have focused on the late 1940s as a time when the current meaning of human rights crystallised,[5] the bulk of the literature has zeroed in on an even more recent period: the 1970s. It was only during this time, a growing number of scholars believe, that human rights came to be seen as a norm that could trump national sovereignty, and it was also only in this decade that human rights came to spur transnational movements.[6]

---

3 Marc Bloch: *The Historian's Craft*. Manchester 1954, 28–29. For Samuel Moyn's quoting Bloch and his critique of the existing literature, see *The Last Utopia. Human Rights in History.* Cambridge, MA 2010, ch. 1 and 311; the books he criticises in particular are Micheline Ishay: *The History of Human Rights. From Ancient Times to the Globalization Era*. Berkeley, CA 2004; Paul Gordon Lauren: *The Evolution of International Human Rights. Visions Seen*. Philadelphia 1998; for assessments of this work similar to Moyn's, see Devin O. Pendas: Toward a New Politics? On the Recent Historiography of Human Rights, in: *Contemporary European History* 21, no. 1 (2012), 95–111, esp. 97–98; Philip Alston: Does the Past Matter? On the Origins of Human Rights, in: *Harvard Law Review* 126, no. 7 (2013), 2043–2081, esp. 2063–2064.

4 An exception is Lynn Hunt's *Inventing Human Rights. A History*. New York 2007. But though Hunt traces the Universal Declaration of Human Rights back to the French revolution, her analysis of the origins of human rights in eighteenth century cultural practices represents a "Blochian" approach to human rights history nevertheless.

5 Mary Ann Glendon: *A World Made New. Eleanor Roosevelt and the Universal Declaration of Human Rights*. New York 2001; Elizabeth Borgwardt: *A New Deal for the World. America's Vision for Human Rights* Cambridge, MA 2005.

6 Hoffmann, Introduction, 13–25; for a focus on the 1970s, see Moyn, Utopia; Jan Eckel and Samuel Moyn (eds.): *The Breakthrough. Human Rights in the 1970s*. Philadelphia 2013; for review articles, see Pendas, Politics; Alston, Past; for broad surveys of the literature, see Kenneth Cmiel: The Recent History of Human Rights, in: *American Historical Review* 109, no. 1 (2004), 117–135; Jan Eckel: Utopie der Moral, Kalkül der Macht. Menschenrechte in der globalen Politik seit 1945, in: *Archiv für Sozialgeschichte* 49 (2009), 437–484; Annette Weinke: Vom "Nie wieder" zur diskursiven Ressource. Menschenrechte als Strukturprinzip internationaler Politik seit 1945, in: Norbert Frei and ead. (eds.): *Toward a New Moral World Order? Menschenrechtspolitik und Völkerrecht seit*

Unsurprisingly, this interpretation has not remained without critics. Most importantly, studies of 1960s human rights discourses in the "global South" and at the UN have focused on the relationship between human rights and the anti-colonial struggle, thus questioning an interpretation of the 1970s as the "big bang" of human rights history. Some of them, most notably Steven Jensen, have taken this criticism a step further. Not only did 1970s discourses have deeper roots than is sometimes acknowledged, he writes, but human rights' actual "breakthrough" had already occurred in the previous decade.[7]

Given how rapidly interest in the history of human rights has evolved, my first aim in this essay is to take stock. The "Blochian" approach to human rights history, I will argue, has spurred an extraordinarily productive array of research, creating an international community of scholars who propose innovative explanations for a crucial process of contemporary history. These scholars, I believe, convincingly show that the 1970s were not merely the next step in a gradual rise of human rights, but that developments peculiar to this decade played a central role in turning human rights into the global norm they are today. But does this research show that the "breakthrough" to our current system of human rights happened in the 1970s? Or do we have to look elsewhere? My second aim is not to answer these questions. Rather, I want to argue that the very quest for such a "breakthrough" may be misguided. Research on the 1970s, to be sure, has shown how human rights gained unprecedented international prominence, but it has also exposed something more fundamental: the historicity of human rights, i.e. the contingent, at times almost accidental nature of their emergence, their enormous malleability and adaptability, the tenuousness of their position both before and after the 1970s. But if this is the case, contemporary meanings of human rights were not simply handed down to us from the 1970s or from any other "breakthrough moment". They remain "the unpredictable results of political contestations".[8]

My argument in this essay, therefore, is that it may be important to move beyond a debate over the "roots" or "breakthrough" of human rights, a debate which at times borders dangerously on doing what we set out to avoid: the creation of a new "idol of origins". Human rights history derives its strength precisely from its consistently historical approach. By looking for a breakthrough moment or decade, cutting it off from previous developments and collapsing the following forty

---

1945. Göttingen 2013, 12–39; for additional important collections of essays, see Akira Iriye, Petra Goedde and William I. Hitchcock (eds.): *The Human Rights Revolution. An International History*. Oxford 2012; Frei and Weinke, Order.

7 Steven L.B. Jensen: *The Making of International Human Rights. The 1960s, Decolonization and the Reconstruction of Global Values*. Cambridge, forthcoming.

8 Hoffmann, Introduction, 4.

years into them, we are in danger of undermining what propels the exciting new project of human rights historiography. Jan Eckel's identification of multiple chronologies of post-war human rights history and Mark Bradley's focus on the great variety human rights vernaculars provide more promising avenues along which to push this project ahead.[9]

The 1970s and the History of Human Rights

The scholar who has argued most forcefully for the 1970s as the crucial decade for the contemporary history of human rights is Samuel Moyn.[10] The continuity between contemporary "rights talk" and previous ideas about rights, even those enshrined in the Universal Declaration of Human Rights (UDHR), his provocative thesis contends, is terminological at best. Current understandings of human rights are rooted not in post-war responses to the Holocaust, but in ideological changes of the 1970s, notably the collapse of modernity's more grandiose schemes of social transformation and revolutionary change. During this decade, social activists discovered human rights as a "minimalist, hardy utopia that could survive in a harsh climate" of ideological disillusionment. They promised to be a fresh source of political idealism, a new path to improving the world, but one whose focus on the liberty and well-being of individuals avoided the violent pitfalls into which other such paths had led. In the process, human rights were transformed "beyond recognition", primarily by being dissociated from questions of sovereignty and self-determination. There are no deep roots of contemporary human rights in Moyn's view, which holds that they originated in processes that occurred just over a generation ago.[11]

There is no doubt that Moyn zeroed in on a crucial decade for the history of human rights. Amnesty International's rise from near-bankruptcy in the late 1960s to Nobel Peace Prize fame in 1977;[12] the use of human rights language by oppo-

---

9 Jan Eckel: *Die Ambivalenz des Guten. Menschenrechte in der internationalen Politik seit den 1940ern*. Göttingen 2014; Mark Philip Bradley: *The United States and the Global Human Rights Imagination*. Cambridge, forthcoming.

10 Moyn, Utopia.

11 Ibid., 42 and 121. Compare, however, Moyn's most recent statement in his *Christian Human Rights*. Philadelphia 2015, 5.

12 Eckel, Ambivalenz, 347–435; Stephen Hopgood: *Keepers of the Flame. Understanding Amnesty International*. Ithaca, NY 2006; Tom Buchanan: "The Truth Will Set You Free". The Making of Amnesty International, in: *Journal of Contemporary History* 37, no. 4 (2002), 575–597.

nents of repressive regimes in Latin America or the Soviet bloc;[13] the transformation of UN institutions, particularly in response to the Chilean coup of 1973, into mechanisms monitoring the human rights compliance of UN member states;[14] the creation of an East-West forum for human rights with the signing of the Final Act of the Conference on Security and Cooperation in Europe (CSCE) in 1975;[15] Jimmy Carter's pledge to turn human rights into the cornerstone of US foreign policy;[16] French leftist intellectuals' celebration of Soviet bloc dissidents[17] – these events are just the best-known indicators of a sudden explosion of interest in human rights during the 1970s.

---

13 On Latin America, see Patrick William Kelly: *Sovereignty and Salvation. Transnational Human Rights Activism in the Americas in the Long 1970s* (PhD thesis, University of Chicago, 2015); Vania Markarian: *Left in Transformation. Uruguayan Exiles and the Latin American Human Rights Networks, 1967–1984.* New York 2005; for the Soviet bloc, see Benjamin Nathans: The Disenchantment of Socialism. Soviet Dissidents, Human Rights, and the New Global Morality, in: Eckel and Moyn, Breakthrough, 33–48; Michal Kopeček: Human Rights Facing a National Past. Dissident "Civic Patriotism" and the Return of History in East Central Europe, 1968–1989, in: *Geschichte und Gesellschaft* 38, no. 4 (2012), 573–602; Robert Brier: Broadening the Cultural History of the Cold War. The Polish Workers Defense Committee and the Rise of Human Rights, in: *Journal of Cold War Studies* 15, no. 4 (2013), 104–127.

14 Patrick James Flood: *The Effectivenes of UN Human Rights Institutions.* Westport, CT 1998, 82–100; Jan Eckel: "Under a Magnifying Glass". The International Human Rights Campaign Against Chile in the Seventies, in: Hoffmann, Human Rights, 321–342.

15 For excellent recent studies of the Helsinki process, see Sarah B. Snyder: *Human Rights Activism and the End of the Cold War. A Transnational History of the Helsinki Network.* Cambridge 2011; Helmut Altrichter and Hermann Wentker (eds.): *Der KSZE-Prozess. Vom Kalten Krieg zu einem neuen Europa 1975 bis 1990, Zeitgeschichte im Gespräch.* München 2012; Hermann Wentker and Matthias Peter (eds.): *Die KSZE im Ost-West-Konflikt. Internationale Politik und gesellschaftliche Transformation 1975–1990.* München 2012; Yuliya von Saal: *KSZE-Prozess und Perestroika in der Sowjetunion. Demokratisierung, Werteumbruch und Auflösung 1985–1991.* München 2014.

16 For accounts of the emergence of Carter's focus on human rights, see Vanessa Walker: *Ambivalent Allies. Advocates, Diplomats, and the Struggle for an "American" Human Rights Policy* (PhD thesis, University of Wisconsin-Madison, 2011); David F. Schmitz and ead.: Jimmy Carter and the Foreign Policy of Human Rights. The Development of a Post-Cold War Foreign Policy, in: *Diplomatic History* 28, no. 1 (2004), 113–144; Jan Eckel: Schwierige Erneuerung. Die Menschenrechtspolitik Jimmy Carters und der Wandel der Außenpolitik in den 1970ern, in: *Geschichte in Wissenschaft und Unterricht* 66, no. 1–2 (2015), 7–24; for a powerful interpretation of the US human rights revolution of the 1970s, see Barbara Keys: *Reclaiming American Virtue. The Human Rights Revolution of the 1970s.* Cambridge, MA 2014; for an in depth account of US human rights policies in the crucial Latin American region, see William Michael Schmidli: *The Fate of Freedom Elsewhere. Human Rights and U.S. Cold War Policy toward Argentina.* Ithaca, NY 2013.

17 Robert Horvath: "The Solzhenitsyn Effect". East European Dissidents and the Demise of the Revolutionary Privilege, in: *Human Rights Quarterly* 29 (2007), 879–907.

Many authors would probably contend that Moyn's focus on intellectual history is too narrow to fully explain this sudden upsurge in human rights-related activities, but many would probably also agree that a crucial factor was that human rights promised moral and political answers where other systems of thought had failed. An important part in the life stories of many Soviet or Central European dissidents entailed, as Ben Nathans has shown, a moment when they first discerned the lies of the official, collectivist ideology and turned to the defence of individual dignity and rights instead.[18] The human rights practices that emerged in and around Latin America in the 1970s, Patrick W. Kelly argues in his impressive multinational study, entailed a shift from a politics of revolution to a "politics of salvation", a minimalist programme of "shin[ing] a spotlight on the rights not to be tortured or disappeared, one victim at a time – what one author called 'salvation in small steps'".[19] In her powerful interpretation of how human rights entered US political discourses, Barbara Keys demonstrates that both conservative and liberal US Democrats seized on human rights language to revitalise American virtue after the disgrace of Watergate and Vietnam.[20] The French Left, finally, portrayed its newfound enthusiasm for dissidents as a collective "exorcism" of Marxist ideas.[21]

As these diverse actors began invoking human rights, the meaning of the term changed. The UDHR had explicitly not been meant to create mechanisms to enforce human rights against the will of sovereign governments.[22] European colonial powers, meanwhile, argued that different levels of economic development merited different applications of human rights. The decolonisation processes of the 1950s and 1960s challenged this view, but tied human rights to questions of collective self-determination.[23] This changed in the 1970s. The work of Amnesty

18 Nathans, Disenchantment. One of Poland's main dissidents, Jacek Kuroń, tellingly titled his autobiography "Faith and Guilt [wina, Schuld]: To Communism and Back". Jacek Kuronì: *Wiara i wina. Do i od komunizmu*. Wrocław ^{4}1995; cf. also the title of the German translation *Glaube und Schuld. Einmal Kommunismus und zurück*. Berlin 1991.

19 Kelly, Sovereignty; Markarian, Left.

20 Keys, Virtue; Schmitz and Walker, Carter.

21 Michael Scott Christofferson: *French Intellectuals Against the Left. The Antitotalitarian Moment of the 1970s*. New York 2004; Sunil Khilnani: *Arguing Revolution. The Intellectual Left in Postwar France*. New Haven, CT 1993.

22 Mel James: The Country Mechanisms of the United Nations Commission on Human Rights, in: Yael Danieli, Elsa Stamatopoulu and Clarence J. Dias (eds.): *The Universal Declaration of Human Rights. Fifty Years and Beyond*. Amityville, NY 1999, 75–84, esp. 75; Thomas G. Weiss, David P. Forsythe and Roger A. Coate: *The United Nations and Changing World Politics*. Boulder, CO ^{3}2001, 180.

23 Eckel, Ambivalenz, 260–339. On this topic, see also below. For the complicated relations between the struggle for human rights and for sovereignty in the thought and activism of Jewish

International and Helsinki Watch, the appeals of Soviet bloc dissidents and Latin American activists, the resolutions and agreements of the UN Commission on Human Rights (UNCHR) and the CSCE as well as the foreign policy of the Dutch or US governments – all began articulating the idea that human rights applied to everyone, everywhere and that they could be, and in emergencies had to be, claimed *against* the sovereignty of nation-states. Human rights as such – rather than the domestic political institutions seen as guaranteeing them – thus became a central topic of western foreign policy and broad non-governmental mobilisation.[24]

As human rights activism surged in the 1970s, moreover, new political styles, images and practices emerged. Americans, for instance, joined Amnesty International for a broad variety of reasons, but the organisation's sudden mass appeal was to a large degree based, Jan Eckel argues, on a widespread desire for less complex forms of political activism. Campaigning against such unquestionable evils as political incarceration or torture thus brought politics from the level of grand ideological schemes down to the level of basic emotions like responsibility and compassion.[25] Transnational solidarity campaigns, based on a shared ideology and geared towards revolution, thus gave way to campaigns against political incarceration, torture and the death penalty, while the figure of the heroic "Third World revolutionary" gave way to that of the innocent "prisoner of conscience".[26]

If emotions like compassion or a sense of global responsibility were crucial factors driving human rights activism, Moyn's focus on ideas, though compelling, is also a little narrow. Mark Bradley identifies a number of economic, technological, cultural and emotional "conditions of possibility" for the human rights explosion of the 1970s, conditions this form of transnational activism shared with its "cousins", the environmentalist, feminist or humanitarian movements. As commodities, information and people began to move across borders and around the globe at unprecedented speed and as a re-globalisation of markets made the nation-state less capable of fending off external influences, a "new global affect" emerged, a sense of the interconnectedness of the world's regions and of a common responsibility for the planet. Following Daniel Rodgers, Bradley also

groups, see Atina Grossmann: Who Guarantees Individual Rights? Jews and Human Rights Debates after World War II, in: Frei and Weinke, Order, 42–52; Nathaniel A. Kurz: *"A Sphere above the Nations?". The Rise and Fall of International Jewish Human Rights Politics, 1945–1975* (PhD thesis, Yale University, 2015).

24 See, for instance, Kelly, Sovereignty, 190–237.

25 Eckel, Ambivalenz, 394–411; on Amnesty, see also Buchanan, Truth; Kenneth Cmiel: The Emergence of Human Rights Politics in the United States, in: *Journal of American History* 86, no. 3 (1999), 1231–1250; Hopgood, Keepers.

26 Markarian, Left; Kristin Ross: *May 68 and its Afterlives*. Chicago 2002.

argues that the human rights explosion of the 1970s was part of a more profound cultural shift: an "age of fracture" in which imaginaries rife with ideas about history, social structures and cultures gave way to social visions centred on the disembedded individual.[27]

Finally, structural changes at the international levels were necessary to allow ideological disillusionment to develop its explosive effects. One of them, as Fabian Klose showed as early as 2009, was that the end of decolonisation both brought a host of new states into UN institutions who would press a human rights agenda and made Europe's former colonial powers more willing to invoke human rights themselves, since they now ceased to be the targets of anti-racist policies.[28] East-West détente was another important political precondition for the rise of human rights during the 1970s.[29]

A "Blochian" approach to the 1970s human rights explosion, in sum, has spurred highly productive and innovative research. Structural changes in the international system, an emergent sense of global "interconnectedness" and an acceleration of worldwide economic and social interactions prepared the ground on which a disillusionment with discredited ideological schemes fired an activism focused on alleviating individual suffering. Seeing human rights within this "moment in time", then, shows how they acquired new meanings and encouraged new forms of political activism.

The 1970s in Context: Decolonisation and Human Rights

If a consensus seems to be emerging on the centrality of the 1970s, a controversial question is how much developments in this decade owed to already ongoing or past causes and processes. In ground-breaking studies, Fabian Klose and Roland Burke have argued that human rights were central to anti-colonial activism, a point Moyn and Eckel disagree with, drawing a sharp distinction between human rights on one hand and the main aim of anti-colonialism on the other: collective

---

27 Bradley, United States; cf. Daniel T. Rodgers: *Age of Fracture*. Cambridge, MA 2011.

28 Fabian Klose: *Menschenrechte im Schatten kolonialer Gewalt. Die Dekolonisierungskriege in Kenia und Algerien 1945–1962*. München 2009. Published in English as *Human Rights in the Shadow of Colonial Violence. The Wars of Independence in Kenya and Algeria*. Philadelphia 2013.

29 Eckel, Ambivalenz, 343–346.

self-determination.[30] A number of authors have recently added fascinating twists to this debate. In an intellectual history of the concept of "self-determination", Eric D. Weitz asks how sharply it can be set off from human rights ideas.[31] Bradley Simpson seems to posit a dialectical relationship between them. Once all former colonies had acquired the "first right", i.e. self-determination, he argues, former colonies and international hegemons like the US strategically appropriated a language of individual rights in order to intervene in the affairs of former colonies and prevent them from extending their quest for self-determination into the economic sphere.[32]

The most substantial recent addition to this debate on the relationship between decolonisation and human rights comes from Steven Jensen. Most authors agree that decolonisation did make a substantial contribution to the rise of human rights. When anti-colonial activists and former colonies aggressively used the language of human rights to push for self-determination, they turned "universality" into a guiding principle of the United Nations. But where Eckel sees this as an instrumental usage of human rights in which *collective* self-determination was the main goal, Jensen argues for a clear link with individual human rights. During the 1960s, he writes, two countries from the global South – Jamaica and Liberia – redefined the UN human rights project around the issues of antiracism and religious liberty. Thus outmanoeuvring the superpowers, they pushed for the adoption of the first legally binding international human rights document: the Convention on the Elimination of All Forms of Racial Discrimination, a crucial step both towards the human rights covenants of 1966 and even the Helsinki Final Act of 1975.[33]

How well Jensen's interpretation will hold up remains to be seen. What is beyond doubt is that, in the sophistication of its argument and the sources it

---

30 Roland Burke: *Decolonization and the Evolution of International Human Rights*. Philadelphia 2010; Klose, Menschenrechte; Steven L.B. Jensen: "Universality Should Govern the Small World of Today". The Cold War and UN Human Rights Diplomacy, 1960–1968, in: Rasmus Mariager, Karl Molin and Kjersti Brathagen (eds.): *Human Rights in Europe During the Cold War*. London 2014, 56–72; Jensen, Making; Jan Eckel: Human Rights and Decolonization. New Perspectives and Open Questions, in: *Humanity* 1, no. 1 (2010), 111–135; Moyn, Utopia, 84–119; for an author agreeing with Eckel, see Marc Frey: A Revolutionary Process? Decolonization and International Law, in: Frei and Weinke, Order, 123–133.

31 Eric D. Weitz: Self-Determination. How a German Enlightenment Idea Became the Slogan of National Liberation and a Human Right, in: *American Historical Review* 120, no. 2 (2015), 462–496.

32 Brad Simpson: Self-Determination, Human Rights, and the End of Empire in the 1970s, in: *Humanity* 4, no. 2 (2013), 239–260; id.: The Many Meanings of National Self-Determination, in: *Current History* 113 (2014), 312–317.

33 Jensen, Making.

draws on, it is nothing short of impressive. Jensen's aims, however, reach much further than laying bare continuities between the 1960s and 1970s or placing the Helsinki Accords into a global context. "The breakthrough and trajectory of international human rights", he argues with regard to research on the 1970s, "has been misdated and misunderstood". If the 1970s appear as the crucial decade for the recent history of human rights, it is because of a time lag separating them from the actual breakthrough of human rights, the Jamaican and Liberian initiatives at the UN.[34]

Couching his argument in these terms, Jensen's work is the latest iteration of a broader attitude in human rights historiography which Mark Bradley has usefully called a "take-no-prisoners competitive sweepstakes" between different chronologies of human rights history, a desire to pinpoint the moment, decade, person or state that turned human rights into the *lingua franca* of our time.[35] Jensen's book is also the latest example of how unusually productive this "sweepstakes" has been. Yet it is worth asking why it has been so productive. The answer, it seems to me, is not that we have identified a definite "breakthrough" but that we have "de-familiarised" human rights, exposing them as historically contingent and politically contested notions. Only by acknowledging that human rights were no natural part of western foreign policy can Steven Jensen bring out the crucial role of Jamaica and Liberia.[36] Only by acknowledging that human rights were something new for Latin American activists and their western sympathisers can Patrick Kelly interpret their interactions as a fascinating story of how the meaning of human rights was negotiated transnationally.[37] The reason, then, why *The Last Utopia* galvanised the debate on human rights history so much is, in my view, not that Samuel Moyn provided a definite answer about the origins of human rights, but that his book was the most radical call yet to look at post-war human rights discourses the same way Marc Bloch had looked at medieval feudalism: as a historical phenomenon that cannot be "understood apart from its moment in time".[38] Teleological notions like "breakthrough", by contrast, turn the past into a part of our present and thus threaten to undermine the very historical attitude that is the source of our field's productivity.

In the remainder of this essay, I will focus on three points that might slip our attention if we conceive of our endeavour primarily as a quest for an elusive "breakthrough" moment: the often subtle ways in which 1970s human rights dis-

34 Ibid., 2.
35 Bradley, Vernaculars, 4.
36 Jensen, Making.
37 Kelly, Sovereignty.
38 Bloch, Craft, 28.

courses were shaped by their past, human rights' contingent and tenuous position even after the 1970s, and the transformations they may have undergone in following decades.

Religion, Politics, and Human Rights in the 1970s and After

Mark Bradley has argued that the quest for "a point of origin, a take-off moment, in which human rights gains the traction that makes it a central presence for present-day state and non-state actors" suggests an account of historical time in which past events figure merely as the pre-history of our own time. What this obscures is that "what human rights were understood to be by actors in the historical moment was always a considerably messier process, one that linear narratives can obscure".[39] "The past", Moyn notes, "is treated as if it simply were the future waiting to happen".[40]

Adopting such a view of historical time, we would miss the second part of Marc Bloch's advice. Condemning the "demon of origins" as "the satanic enemy of true history", Bloch also wrote about the "'solidarity' of ages" to underline how deeply every "moment in time" is shaped by its past.[41] The human rights moment of the 1970s is no exception. While human rights seem to have acquired a distinct meaning during the 1970s – a new-found focus on individual rights as such – this meaning was so abstract and broad that activists and politicians could (in fact, had) to fill it with more particular meanings to turn it into a mobilising force. And as they did, a broad variety of what Bradley calls "human rights vernaculars" emerged: local interpretations of human rights which were laced with the ideas historical actors brought to them.[42]

There are two particularly striking examples for how old and new ideas co-existed in these vernaculars. First, a significant number of the vernaculars were profoundly shaped by religious ideas and symbols. This could take an overt form, like when Brazil's Catholic bishops used quotations from scripture to explain the UDHR or when John Paul II called Auschwitz the "Golgotha of the modern world", demanding that "*the Declaration of Human Rights* must have all its just

39 Bradley, Vernaculars, 4.
40 Moyn, Utopia, 11.
41 Bloch, Craft, 26 and 36.
42 Bradley, United States.

consequences drawn from it".[43] But there was also a more subtly religious dimension to large chunks of human rights activism. The Polish intellectual Jacek Kuroń and British activists from Amnesty International both subscribed to a "religionless" Christianity they derived from the work of Protestant German pastor Dietrich Bonhoeffer. Religious echoes are also clear in central practices of human rights activism, such as that of "bearing witness" to other people's suffering or in the figure of the "prisoner of conscience": someone who creates community and inspires activism through his innocent suffering.[44] To be sure, human rights activism was no automatic outgrowth of religious practices and especially the Catholic Church's position on human rights remained highly ambiguous. Religious notions were often secularised and amalgamated with human rights ideas and countercultural individualism to forge a distinctly novel way of understanding suffering.[45] But the continuing presence of religious notions is noteworthy nonetheless.

Second, underneath claims about the anti-political nature of human rights, activists often carried decisively political concerns into their newfound adherence to human rights. This, too, could take more or less overt forms. Latin American activists and their international supporters adopted the practices and language of Amnesty International, but grafted human rights on to older concerns for political solidarity and social change, as Patrick Kelly and Jessica Stites Mor show.[46] US (neo)conservatives, Barbara Keys and Carl J. Bon Tempo show, appropriated human rights for their anti-Communist views.[47] Trade unions, meanwhile, began recasting their activism on behalf of the material interests of employees as a struggle for the universal right of freedom of association.[48]

But even as human rights were explicitly interpreted as anti-political, they often remained related to questions of civil liberties, citizenship and democracy. In his famous essay "The Power of the Powerless", Czech playwright Václav Havel did advocate a shift from traditional politics to an activism evolving out of the individual choice to "live in truth". But even if this move was based on what Havel

43 Patrick Kelly: Situating the Southern Cone in Global Human Rights Politics in the 1970s. Presentation at "Does Human Rights Have a History", Chicago, 11 Apr. 2015.

44 On Amnesty, see Hopgood, Keepers; on Kuroń, see Dariusz Gawin: *Wielki zwrot. Ewolucja lewicy i odrodzenia idei społeczeństwa obywatelskiego*. Kraków 2013.

45 Bradley, United States.

46 Kelly, Sovereignty, 132–189; Jessica Stites Mor (ed.): *Human Rights and Transnational Solidarity in Cold War Latin America*. Madison, WI 2013.

47 Keys, Virtue, 103–126.

48 Robert Brier: *A Contested Icon. Poland's Solidarity Movement and the Rise of an International Human Rights Culture* (unpublished manuscript).

cryptically called a "hidden sphere", "life in truth" was not meant to be an escape from politics into an abstract morality. In both East and West, Havel argued, the powerful had colonised the public sphere: in the East by plastering it with the empty slogans of post-totalitarian ideology and in the West through the false promise of consumerism. Life in truth was meant to expose these lies for what they were and thus awaken a longing for authenticity which Havel believed was slumbering in every human being. "Life in truth" therefore made sense only as a public act, for its aim was to reclaim the public space from empty ideological or consumerist slogans, thus allowing citizens to shape their collective life. Morality was no escape from politics, but a means of reclaiming politics.[49]

This was a politics, to be sure, which was to be different from the traditional politics of parties and parliaments, focusing instead on individual self-realisation, social self-organisation and deliberative forms of democracy, but it was political nonetheless. Both in theory and practice, a central condition for implementing this political project was for Czechoslovakia to reacquire full sovereignty. For Central European dissidents, the struggles for human rights and self-determination were closely aligned, thus drawing into question too sharp a distinction between the 1960s and 1970s.[50]

If Havel's views differed from those of the members of Amnesty International in the US, this was not only a matter of different cultures, but also of different concerns associated with human rights. Havel, after all, invoked human rights not to help people abroad or counter an abstract sense of impotence towards the evils of the modern world; he did so to protect himself and his compatriots against repression. For western members of Amnesty International, human rights were strongly anti-political, an attitude expressed in the famous own-country-rule which forbade activists to work for political prisoners in their homeland. "[D]etaching Amnesty from the business of political agitation", Stephen Hopgood observes, the own-country-rule "reinforced [Amnesty's] own sense of a separate, distinct, and sacred identity". Yet for an aspiring Amnesty activist from an authoritarian country in Africa, the own-country-rule was "bullshit [...] a misunderstanding of what human rights is. Human rights in the south is domestic. Human rights in the north is foreign policy".[51] The interests of victims of repression and those of their supporters pulled human rights into different directions and the former pulled human rights into a decisively political one.

---

49 Václav Havel: The Power of the Powerless, in: *International Journal of Politics* 15, no. 3–4 (1985), 23–96; cf. Jonathan Bolton: *Worlds of Dissent. Charter 77, the Plastic People of the Universe, and Czech Culture under Communism*. Cambridge, MA 2012.

50 Kopeček, Human Rights.

51 Hopgood, Keepers, 98.

The Contingent and Tenuous Position of Human Rights

The term "breakthrough" suggests a certain finality of events and processes. Once someone or something has "broken through", say, a wall, she or it is here to stay. This metaphor thus contrasts markedly with a contemporary history of human rights which, as Eckel argues, does not lend itself to grand narratives, but evolved in fits and starts, at times even in an almost accidental fashion. The adoption of the human rights covenants of 1966 and the Year of Human Rights in 1968 later greatly inspired Soviet dissidents to shift their attention from the Soviet constitution to international human rights. Yet both of these events were, as Jensen shows, the result of completely unrelated developments, i.e. the diplomatic shrewdness of Jamaica and Liberia at the UN.[52] The international campaign against Augusto Pinochet, a paradigmatic case for the international human rights movement, was the result of a rather exceptional constellation in which members of both NATO and the Warsaw Pact could agree on condemning violence in Chile.[53]

If such bursts in human rights activism were often the result of almost accidental constellations, the international position of human rights afterwards could remain highly tenuous. The CSCE process is a case in point. The signing of the Helsinki Final Act is often cited as a central event in human rights history because the subsequent meetings to review the Act's implementation created a new forum to denounce repression. Yet this had not been the intention of the CSCE's authors, but was the achievement of recent converts to the cause of human rights: Soviet bloc dissidents, their western supporters and the Carter administration.[54]

Yet this achievement was highly tentative. In March 1982, the members of NATO took to the floor at the review conference in Madrid to vigorously condemn human rights violations in Poland where a military government had just taken power. This was a stark contrast to the first review meeting in Belgrade, where the Dutch-American human rights crusade had caused consternation in Bonn and Paris, but it is no evidence of a "human rights breakthrough". The three largest European members of NATO – Britain, France and West Germany – believed that the CSCE process should be made to serve its original purpose, East-West détente, rather than being a human rights forum. The newly elected US government under Ronald Reagan rejected the entire CSCE process as based on dangerous illusions

52 Jensen, Making.
53 Eckel, Glass.
54 Snyder, Activism.

about Soviet foreign policy. The Western Europeans' initial response to martial law in Poland was thus to quote the Final Act's provisions of non-interference in a signatory's internal affairs in order to keep Polish events off the agenda of the CSCE. For Washington, on the other hand, repression in Poland was a pretext to pull out of the CSCE process altogether. It was only against the latter prospect that the Western Europeans suggested to use the CSCE to condemn Warsaw's human rights violations in Madrid. Human rights, then, were not the basis of a broad value consensus, but a way to paper over the lack of such a consensus. And while the Madrid conference established a fairly robust human rights agenda, western governments were repeatedly more than willing to write off a dissident movement which, by most accounts, appeared to have been crushed.[55]

Another example for the tenuousness of human rights even after their seeming "breakthrough" is the fate of Amnesty International in the 1980s, as sketched by Eckel. By the middle of the decade, it seemed to have run out of steam: its second campaign against torture did not catch on, it appeared incapable of solving its internal problems, and the gulf between its leadership and rank-and-file seemed to widen. If the organisation made a spectacular comeback, it was only at the prize of organising an actual spectacle, a tour of rock concerts called *Conspiracy of Hope* and *Human Rights Now!* But by striking an alliance with the shrill world of 1980s pop culture, Amnesty was effectively turned into a youth organisation and entered a sphere that was worlds apart from the sternness and "culture of suffering" that had hitherto been the organisation's hallmark.[56]

Amnesty's travails in the 1980s lead us to a final point which the finality of the breakthrough metaphor threatens to obscure: the many ways in which human rights seem to have changed since the 1970s.

The Changing Meaning of Human Rights

An important impetus for the quest for a breakthrough is the aim to explain the current position of human rights. Yet as we strive to answer this question, it is worth noting that almost forty years have passed since the symbolic year of 1977. And much as developments in the 1970s helped human rights burst onto the global stage, it was only in these forty years, Hoffmann and Moyn argue, that

---

55 Brier, Icon.
56 Eckel, Ambivalenz, 423–434.

a "'global human rights revolution' [...] has occurred, when a variety of groups around the world, and all governments, learned to speak the language".[57]

In these years, human rights did become the foundation of a certain value consensus – though this was no foregone conclusion caused by their "breakthrough" – but the meanings and practices associated with human rights were changed again. A central question in analysing these changes seems to me how human rights became entangled with two processes: the wave of democratisation that swept the globe since the late 1970s and the worldwide spread of neoliberal economic models.

The conservative governments that had taken power across Europe and America in the 1980s realised that they could not simply dismiss human rights concerns. Adopting them, though, they also interpreted them in new ways. The most effective way of struggling for human rights, the Reagan administration argued, was "democracy promotion": fostering the "democratic infrastructure" of the world's societies, such as political parties, parliaments, trade unions, the free press etc. This was an only thinly veiled way of putting human rights into the imagery of an East-West "war of ideas". In a famous speech in Westminster, in which he announced the policy of democracy promotion in June 1982, Reagan painted the vision of a worldwide "march of freedom and democracy which will leave Marxism-Leninism on the ash-heap of history as it has left other tyrannies which stifle the freedom and muzzle the self-expression of the people".[58]

Associated with a specific political system, human rights were thus re-politicised, a major difference to the 1970s when Amnesty International claimed to oppose political repression not political systems, and when Soviet bloc dissidents sought to constitute a politics that was to be different from the systems in East and West. After the fall of Communism, EU accession seems to have strengthened this politicisation when human rights compliance and the creation of a specific domestic political and economic model became a precondition for post-Communist states to join the EU.[59]

"Democracy promotion", however, entailed more than instrumentalising human rights for Cold War policies; it was also part of a redefinition of the stakes of the Cold War. At Westminster, Reagan drew a specific picture of the Cold War.

57 Moyn, Utopia, 218; Hoffmann, Introduction, 2.

58 Ronald Reagan: Address to the Members of British Parliament, Westminster, 8 June 1982, in: *The Public Papers of President Ronald Wilson Reagan (1982)*. URL: *http://www.reagan.utexas.edu/archives/speeches/1982/60882a.htm* (31 Aug. 2015); on the following see, Eckel, Ambivalenz, 540–583.

59 Robert Brier: Historicizing 1989. Transnational Culture and the Political Transformation of East-Central Europe, in: *European Journal of Social Theory* 12, no. 3 (2009), 337–357.

"Consensus liberalism", the West's common ideological denominator of the 1950s and 1960s, had combined a preference for representative democracy with broad welfare policies. In his Westminster address, by contrast, Reagan characterised the struggle with totalitarian tyranny as only the most extreme expression of man's general struggle with "the enormous power of the modern state. History", he went on, "teaches the dangers of government that overreaches – political control taking precedence over free economic growth, secret police, mindless bureaucracy, all combining to stifle individual excellence and personal freedom".[60] The Westminster address, then, is also an example of Reagan's rhetorical habit of displacing "the totalitarian nightmare from the world scene to the stealthy, creeping, insidious growth of government at home".[61] The struggle for human rights and democracy, his speech suggested, was of one cloth with the struggle to unleash the creative power of free enterprise.[62]

This association of human rights with market fundamentalist ideas – an association strengthened when the World Bank integrated human rights concerns into its work – has led some authors to argue that there was something of an elective affinity between the two.[63] This interpretation would run counter to the malleability of human rights ideas which the recent historiography has brought to the fore. Yet it could be worth asking whether human rights' association with a "politics of truth" – the belief that the "bare facts" reveal a higher form of political truth than seeming ideologies, that politics and morality are necessarily in conflict[64] – has not helped paving the way for the technocratism of neoliberal ideas.[65]

60 Reagan, Westminster Address.

61 Rodgers, Age, 22.

62 Brier, Icon; Carl J. Bon Tempo: Antikommunistische Menschenrechte. Die Republikanische Partei und die Menschenrechtspolitik in den späten 1970er Jahren, in: Jan Eckel and Samuel Moyn (eds.): *Moral für die Welt? Menschenrechtspolitik in den 1970er Jahren*. Göttingen 2012, 290–315; id.: From the Center-Right. Freedom House and Human Rights in the 1970s and 1980s, in: Iriye, Goedde and Hitchcock, Revolution, 223–244; Robert C. Rowland and John M. Jones: *Reagan at Westminster. Foreshadowing the End of the Cold War*. College Station, TX 2010.

63 Nicolas Guilhot: *The Democracy Makers. Human Rights & International Order*. New York 2005; Mary Nolan: Gender and Utopian Visions in a Post-Utopian Era. Americanism, Human Rights, Market Fundamentalism, in: *Central European History* 44, no. 1 (2011), 13–36.

64 Eckel, Ambivalenz, 418.

65 Cf. Wendy Brown: "The Most We Can Hope For ...". Human Rights and the Politics of Fatalism, in: *South Atlantic Quarterly* 103, no. 2-3 (2004), 451–463; Jean L. Cohen: Rethinking Human Rights, Democracy, and Sovereignty in the Age of Globalization, in: *Political Theory* 36, no. 4 (2008), 578–606.

Conclusions

The 1970s were a time when the term "human rights" acquired an unprecedented prominence in international politics. The reason for this prominence was to a large extent, though not solely, that human rights provided political and moral answers where other systems of thought had failed. As a result, a novel – very broad and vague – understanding of human rights emerged, turning them into a rallying point for transnational activism.

And yet the perspective sketched in this article also suggests that the 1970s were no more and no less the time of "the breakthrough" of human rights than the late eighteenth century, the late 1940s or the 1960s. When people around the globe began turning massively to human rights in the 1970s, they translated human rights into a broad variety of human rights vernaculars which had as much to do with the ideas and concerns people brought into the 1970s as with the ideas they left behind for future generations. Rather than distilling an essential meaning of human rights, Jan Eckel's discerning of multiple chronologies, Mark Bradley's focus on different vernaculars, or the analysis of what Stefan Hoffmann calls "competing universalisms", many of which referred to human rights, all provide useful tools for seeing the 1970s in a broader historical context.[66]

But if historical human rights vernaculars can only be understood from within their own dynamic, why should we bother analysing them? One of the reasons why human rights history has become so popular is that they are part of contemporary history, which is concerned, Stefan Hoffmann writes, with the emergence of the problems that concern us today.[67] Unlike medieval feudalism, human rights continue to exert huge influence in our own time. Is the approach proposed here not an escape into historicism and relativism?

There are three answers to this question. First, as for relativism, to say that values emerge in response to particular historical experiences and that they change over time does not mean, as Hans Joas argues, that these values are meaningless. It merely explains how they emerged.[68] Second, in a time when global interconnections have intensified compared to the 1970s, when people and information travel even more rapidly around the globe than they did forty years ago, it may be even more important to interpret different vernaculars of human rights, and history may provide the tools to do just that. Finally, to say that the human rights

---

66 Eckel, Ambivalenz; Bradley, United States; Hoffmann, Introduction, 13–25.

67 Hoffmann, Introduction, 2.

68 Hans Joas: *The Genesis of Values*. Chicago 2000; id.: *The Sacredness of the Person. A New Genealogy of Human Rights*. Washington, DC 2013.

ideas of a time can only be understood within their "moment in time" does not mean at all that these ideas cannot be relevant for contemporary political theory or social thought. On the contrary, uncovering the many meanings human rights ideas acquired in the past could open the way for a productive reinterpretation of them in our own. History would then be a source of innovation.

Acknowledgements

I would like to thank Jan Eckel, Patrick W. Kelly and the anonymous reviewer of the *European History Yearbook* for helping me to improve an earlier version of this essay with their excellent comments. I am also indebted to Kelly, Steven Jensen and Mark Bradley for sharing unpublished manuscripts with me.

List of Contributors

Dr. Cornelia Aust,
Research Associate,
Leibniz Institute of European History,
Mainz.
aust@ieg-mainz.de

Dr. Robert Brier,
LSE Fellow in International History,
London School of Economics and
Political Science.
R.Brier@lse.ac.uk

Prof. Dr. Thomas David,
Director of the College of Humanities,
École Polytechnique Fédérale
of Lausanne.
Thomas.David@unil.ch

PD Dr. Simone Derix,
Senior Lecturer *(Privatdozentin)*,
University of Munich,
currently Visiting Professor
in Contemporary History,
University of Gießen.
simone.derix@lrz.uni-muenchen.de

Dipl.-Pol. Lucas Geese,
Doctoral Research Fellow,
Chair of Comparative Politics,
University of Bamberg.
lucas.geese@uni-bamberg.de

Dipl.-Pol. Wolfgang Goldbach,
Lecturer *(Wissenschaftlicher Assistent)*,
Chair of Comparative Politics,
University of Bamberg.
wolfgang.goldbach@uni-bamberg.de

Dr. Alix Heiniger,
Research Associate and Lecturer,
University of Lausanne.
Alix.Heiniger.1@unil.ch

Prof. Dr. Rainer Liedtke,
Professor of European History,
University of Regensburg.
**Rainer.Liedtke@geschichte.
uni-regensburg.de**

Dr. Sarah Panter,
Research Associate,
Leibniz Institute of European History,
Mainz.
panter@ieg-mainz.de

Prof. Dr. Johannes Paulmann,
Director,
Leibniz Institute of European History,
Mainz.
paulmann@ieg-mainz.de

Dr. Nico Randeraad,
Lecturer in Modern History,
University of Maastricht.
n.randeraad@maastrichtuniversity.nl

Prof. Dr. Thomas Saalfeld,
Professor of Comparative Politics,
University of Bamberg.
thomas.saalfeld@uni-bamberg.de

Prof. Dr. Margit Szöllösi-Janze,
Professor of Modern and
Contemporary History,
University of Munich.
margit.szoelloesi-janze@lmu.de

Jun.-Prof. Dr. Gesa zur Nieden,
Assistant Professor *(Juniorprofessorin)*
of Musicology,
University of Mainz.
znieden@uni-mainz.de

Bei Fragen zur Produktsicherheit wenden Sie sich bitte an:
If you have any questions regarding product safety,
please contact:

Walter de Gruyter GmbH
Genthiner Straße 13
10785 Berlin
productsafety@degruyterbrill.com